Certification Manual

LEAN SIX SIGMA GREEN BELT

Collection: GESTIONA
Publishing director: David Soler

LEAN SIX SIGMA GREEN BELT. CERTIFICATION MANUAL
1st Edition, 2022

© 2022, Luis Vicente Socconini Pérez Gómez
© of this Edition: ICG Marge, SL

Publisher: Marge Books
València, 558 – 08026 Barcelona (Spain)
Tel. + 34 931 429 486 – marge@margebooks.com
www.margebooks.com

Edition: Núria Gibert
Edition coordination: Karina Ahumada Serrano
Make-up editor: Mercedes Lara
Printed by: Safekat, SL (Madrid)

Paper Edition ISBN: 978-84-18532-91-7
Digital Edition ISBN: 978-84-18532-92-4
Legal Deposit: B 5596-2022

The paper used in this books has not been bleached with elemental chlorine (CI_2).

The author

ABOUT LUIS SOCCONINI

He holds a bachelor's degree in Industrial Engineering and a master's degree in Quality and Productivity from Monterrey Tec. He is also a Master Black Belt in Lean Six Sigma and a distinguished professor at several prestigious universities in Mexico.

Luis is certified in Strategic Management by Stanford University, in Leading Product Innovation by Harvard University, and in Industry 4.0 by MIT.

He has worked as a business consultant for the Wharton Business School in Pennsylvania, as a process engineer for Grolsch Brewery in the Netherlands, and as a manufacturing engineer at IBM.

As director of Lean Six Sigma Institute, Luis develops high-impact projects for companies such as Abbott Laboratories, Kraft Heinz, Coca-Cola, BMW, Bimbo, and Fender – to name a few. He has a broad base of experience and is continually developing productivity applications in diverse industries such as construction, mining, agriculture, government, energy, service, and more.

Luis is the author of **Lean Six Sigma Yellow Belt, Certification Manual, Lean Company, Lean Manufacturing, The Process of the 5's in Action,** as well as co-author of **Lean Six Sigma Management System** and **Lean Energy 4.0.**

SOCCONINI

www.socconini.com

Index

LSSI
LEAN SIX SIGMA INSTITUTE

Preface

Dear Reader,

I warmly welcome you on this journey to obtain the **Lean Six Sigma Green Belt Certification** and I wish to congratulate you because having this certification manual in your hands means that you seek to contribute to social development through the improvement of people, processes, and organizations – which ultimately leads to the well-being of our communities.

This certification manual is born from the need to share what we at Lean Six Sigma Institute (LSSI) teach people who participate in organizational processes – including managers, business owners, government officials, engineers, operators, and students. All of them receive training to transform today's key processes and design the organizations of the future.

At first, this manual was part of the material delivered to LSSI course participants across the world. Until one day, our regional Director in Spain suggested that our manuals could also be distributed in bookstores – allowing anyone to access the knowledge that is revolutionizing business thinking and the way organizations work today. We know that as long as people are trained and – above all – committed to a new spectrum of design and improvement possibilities, organizations will grow stronger as they face the new challenges posed by the ever-changing world we live in.

In this manual you will find a particularly useful toolbox that will help you successfully develop and continuously improve organizational activities. This toolbox is the result of decades of best practices proven to help organizations maximize value and achieve their goals.

You will find management tools that leaders must understand and implement in order to plan and execute strategies, analyze results, design organizational structures, nourish new talent, and develop a new financial thinking that accurately reflects real costs.

Throughout the Green Belt certification course you will learn to utilize different tools to improve quality by eliminating variation which stem from different factors. These factors increase the company's quality cost and therefore reduces the company's competitive advantage.

You will be presented with several tools through a methodology which presents a step by step process for implementing and developing high impact projects.

It's highly critical that you continuously develop improvement projects utilizing your new understanding. The improvement process is a path that has a beginning but it knows no end. It requires that we develop good habits created by constantly repeating and performing Lean Six Sigma exercises.

The objectives for these tools are that you can understand, apply, and teach your collaborators new work methods, so that the subsequent generation can be well equipped in an effective manner to confront the complex and ever changing environments businesses are faced with everyday.

I want to thank you for trusting me by giving me the opportunity to present to you a widely contrasting method to address current business complications and for granting me the responsibility to help you in your improvement path. Specially in a world where the decision to continuously improve is in one's hands.

Luis Socconini
CEO and Lean Six Sigma Master Black Belt

Certification Manual

LEAN SIX SIGMA
GREEN BELT

Introduction to Green Belt

Six Sigma: Transform data into valuable information

Objectives

1. Learn the basic Six Sigma concepts.
2. Understand the DMAIC methodology.
3. Apply improvements in all kinds of internal processes (sales, purchasing, logistics, personnel, finance, service, manufacturing, etc.) and make the most out of their data.

Content

> Background
> What is Six Sigma?
> Tools and methodology
> Six Sigma structure

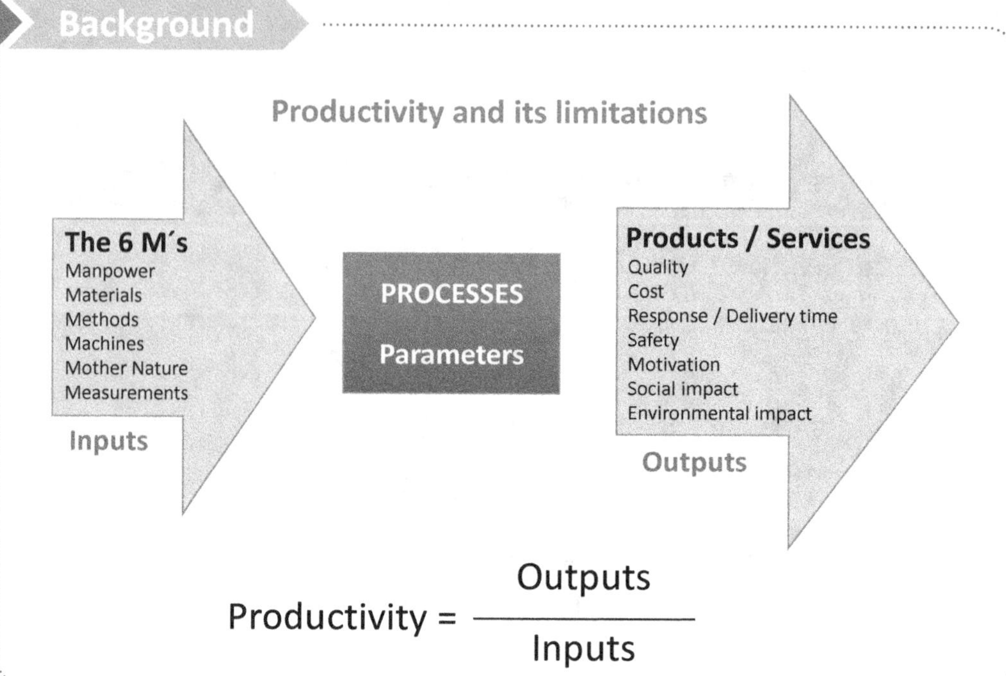

$$\text{Productivity} = \frac{\text{Outputs}}{\text{Inputs}}$$

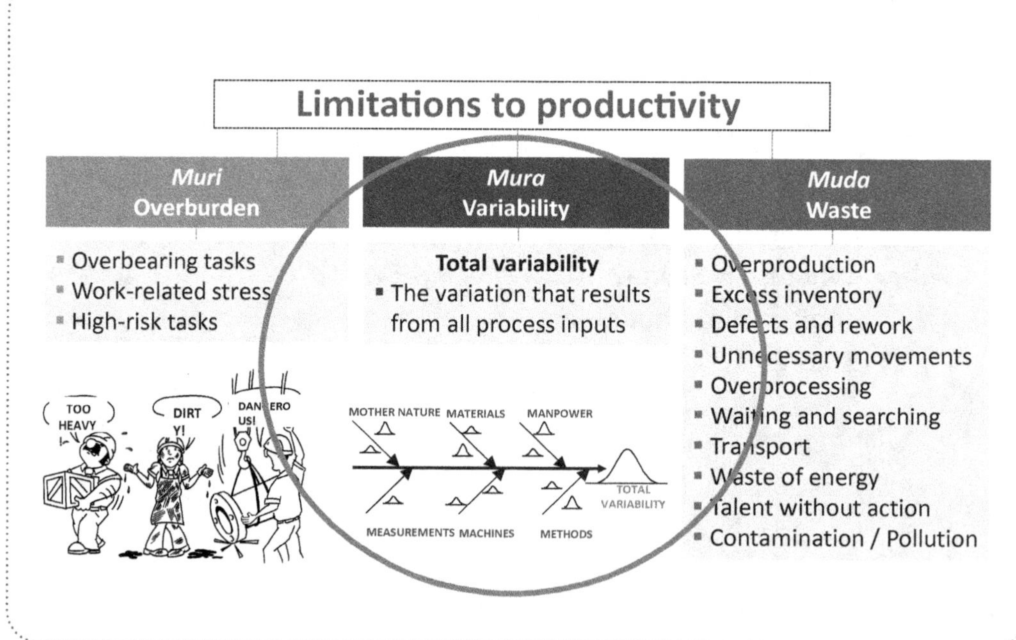

Variation around a target value

Variation around a target value affects cost in four important ways:

1. Fluctuations around the target value increase the cost of existing operations.
2. Fluctuations around a target value increase the cost of subsequent operations in the process.
3. Variation "bulges" processes in terms of tolerance, resources, raw materials, and the number of units started.
4. Variation decreases the efficiency of a process due to the need for increasing process complexity (e.g. rework or inspection).

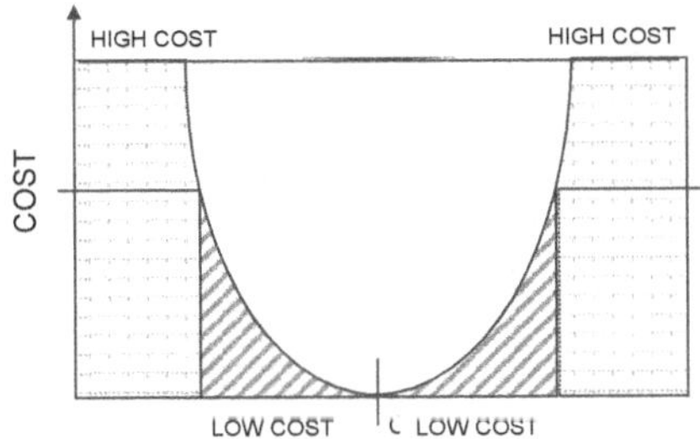

Start of Six Sigma

- In 1980, Motorola established a goal to improve quality levels by 10 times over the next 5 years. By 1989, they were able to improve the quality of their products and services by 100 times (as compared to its goal in 1980). Motorola achieved approximately $4.5 billion USD in savings between 1997 and 1999. In recognition of their developing and implementing the Six Sigma initiative, Motorola received the Malcolm Baldrige Quality Award in 1988.
- Allied Signal achieved more than $2 billion in savings from 1994-1999.
- GE achieved more than $3 billion in savings in two years (1998 and 1999).

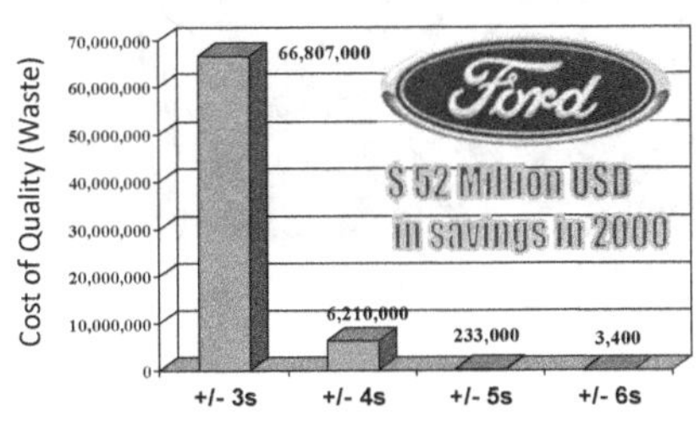

Lean Six Sigma integration

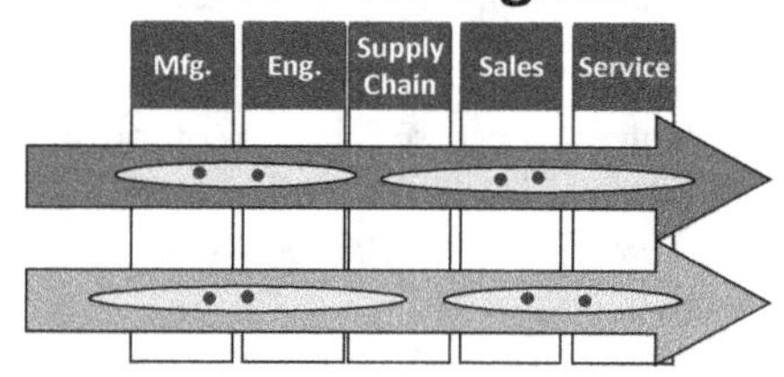

- Discrete projects targeting specific problems.
- Focus on individual projects.
- Reduction of variability to ensure quality and productivity.

- Value Stream Map (VSM) processes.
- Focus on cross-functional teams.
- Reduction of "waste" to ensure quality and speed.

What is Six Sigma?

- **A** work philosophy

- **A** metric

- **A** goal

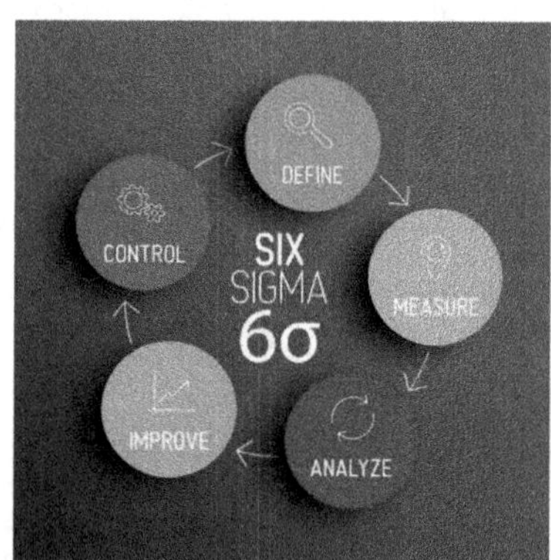

What is Six Sigma?

- As a work philosophy, Six Sigma means *continuous improvement* of processes and products supported by the implementation of the DMAIC (define, measure, analyze, improve, and control) methodology, which primarily includes the use of statistical tools and methods.

- As a metric, Six Sigma represents a way of measuring process *performance* and *out-of-spec* level of products or services.

- As a goal, a process with a *Six Sigma quality level* statistically translates to having world-class quality and not producing defective products or services.

Six Sigma Chart

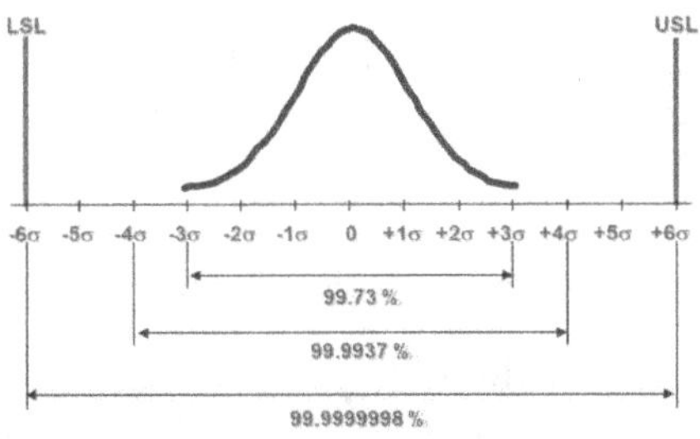

Sigma Level	Defect per million Opportunities (DPMO)	Yield
6	3.4	99.9997%
5	233	99.997%
4	6,210	99.379%
3	66,807	93.32%
2	308,537	69.2%
1	690,000	31%

Other meanings for sigma levels

Sigma Level	Parts per million (PPM)	Quality Cost	Classification	# of mispelled words
6	3.4	<10% of sales	World-Class	1 in a small bookstore
5	233	10-15% of sales		1 in several books
4	6,210	15-20% of sales	Average	1 in 31 pages
3	66,807	20-30% of sales		1.35 per page
2	308,537	30-40% of sales	Non-competitive	23 per page
1	690,000			159 per page

Harry (1998) & McFadden (1993)

"Six Sigma is about solving business problems by *improving processes." (Snee 2001)*

The importance of data

- In recent years, organizations have acquired modern information systems to control all key functions and have generated an enormous amount of **data** on.

- These massive amounts of data come from various areas, including:

  - Human Resources
  - Sales
  - Logistics
  - Services

  - Rejects
  - Manufacturing
  - Investments
  - Finance

  - Purchases
  - Marketing
  - Inventory
  - Maintenance

Big data  **Industry transformation**

LSSI
LEAN SIX SIGMA INSTITUTE

Competitive advantages

- **Six Sigma** transforms data into information and valuable decisions, increasing productivity and profitability.

Define
- Define the problem, document the project, select and gather the team, and build leadership support.

Measure
- Define and describe the process.
- Evaluate measurement systems.
- Gather and graph data to understand behavior, cycles, and patterns.
- Evaluate process capability and compare it to the objectives.

Analyze
- Determine key variables that generate variability and that represent root causes for the defined problem.

Improve
- Optimize the process and make it robust.
- Validate improvements.

Control
- Control and monitor the process.
- Improve continuously.

Six Sigma tools

1. Introduction	Introduction to Green Belt
2. Define	Project Definition
	VoC (Voice of the Customer)
	Kano Model
	Critical-to-Quality Tree
	Quality Function Deployment (QFD)
3. Measure and Map	Process Maps
	Measurement Systems Analysis (MSA)
	Basic Statistics
	Sampling
	Histograms
	Process Capability
	Process Performance
4. Analyze	Box Plots
	Analysis of Variance (ANOVA)
	Correlation
5. Improve	Design of Experiments (DOE)
6. Control	Statistical Process Control (SPC)
	Control Plan

Six Sigma structure

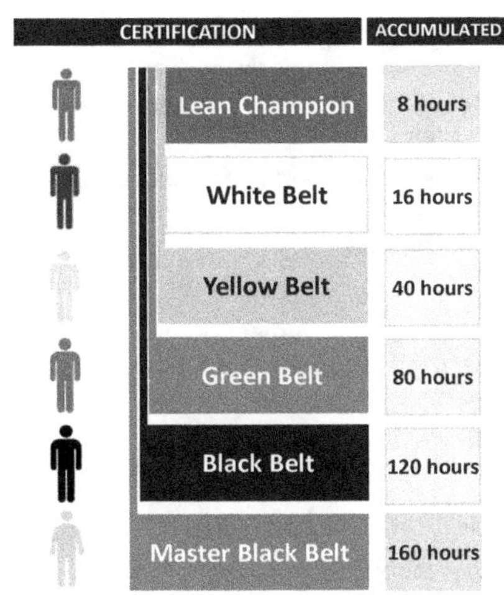

Problem and project selection

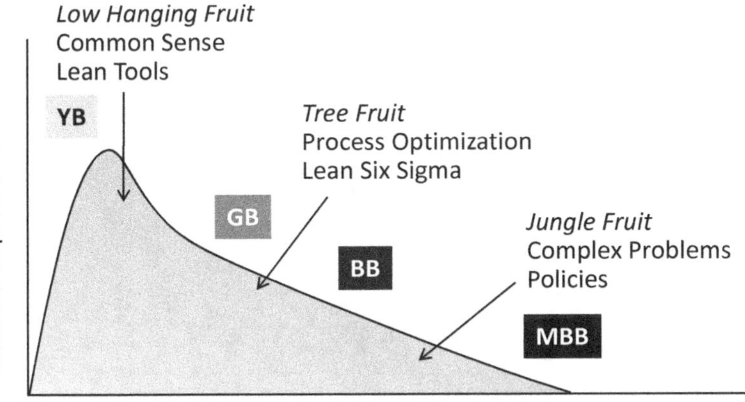

Responsibilities of a Green Belt

10 to 20 GBs for every 100 employees.

Experts in the Lean and Six Sigma tools and methodologies.

As an individual contributor

- Maintain a clean and orderly work area, standardize work to ensure speed and quality in their work.
- Utilize both Lean and Six Sigma tools in order to solve problems and implement continuous improvement.

As a team leader

- Leaders in basic improvement projects and provide specific support in the solution of problems.
- Train Yellow Belts and White Belts.

Knowledge

- Lean tools for speed and quality.
- DMAIC methodology.
- Statistical tools and administrative improvement.

Project definition

High-value Six Sigma Projects

Objectives

1. Understand the key elements that form part of the project charter.
2. Achieve successful project planning, documenting, execution, and completion.
3. Improve project planning to obtain project funding and management approval.

Content

> Project planning and documenting
> Project charter
> Project Gantt chart

Project planning and documenting

- All details on the definition of the project are documented in the project charter, which is revised and updated regularly if needed.

- Key activities in the development of a project charter are:

  - Define the business case or problem statement.
  - Describe the purpose of the project (CTQs to improve).
  - Describe the project objective and deliverables.
  - Define the scope of the project.
  - Define team member roles and responsibilities.
  - Determine the necessary resources to complete the project.
  - Define project metrics.
  - Create a preliminary implementation plan.

Project definition

Inputs

- Business cases
- Preliminary quantitative information
- Results
- Qualitative information

Project definition process

Outputs

- Area(s) of opportunity
- Current state
- Objective
- Scope
- Stakeholders
- Preliminary plan

Facilitator / Process owner → Team

Characteristics of a good project

- Aligned with business goals and priorities, as well as with customer needs, known as Critical-to-Quality[*] (CTC) characteristics.
- Highly important and easily understood and communicated.
- Achievable and within scope.
- Understood by all team members.
- Includes appropriate metrics (i.e., measurable).
- Supported and approved by the management team.
- Financial impact validated by the finance area.

[*] *Source:* Hosotani (1992) and Snee (2001)

Project identification

Methodology

- Ensure that the improvement projects are aligned and prioritized relative to the *strategy*.

- *Standardize* how the organization *identifies* improvement projects to avoid making decisions that are not based on data or that depend on specific individuals.

- Avoid situations where the number of projects assigned to a process or area exceed the allocated *human resource capacity*.

- Construct a *system* that leads the organization to periodically identify improvement opportunities in all business processes.

Project charter

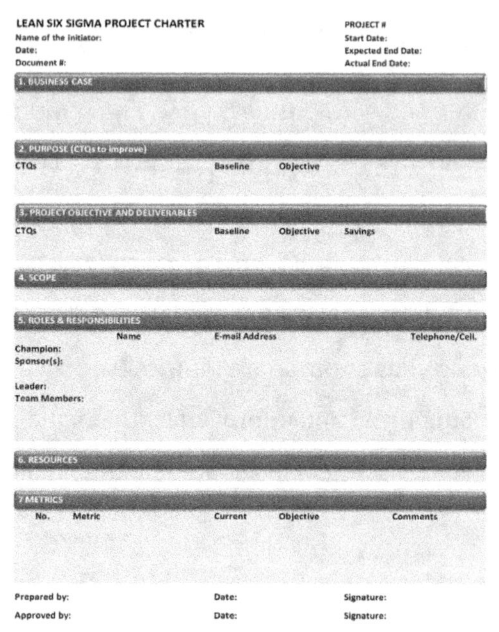

- This project charter template will be useful to document any improvement project.

- An A3 template can also be included in the overall project documentation.

1. Define the business case

- The business case helps to identify areas where there are problems or potential improvement opportunities.

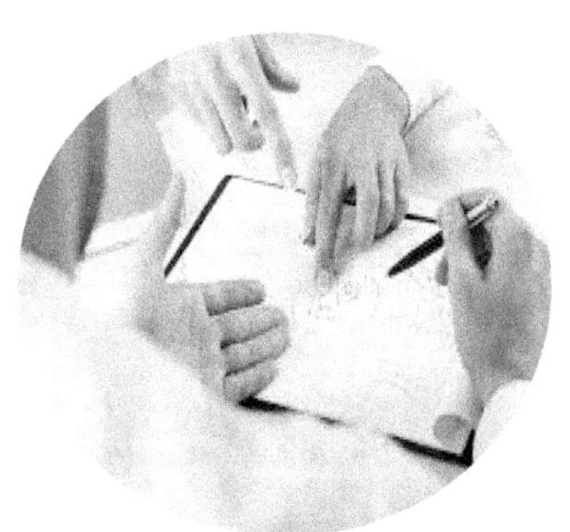

- It provides a summarized description of the characteristics of a situation.

- It is used to estimate the potential value of implementing a Lean Six Sigma project.

LSSI
LEAN SIX SIGMA INSTITUTE

Business case (template)

What is a business case?

It is a general definition of the area of opportunity assigned to the project team.

> As a company, the performance of our________________ in the area of____________ is not meeting ___________. This is causing problems like____________, which cost(s) approximately_______________ per year.

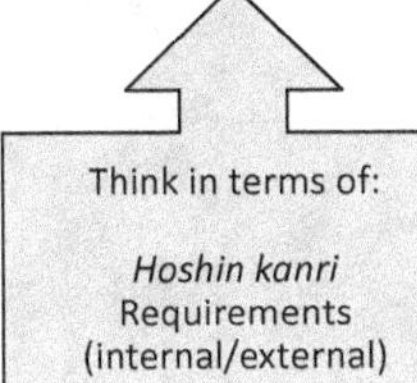

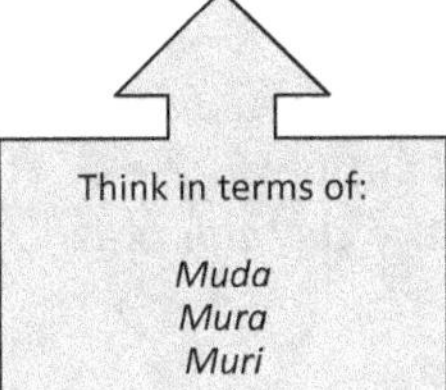

Business case example

Juliana Wilson is a chemical engineer and Master Black Belt at Chemical Manufacturing, a manufacturer of fertilizers. She developed the following business case:

LEAN SIX SIGMA PROJECT CHARTER

Name of the initiator:	Juliana Wilson	PROJECT #	LSSI - 001
Date:	1/6/2020	Start Date:	1/6/2020
Document #:	LSSI - 001 - 001	Expected End Date:	4/13/2020
		Actual End Date:	

1. BUSINESS CASE

As a company, the performance of our net weight of products in the bottling area is not meeting our goal of 100% and 104% of the weight. This is causing problems such as customer complaints and excess weight, which cost approximately $800,000 USD per year.

2. Determine CTQs to improve

- Based on the Voice of the Costumer (VOC) analysis already performed (which is explained in detail in the next topic), we evaluate all CTQs that will be improved according to the business case or any other priority established by the customer or the organization.

- All CTQs are now documented as a function of the established business case or as a priority established by the client or organization.

CTQs to improve

We assign the CTQs (Y) obtained from the VoC*

TOOLS:

- Kano model
- Customer Needs Map (CNM)
- Quality Function Deployment (QFD)

*VoC = Voice of the Customer

Determine the performance baseline

- At this point, we can have an idea of the magnitude of the problem or improvement area.
- The magnitude should be expressed in measurable units: hours, order quantities, percentage of late, …
- Show the current performance level (baseline) and the desired performance level (objective/goal).
- Verify that we are using long-term information when estimating the baseline.

Determine the performance baseline for CTQs

2. PURPOSE (CTQs to improve)	
CTQs	**Baseline**
Weight of packaged product	98 to 108 %
Process peformance	89%

3. Define project objective(s)

The objective is a more specific statement of the results expected from the project.

Examples:

- Reduce DPMO* from 1,000 to 500 within 6 months.
- Improve lead time from 20 days to 5 days.
- Increase OEE** from 67 % to 75% within 12 months

Project objectives

3. PROJECT OBJECTIVE AND DELIVERABLES		
CTQs	**Baseline**	**Objective**
Weight of packaged product	98 to 108 %	100 to 104 %
Process peformance	89%	98%

*DPMO: Defects per Million Opportunities. **OEE = Overall Equipment Effectiveness.

Specify the savings that can be obtained

Describe (in monetary terms) the savings that can be achieved up until this point and based on the project definition.

Savings

3. PROJECT OBJECTIVE AND DELIVERABLES

CTQs	Baseline	Objective	Savings
Weight of packaged product	98 to 108 %	100 to 104 %	$800,000 USD/year
Process peformance	89%	98%	

4. Scope

Projects like "Eliminating world hunger":

- The scope is so big that it is extremely difficult to manage.
- Discourages the team.
- Makes it difficult to correlate results with activities.

Projects with an appropriate scope:

- The project is large enough to present a challenge for participants.
- The team feels that the solution is within their area of responsibility.

4. SCOPE

Bottling and packaging process of sulfate products.

LSSI
LEAN SIX SIGMA INSTITUTE

5. Assembling the team

- Effective team formation is *crucial* so that process owners buy into the project.

- *Multiple* and *complimentary* skills to reach the common goal (multidisciplinary).

- *Number* of team members as a function of project complexity and scope.

- Invite *experts* (occasionally) and *process owners* (mandatory) to join the team.

- *Interaction* between members is a function of the number of team members. It is recommended to review the number of team members, so it is not excessive regarding the number of project objectives.

- Earn the support of the *external* members who will question the hypotheses and contribute a new perspectives.

Roles and responsibilities

The roles that should be defined include:

- **Champion:** Owner of the process in which the project will be implemented and main beneficiary of its results. His/Her responsibility is to keep the team focused on achieving the project's objectives and be the link with the organization's executive team. Participates in all meetings.

- **Sponsor(s):** Member(s) of the organization's executive team, whose responsibility is to remove any obstacles and make strategic decisions that enable the team to achieve the project's objectives. Participates in meetings as requested.

- **Leader:** Guides the team and ensures that the project's objectives are met. Coordinates meetings, plans activities and reports progress to the champion and sponsor(s). Provides the means that enable all team members to perform assigned tasks and monitors these.

- **Team Members:** Selected according to the previously mentioned guidelines.

Assembling the team

Team members

5. ROLES & RESPONSIBILITIES			
	Name	**E-mail Address**	**Telephone/Cell.**
Champion:	Seth Gordon	s.gordon@chemicalmanufacturing.com	(413) 000 - 0000
Sponsor(s):	Monica Parks		
	Miles Campbell		
Leader:	Juliana Wilson		
Team Members:	Patrick Clark		
	Diana Williams		
	Oscar Jones		
	Melissa Newton		

6. Resources and needs

The resources are based on the needs of the:

- Team
- Databases
- External experts (who may represent a cost)

Examples:

- Accounts payable database
- Equipment maintenance records

6. RESOURCES
Access to the accounts payable database for this year's orders.

7. Metrics

Other metrics can also be added to the previously defined CTQs. These metrics are also meant to be improved once the project is completed – or they can be included so they are monitored and not affected in a negative way throughout the project's implementation.

Common metrics in the projects:

- Material, maintenance, and labor costs.

- Meeting the sales budget.

- Work-in-Process (WIP) inventory.

- Reduction in workplace accidents.

- Cost of consumables (paper, oil, glue).

- Delivery time.

- Improvement in employee morale and job satisfaction.

7 METRICS

No.	Metric	Current	Objective
1	Weight of packaged product	98 to 108 %	100 to 104 %
2	Process performance	89%	98%
3	Required personnel	12	10
4	Percentage decrease	8.50%	0.50%
5	Distance covered	186 mts.	150 mts.

Project Gantt chart

- The project should be *documented* and *updated* on a weekly report that analyzes the activities performed, their duration, and – above all – the level of progress according to the established plan.

- The plan should be *communicated* and *analyzed on a weekly basis* because it is critical to the success of the project.

- Process owners (champions), team members, and project sponsors should participate as needed for decision-making purposes.

- The following Gantt chart shows a list of suggested activities for the phases of the DMAIC methodology. This list can be modified according to the specific objectives of each project.

LEAN SIX SIGMA PROJECT GANTT CHART
PROJECT #

	Duration	Start	End	1	2	3	4	5	6	7	8	9	10	11	12	13	14	15	16	17	18	19	20
DEFINE	**13**	**1/6/2020**	**1/19/2020**																				
Define the project, create a project charter	7	1/6/2020	1/13/2020																				
Define the process and problem metrics	3	1/13/2020	1/16/2020																				
Form the team	2	1/16/2020	1/18/2020																				
Project approval	1	1/18/2020	1/19/2020																				
MEASURE	**16**	**1/18/2020**	**2/3/2020**																				
Describe the process	2	1/18/2020	1/20/2020																				
Measure process performance	2	1/20/2020	1/22/2020																				
Measurement systems analysis	2	1/22/2020	1/24/2020																				
Define the baseline	10	1/24/2020	2/3/2020																				
Revise and update project status	0	2/3/2020	2/3/2020																				
ANALYZE	**28**	**2/3/2020**	**3/2/2020**																				
Analyze the process	8	2/3/2020	2/11/2020																				
Analyze the sources of variation	10	2/11/2020	2/21/2020																				
Determine significant variables	10	2/21/2020	3/2/2020																				
Revise and update project status	0	3/2/2020	3/2/2020																				
IMPROVE	**25**	**3/2/2020**	**3/27/2020**																				
Determine new operating conditions	10	3/2/2020	3/12/2020																				
Estimate the benefits of the improved process	5	3/12/2020	3/17/2020																				
Determine and adjust the failure modes	5	3/17/2020	3/22/2020																				
Implement and verify process changes	5	3/22/2020	3/27/2020																				
Revise and update project status	0	3/27/2020	3/27/2020																				
CONTROL	**17**	**3/27/2020**	**4/13/2020**																				
Implement control actions	9	3/27/2020	4/5/2020																				
Implement a control plan with the process owner	2	4/5/2020	4/7/2020																				
Implement a monthly achievements plan analysis	5	4/7/2020	4/12/2020																				
Document lessons learned	1	4/12/2020	4/13/2020																				
Formal project completion	0	4/13/2020	4/13/2020																				

Voice of the customer

Kano model, critical to quality tree and quality function deployment

Objective

1. Implement tools to translate customer needs into technical requirements.

Content

> Voice of the Customer (VoC)

- Kano model
- Critical to Quality (CTQ) Tree
- Quality Function Deployment (QFD)
- Checklist: Reviewing the define phase

Voice of the Customer (VoC)

We must answer three critical questions when listening to the voice of the customer:

1. **Who** are my customers?

2. **What product or service** must I provide to my customers?

3. What do my customers believe is **critical to quality**?

Voice of the Customer and CTQs

- A CTQ is a characteristic of a product or service that meets a critical customer requirement.

- CTQs are the basic requirements used for measuring the improvement and control processes.

- It is critical to ensure that CTQs represent exactly what is important to the customer (VoC).

LSSI
LEAN SIX SIGMA INSTITUTE

How to listen to the VoC

- **Interviews:** In-person visits or contact via telephone to collect information directly from the customer.

- **Surveys and questionnaires:** Can be conducted in-person or via email and telephone.

- **Focus groups and panels:** Select a representative group of your customers to collect data virtually or in person.

- **Exhibitions:** Participate in expos and exhibitions and use such opportunities to listen to your customers.

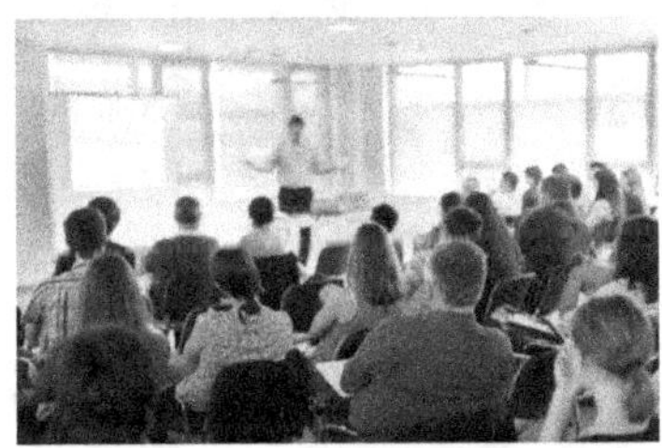

- **Customer complaints:** Provide customers with a phone number, email address, or any easy-to-use method that allows them to effectively communicate complaints about your product or service.

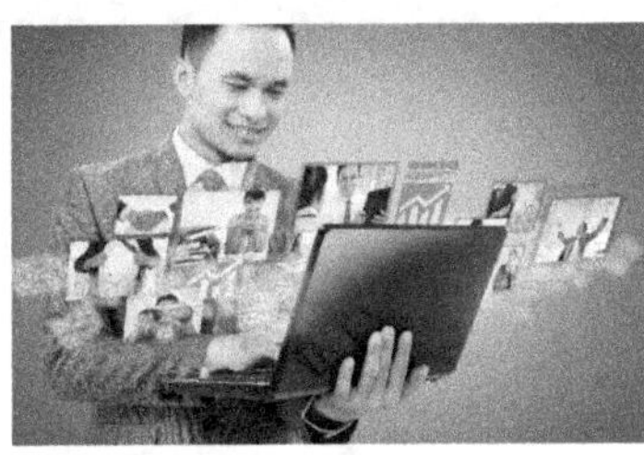

- **Market research:** Hire a professional to conduct it. The downside is that costs are higher, but these kind of services generally represent rich data that can be used as a good starting point.

How do we translate customer requirements?

**Customers are not sure about
what they want, and sometimes
provide conflicting requirements.**

We need to use methods that will help us
understand customer requirements and
translate them into internal requirements.

Tools:

- **Kano model**
- **CTQ Tree**
- **QFD**

Once customer requirements are
translated into internal
requirements, we must be able
to measure and evaluate the
quality of the product or service
as well as process performance.

LSSI
LEAN SIX SIGMA INSTITUTE

Voice of the customer
Kano model

Objective

1. Use the Kano model to understand the customers' CTQ
   requirements and meet their needs.

Content

> Background
> What is the Kano model?
> What is it used for?
> Procedure
> Example
> Exercise

Background

- During the 1980s, Professor Noriaki Kano developed a theory of product development and with it an evaluation of customer satisfaction – a framework that came to be known as the Kano model.

- The Kano model focuses on the differentiation of product or service characteristics instead of initially focusing on customer's requirements.

Noriaki Kano

What is the Kano model?

- A tool that helps us understand, analyze, and classify customer requirements according to their priority.

- The Kano model offers an idea of the characteristics of the products or services perceived as important to customers.

- The purpose of the tool is to support the product or service specifications and to facilitate debate through a better development of the team's understanding.

Dimensions of quality

1. Performance level of a product or service.

Performance

Low   High

2. Level of customer satisfaction.

Customer satisfaction

Low   High

Kano model

Two dimensions

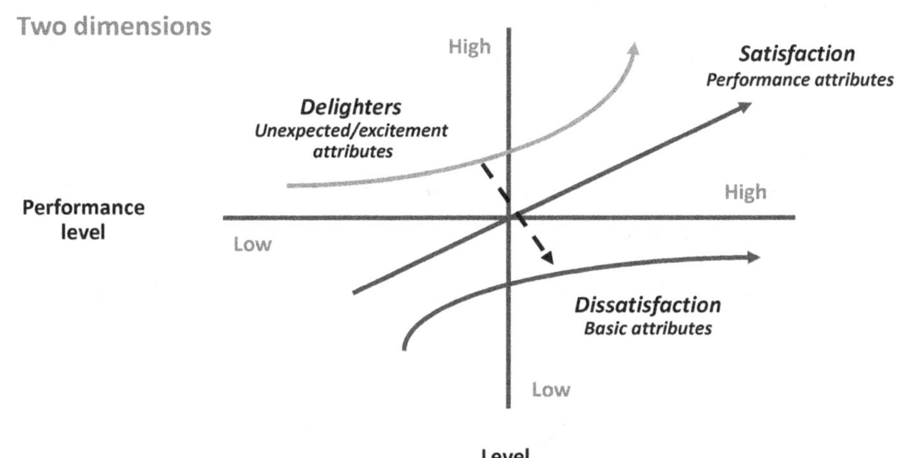

What is it used for?

- To identify customer requirements.

- To develop new products and services.

- To determine functional requirements.

- To perform comparative analysis of products and services against competitors.

Procedure

1. Collect information to identify customer requirements.

2. List the potential requirements identified.

3. For each potential requirement, ask your customers the following questions:

   - Q1: Rate your level of satisfaction if the product or service were to have this attribute (potential requirement)?
   - Q2: Rate your level of satisfaction if the product or service did not have this attribute (potential requirement)?

4. The customer or end user can choose his or her answer from the following options:

   a) Satisfied.
   b) Neutral (since this attribute is expected from the product or service).
   c) Don't care.
   d) Dissatisfied.

Classification of responses

Classify the responses as basic, performance, or unexpected/excitement attributes.

Basic attributes generally receive:
- **Neutral** as a response to question 1.
- **Dissatisfied** as a response to question 2.

Performance attributes usually relate to the following question: "How much would you be willing to pay for this attribute or more of it?" They generally receive:
- **Satisfied** as a response to question 1.
- **Dissatisfied** as a response to question 2.

Unexpected/excitement attributes generally receive:
- **Satisfied** as a response to question 1.
- **Don't care** as a response to question 2.

> Example

Paul Evans from **Logistics Company** conducted a survey among 237 of his customers by using the Kano model. The following table summarizes the results he obtained:

POTENTIAL NEEDS / REQUIREMENTS	Level of satisfaction if the product/service has this attribute	Level of satisfaction if the product/service does NOT have this attribute	TYPE OF NEED OR REQUIREMENT
On-time deliveries	Neutral	Dissatisfied	**BASIC**
Fulfilled and accurate orders	Neutral	Dissatisfied	**BASIC**
Last-mile delivery	Satisfied	Dissatisfied	**PERFORMANCE**
Discount codes for repeat customers	Satisfied	Don't care	**DELIGHT**
Special packaging for fragile products	Satisfied	Dissatisfied	**PERFORMANCE**
Accurate and on-time invoicing	Neutral	Dissatisfied	**BASIC**

- An entrepreneur decides to open a coffee shop and needs to understand her key customer requirements.

- Use the Kano model to identify and classify at least five basic, four performance, and three unexpected/excitement attributes of the product and service that will be offered.

  - Form teams.
  - Perform a Kano Model analysis.
  - Express your results in a matrix and present your conclusions.

Voice of the customer
Critical to Quality (CTQ) Tree

3.2

Objective

1. Use the Critical to Quality (CTQ) tree to understand customers' CTQs.

Content

> Background
> What is a CTQ tree?
> What is it used for?
> Procedure
> Example
> Exercise

Background

- When we are developing new products and services, quality is key not only to satisfying customers' needs but to building competitive advantage as well.

- The definition of quality, however, can be a challenge. It is easy to overlook the factors that concern or matter to customers the most.

- A **Critical to Quality [CTQ] tree** helps us understand what drives quality in the eyes of customers, and in this way helps us meet their requirements.

What is a CTQ tree?

- It is a tool used to translate general customer needs into specific, achievable, and measurable performance requirements.

- A critical to quality tree is also known as a quality needs tree.

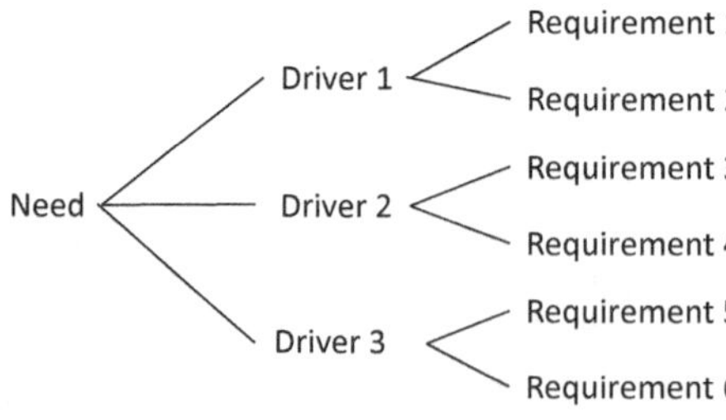

LSSI
LEAN SIX SIGMA INSTITUTE

What is it used for?

- A **CTQ tree** helps us identify the needs of customers and translate these into the specific requirements for a product or service.

- This is what a product or service must provide in order to satisfy customers' needs.

For example, if we are launching a new website, a need might be: "It must be accessible on a smartphone."

Procedure

1. Identify critical needs.

2. Identify drivers of quality.

3. Identify performance requirements.

1. Identify critical needs

- First, we need to identify the critical needs that the product or service must meet. We must develop a CTQ tree for each critical need identified.

- During this first step, we essentially ask: "What is critical for this product or service?"

- It is important for needs to be defined in generic terms; this helps ensure that important aspects are not lost or forgotten during the next steps.

- If we cannot ask our customers directly about needs, then we can *brainstorm* with salespeople, customer service representatives, and internal teams.

- We must transition from an engineering mentality or point of view to a *customer mindset*.

2. Identify drivers of quality

- Next, we must identify the specific drivers of quality that meet the needs we identified in the previous step. These drivers must be present so that customers consider our products and services as high-quality value.

- Do not rush; it is important that we invest time in identifying all the drivers that are important to our customers.

- Tools such as Kano model and QFD are useful during this step; they help us identify the characteristics and features that will delight our customers.

3. Identify performance requirements

- Finally, it is necessary to identify the minimum performance requirements that must be met for each quality driver. This allows us to measure requirements, which helps us provide high-value products and services.

- There are some factors that will affect the ability to deliver the expected results. For example: Do we have enough resources or the right technology? We should also consider any action that must be done in other parts of the organization to meet these requirements.

> Example

- Elizabeth is launching a newborn baby clothing store.

- After talking with potential customers, one of the critical needs that she identifies is: **"Excellent customer service."**

- Therefore, she uses a CTQ tree to create a list of measurable performance requirements that will help her achieve this critical need.

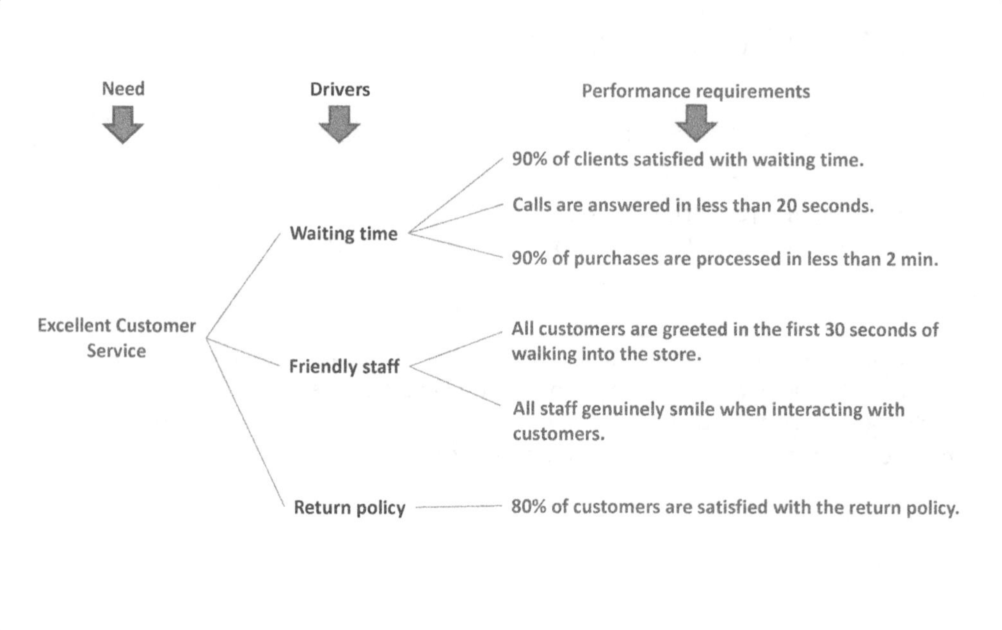

Exercise

- Choose a new product or service that your organization – or a fictional organization – will develop.

- Develop a CTQ tree for one of the product's or service's critical needs.

Voice of the customer
Quality Function Deployment (QFD)

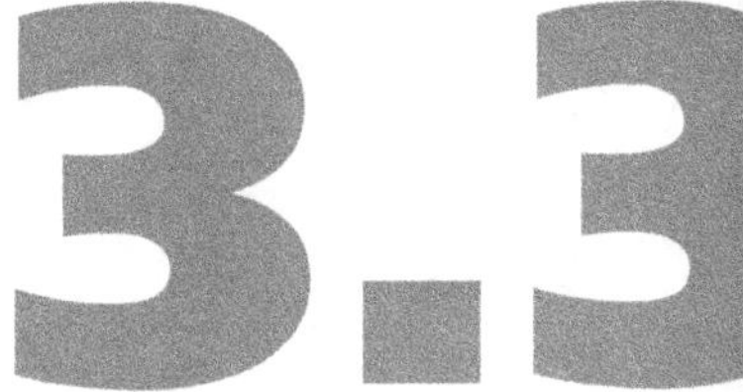

Objectives

1. Understand the basic concepts of QFD (Quality Function Deployment).
2. Develop QFDs for your projects.
3. Interpret the results correctly and use them to make decisions.

Content

> Background
> What is QFD?
> What is it used for?
> Procedure
> Example
> Exercise

Background

- QFD was introduced in Japan by Yoji Akao in 1966 and was first implemented in Mitsubishi Heavy Industries, Ltd., in 1972.

- Its implementation in Western companies did not occur until the mid-1980s, when Rank, Xerox, and Ford applied the technique to their new product development processes (Zairi and Youssef, 1995).

Yoji Akao

What is QFD?

- QFD (Quality Function Deployment) is a method used to translate customer requirements, or "What's", into multiple levels of internal requirements, or "How's."

Identify customer requirements

- QFD is a process used to plan and redesign products and services. The essential input for QFD is the Voice of the Customer (VoC).

VoC → Surveys, interviews, focus groups, market research, and benchmarking

- A QFD matrix shows the relationship between the Voice of the Customer (VoC) and the corresponding technical requirements.

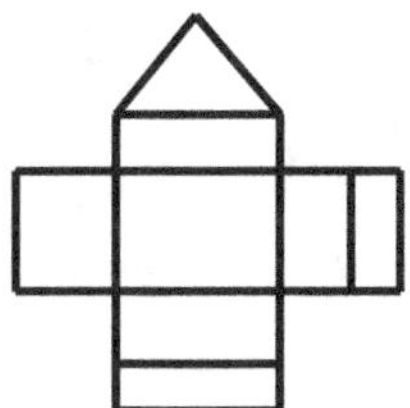

What is it used for?

- To identify the requirements that impact and satisfy the needs of customers.

- To define the technical requirements that meet all customer needs.

- To define the requirements of the process design.

- To define the requirements needed to control the process and ensure the best quality.

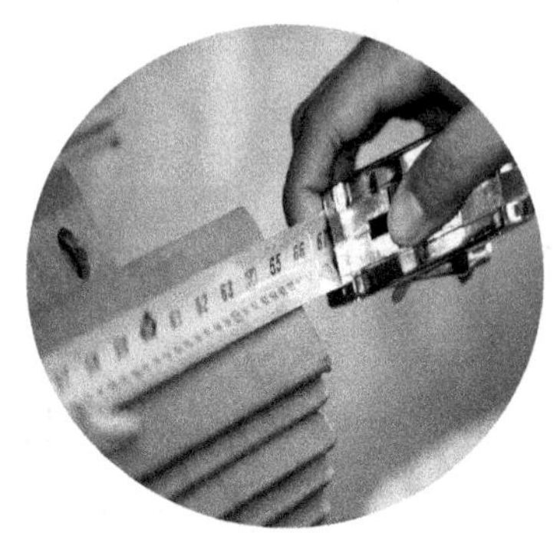

Procedure

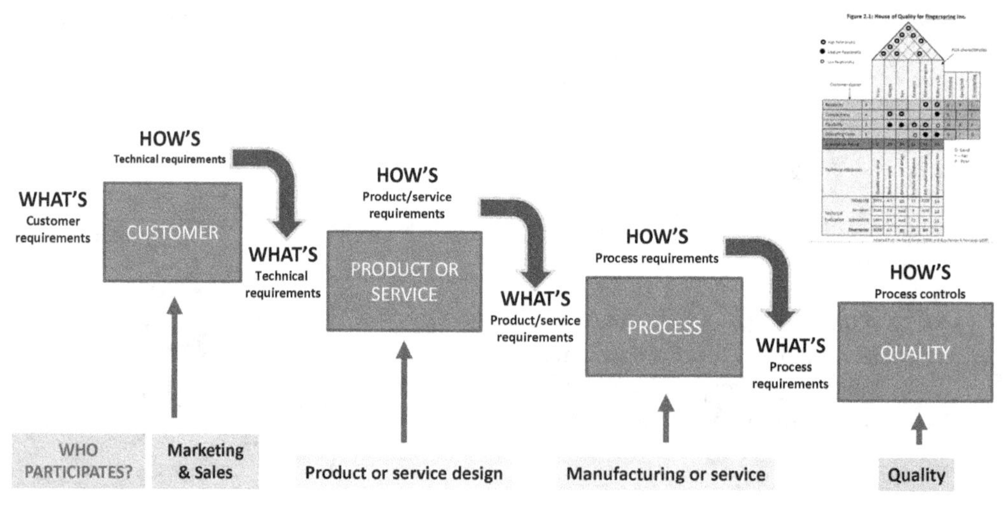

LSSI
LEAN SIX SIGMA INSTITUTE

Elements of the QFD matrix

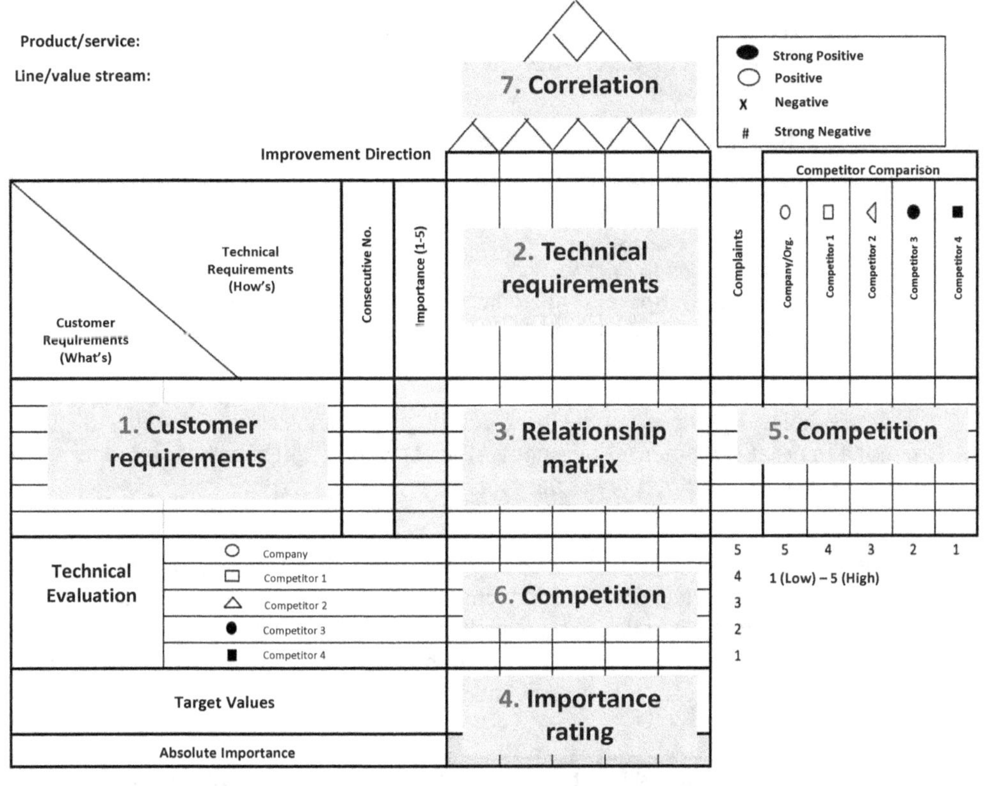

Procedure

1. In the **Customer Requirements** section, write the customer needs per category along with their level of importance (1 - 5), classified as follows:

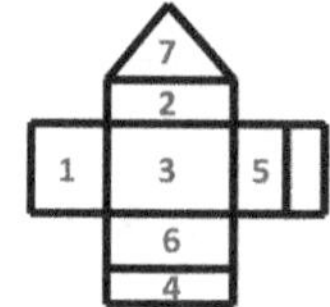

   A. Perform data collection; ask customers to answer the following questions:

   - **What are the features/characteristics that you expect from our products/services?**
   - **What is the level of importance that you would assign to each feature/characteristic?**

   B. For Question 2, customers can choose their answer from the following options:

   * 5 points: Critical.
   * 4 points: Important.
   * 3 points: Nice to have.
   * 2 points: Not very important.
   * 1 point: Does not matter.

2. In the **Technical Requirements** section, describe the technical requirements needed to meet customer requirements. These can be suggestions or elements that already exist or form part of the process, product, or service.

3. In the **Relationship Matrix** section, establish degrees of relationship between customer requirements (What's) and technical requirements (How's). These degrees of relationship measure how much each technical requirement influences each client need (i.e., the effect or ability of the technical requirement to meet the client need). These degrees can be defined as follows:

   0 points: No existing relationship between the client need and the technical requirement.
   1 point: A weak relationship exists between the client need and the technical requirement.
   3 points: A moderate relationship exists between the client need and the technical requirement.
   9 points: A strong relationship exists between the client need and the technical requirement.

4. In order to obtain the **Importance Rating** for each technical requirement, we must multiply the value of the relationship times the level of importance of the corresponding characteristic and add the values for each column.

5. In the **Competition** section (on the right-hand side of the matrix), benchmark the fulfillment of needs with respect to the most important competitors. This can be performed through customer or end user survey.

6. In the **Competition** section (in the middle part of the matrix), benchmark the technical requirements with respect to the most important competitors. Generally, we should compare our products and services with the competition.

7. In the **top pyramid**, use symbols to evaluate the correlation between technical requirements. This correlation can be:

   - Strong positive: By increasing or improving the technical requirement, the second requirement (the one with which the first is being compared) also increases or improves to a strong degree. The same is true for an inverse scenario (for a decrease instead of an increase).
   - Positive: By increasing or improving the first technical requirement, the second one also increases or improves to a lower degree. The same is true for an inverse scenario (for a decrease instead of an increase).
   - Negative: If the first requirement increases, then the second requirement decreases – and vice versa.
   - Strong negative: Similar to the previous description, but to a stronger degree.
   - Null: There is no correlation between the requirements being compared.

8. Repeat the same procedure for the second matrix (the Design Matrix) – using the technical requirements as inputs (the "How's" become the "What's") and assigning the product or service requirements that meet such technical requirements.

Continue this procedure in order to obtain the third matrix (the Process Matrix) and the fourth matrix (the Control Matrix).

Example

- An improvement team at Chemical Manufacturing conducts a QFD analysis to determine the technical requirements that must be established in order to meet customer needs for the product: powdered fertilizer.

- In conclusion, the most important technical requirement is to have an agile and reliable process, since this requirement is the one with the highest importance rating (129 points) and, even when the comparative analysis shows that we are better than our competitor (level 3 compared to level 2), the are existing areas of improvement.

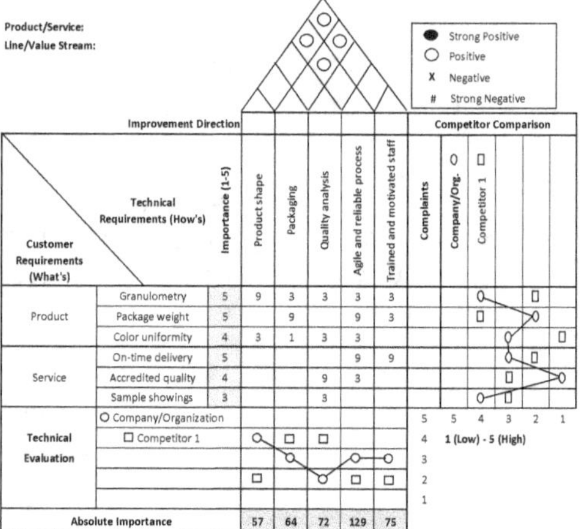

Exercise

Quality Function Deployment (QFD):

- Using the information gathered in the Kano Model for the customer (the "What's"), create a QFD matrix for the preparation of coffee in its first stage (QFD 1).

Checklist: Reviewing the define phase

Once the activities for the Define Phase have been completed – and before moving into the Measure Phase – the improvement team must verify if the objectives were met. The following checklist can be used to do so:

Review: Define Phase

Project: ____ Date: __________

	Yes	No
1.- We have confirmed that the Project aims to solve an area of opportunity that is important, and the Project has the support of the company's or organization's management team.	☐	☐
2.- The Business Case has been defined, and it explains the potential impact the Project has on the overall performance and results of the company / organization, as well as its alignment with the strategic plan.	☐	☐
3.- The area of opportunity has been defined, and such definition is solely focused on the symptoms of the problem (not on causes nor solutions).	☐	☐
4.- The expected results that the Project is meant to achieve have been clearly defined - including objective(s) and deadline.	☐	☐
5.- Key elements of the DMAIC process have been defined, including: Preliminary plan, work team(s), roles and responsibilities for every team member, Project scope, etc.	☐	☐
6.- Project documentation (including the Project charter) has been reviewed with the project facilitator, and management approval for such documentation has been confirmed.	☐	☐
7.- The customers and end users, as well as their critical requirements (CTQ's), for the product, service, or process that we seek to identify - have been identified.	☐	☐

Process maps

Knowing the process is the key to understanding its tendencies

Objectives

1. Understand the elements that form part of the different types of process maps.
2. Develop different types of process maps for any process in an organization.
3. Integrate process maps to Lean Six Sigma projects.

Content

> Background
> What are process maps used for?
> Types of process maps
> Conclusions
> Exercise

Background

- For an organization to work in an effective way, it has to identify and manage numerous interrelated activities.

- An activity that uses resources and is managed so that inputs are transformed into results is considered a process.

- Frequently, the result of a process is the direct input to the next process.

What is a process?

A *process* is a combination of activities that uses one or more types of inputs and that creates an output that is of value to the customer.

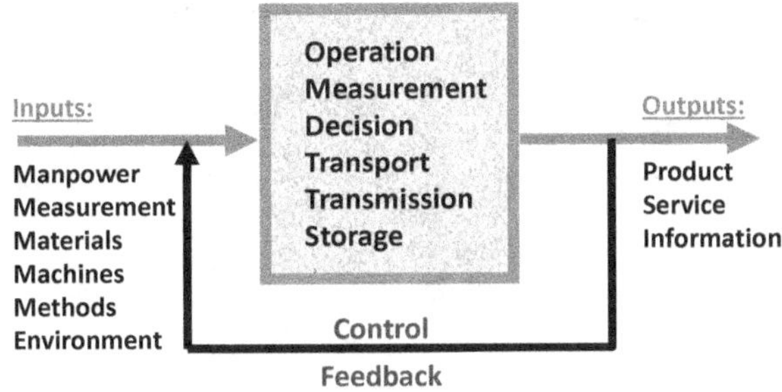

Everything we do is a process!

It is key to:

- Identify and measure the critical inputs and outputs.
- The critical inputs (X's) are causes for the critical outputs (Y's) or effects:
  $$Y = f(X_1) + f(X_2) + \ldots + f(X_n)$$

If X is …	Then Y is…
Cycle time	On-time deliveries
Amount of sugar	Cake sweetness

It is key to:

- Establish **control** over the critical inputs and outputs.
- Use critical outputs to provide **feedback** to the process and guide it towards target performance levels.

What are process maps used for?

- To manage the improvement process and to have a high level of awareness of all company activities.

- To understand the process at a detailed level and identify opportunities to:
  - Eliminate steps
  - Perform process steps faster
  - Perform steps simultaneously (in parallel)
  - Rearrange steps
  - Simplify steps

- To define critical-to-quality (CTQ) factors through process inputs and outputs.

- To define the current state or condition of the process.

- To identify potential problems and root causes in the process and to generate alternative solutions.

Types of process maps

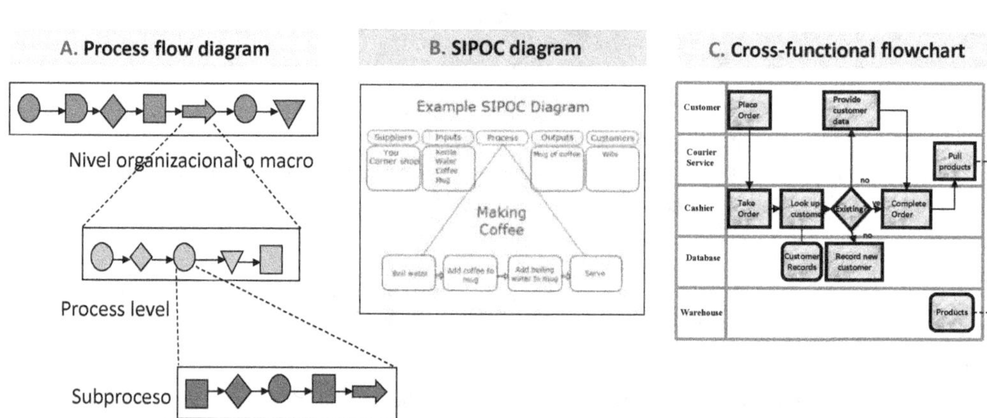

A. What is a PMAP?

A **Process Map** or **PMAP** is a graphical tool that is used to document process flow:

- It is similar to a process flow diagram.

- A Process Map includes the input (X) and output (Y) variables of each operation and classifies these as either **noise**, **controllable**, **standard**, or **critical variables**.

- It can be used to show the value stream of a process, including information and services.

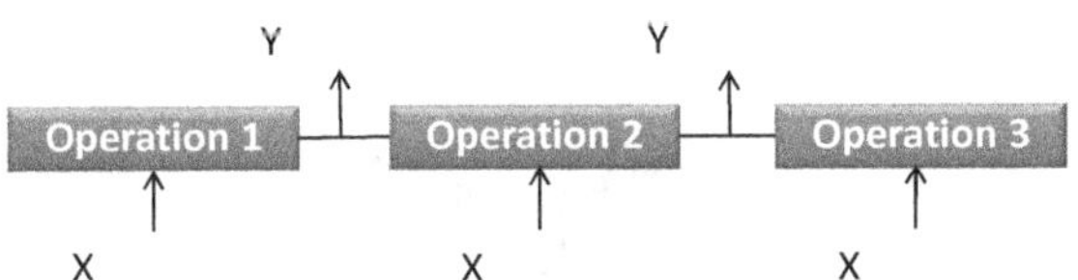

A process map is a *visual representation* of a process that transforms a set of inputs into outputs.

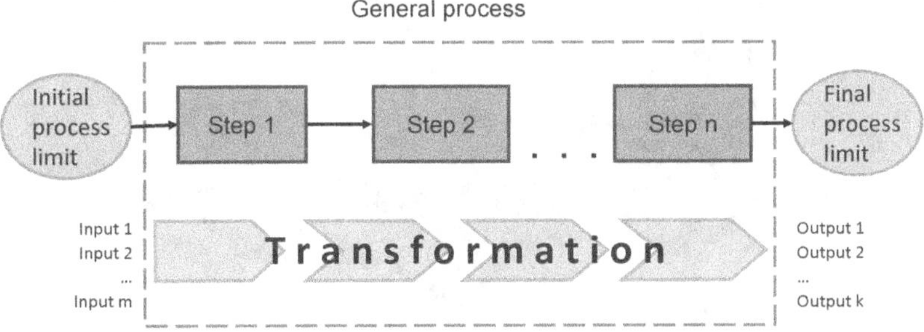

Process map procedure

1. Identify all steps in the process.

2. List the inputs and outputs for each step in the process.

3. Classify the inputs.

4. Determine input and output variable requirements.

5. Validate the process map.

Process map symbols

 Start or end points in a process

 **Operation:**
Activity, Inspection, Testing, etc.

 **Decision:**
A step in the process where process flow may change.

 **Transport:**
Movement of information or materials.

 **Storage:**
Storage for future use.

 **Delay or wait:**
Waiting for the next operation.
Does not add value.

 **Connector:**
Shows a jump from one process flow to another.

1. Identify all steps in the process

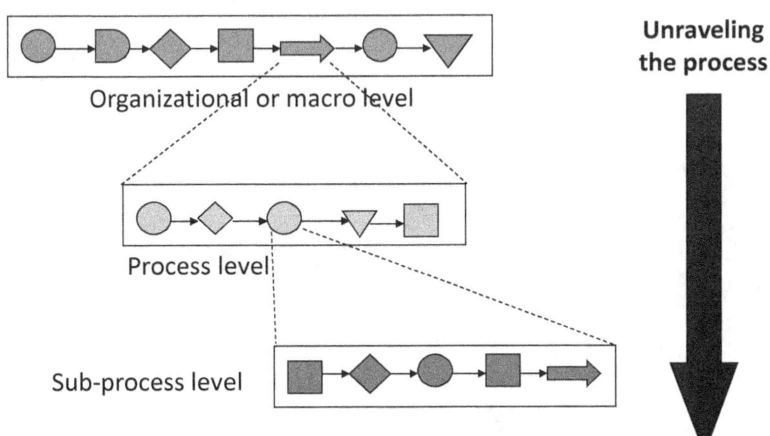

Include all activities: value-added and non-value added.

2. List the inputs and outputs for each step in the process

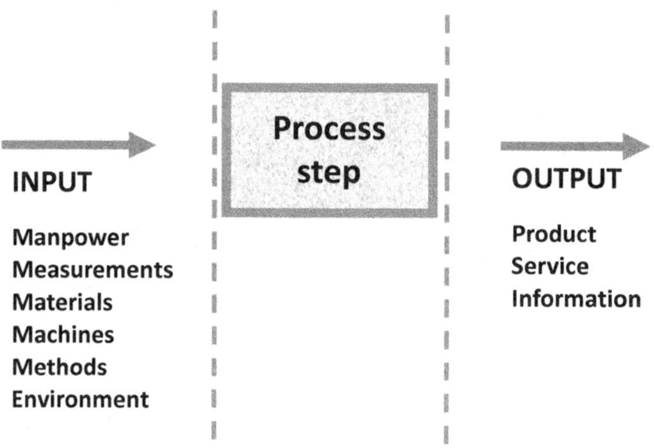

Parts cleaning process

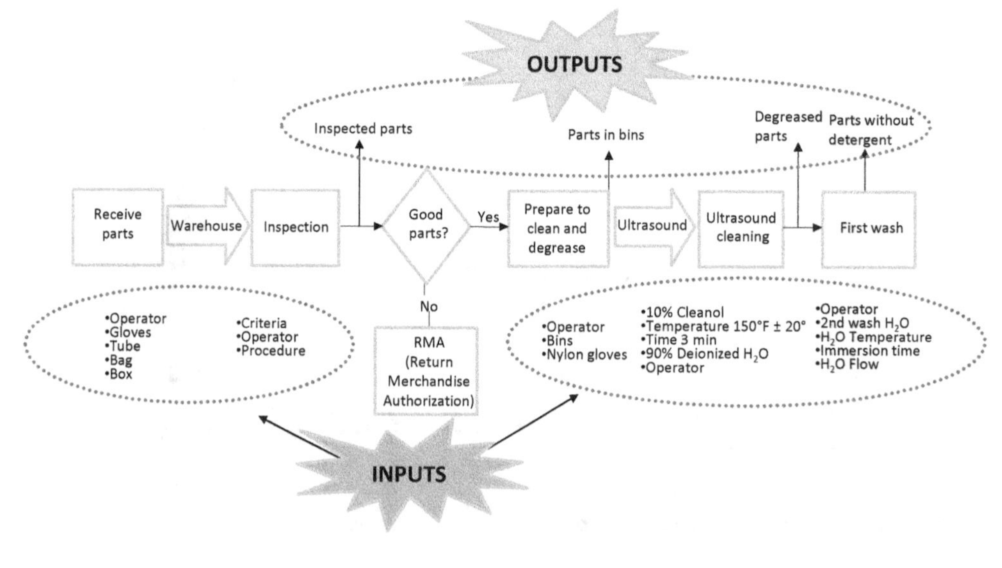

3. Classify the inputs

Inputs can be classified into four categories:

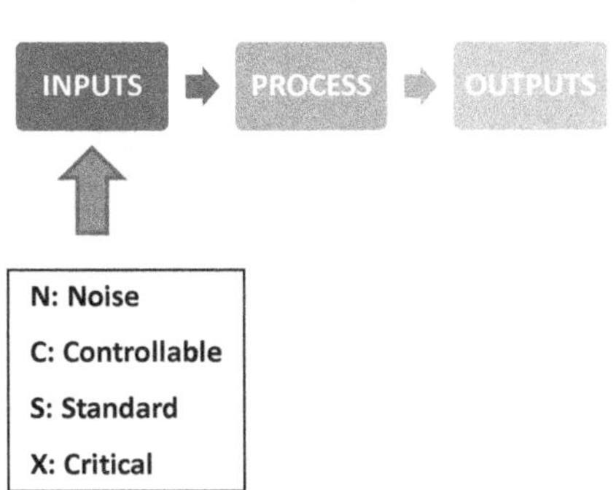

- **Noise (N) inputs:** Those that are hard or impossible to control. Example: Climate/Environment (humidity, age, outside temperature, etc.)

- **Controllable (C) inputs:** Those that can be changed to see what effect they have on output variables.

- **Standard (S) inputs:** A standard procedure to run the process.

- **Critical (X) inputs:** Those that have been statistically proven to have an impact on output variables.

Parts cleaning process

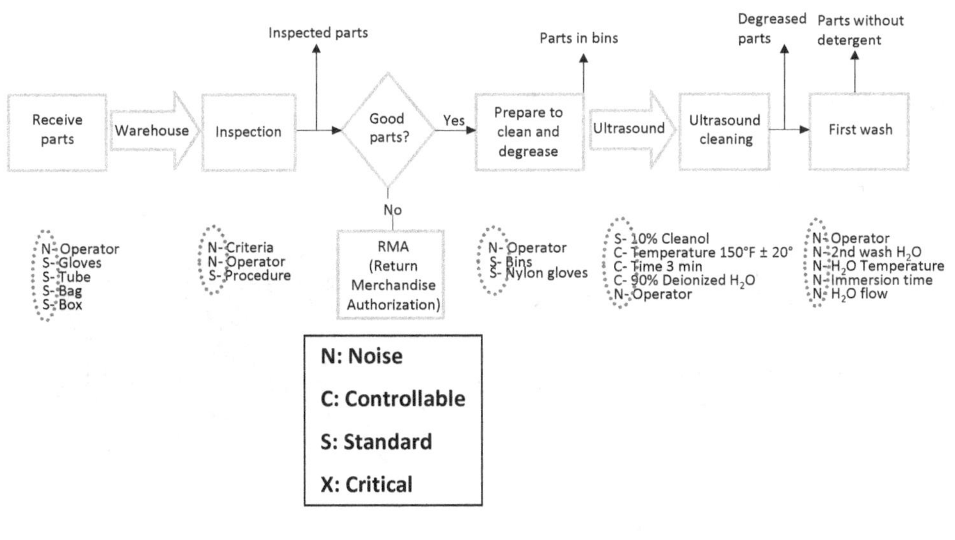

4. Determine the requirements

Include:

- Controllable and critical input variable requirements.

- Output variable requirements.

Input	Classification	Requirement
Water Temperature	Controllable	150°F ± 20°
Time	Controllable	3 min
Gloves	Standard	Nylon
Boxes	Standard	Stainless steel

5. Validate the process map

Validate the accuracy of the process map you have created.

- Walk through the **real process.**

- Include people that go through the process on a daily basis – process **experts.**

- **Update** the process map when you make changes to the process.

B. What is a SIPOC diagram?

- It is a tool that provides a graphical representation of the steps in a process in conjunction with suppliers, inputs, outputs, and customers.

- It is a tool that helps us analyze a process relative to these parameters to understand its impact on the value stream.

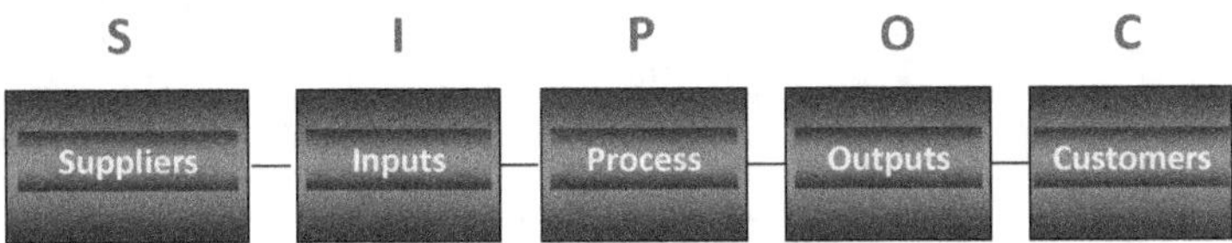

SIPOC elements

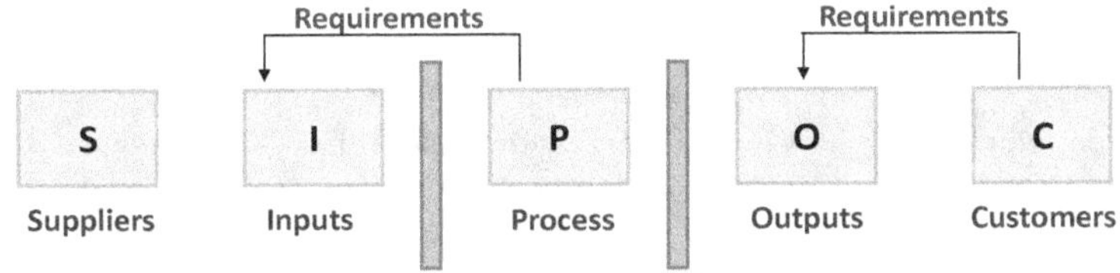

- **Suppliers**
  Provide the inputs to the process.
- **Inputs**
  Resources required by the process.
- **Input Requirements**
  What the process requires from the inputs (measurable, quantifiable).
- **Process**
  The activity that modifies or transforms the inputs into outputs.

- **Outputs**
  Resulting product or service.
- **Customers**
  Stakeholders who determine output requirements.
- **Output Requirements**
  What the customer expects and requires from the outputs (measurable, quantifiable).

SIPOC diagram procedure

1. Define the process and its boundaries.
2. Identify process outputs.
3. Identify customers for each output.
4. List the requirements for each output.
5. Identify the inputs.
6. Identify the supplier for each input.
7. List the requirements for each input.
8. Perform an analysis and form conclusions.

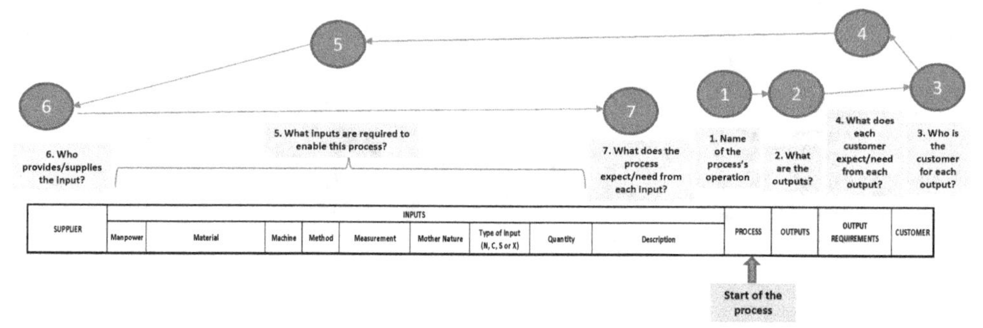

SUPPLIER	INPUTS									PROCESS	OUTPUTS	OUTPUT REQUIREMENTS	CUSTOMER
	Manpower	Material	Machine	Method	Measurement	Mother Nature	Type of Input (N, C, S or X)	Quantity	Description				

1. Define the process and its boundaries

Name the process

- Short, but descriptive.
- Should declare an action.
- Should encompass the entire process.

Identify process boundaries

- Make sure that the sponsor has control over the entire process.
- Make sure that the problem is within the process boundaries.
- Process boundaries define the scope of the improvement opportunity.

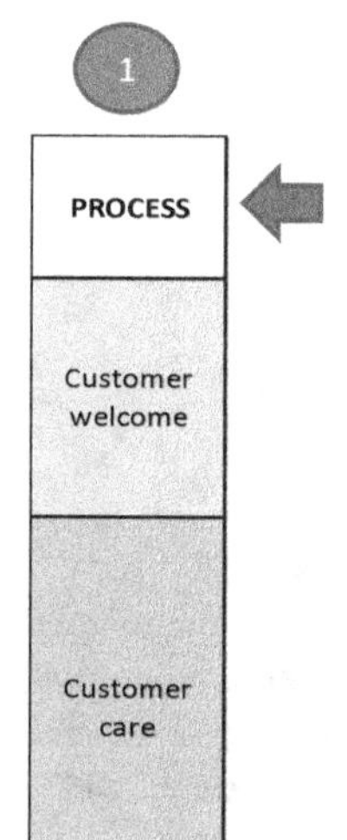

Example

James Roberts' improvement team at Bank of the Atlantic is drawing a SIPOC diagram for its customer care service at bank teller windows, and has identified two operations for the process:

2. Identify process outputs

- Make a list of what the process provides:
  - Product
  - Service
  - Documentation
  - Information
  - Waste (undesirable output)
- You must list current outputs (not desired or future outputs)...
- These are the Y's of the process.

PROCESS	OUTPUTS
Customer welcome	Instructions on where to request service
Customer care	Service provided

3. Identify customers for the outputs

- List the customers for the outputs established in step 2:
  - Can be internal or external customers
  - Can be different departments
  - Can be management
- Respective customers and outputs should be aligned horizontally.

PROCESS	OUTPUTS	OUTPUT REQUIREMENTS	CUSTOMER
Customer welcome	Instructions on where to request service		External customer
Customer care	Service provided		External customer

4. Identify customers requirements

- List the requirements of each customer for each output.

- Requirements should be:

  - Numerical

  - Specific

  - Quantitative

- Highlight a requirement when:

  - It is not being met

  - It doesn't exist

PROCESS	OUTPUTS	OUTPUT REQUIREMENTS	CUSTOMER
Customer welcome	Instructions on where to request service	Detailed instructions Less than 2 minutes	External customer
Customer care	Service provided	Less than 6 minutes	External customer

Listen to the voice of the customer

- **To obtain customer requirements...**

  - Observe how the product is used.
  - Use the product yourself.
  - Survey the customers or create focus groups.
  - What are the customers saying? What are they doing?

- **Be careful...**

  - Don't ask "yes" or "no" questions (too little information is obtained).
  - Don't assume that everyone will ask the same questions.

- **This is a continuous process...**

  - What are the customers' future needs?
  - Know your customers and market, as well as your current and future opportunities.

5. Identify the process inputs

- List what the process needs in order to generate the outputs.

- Should be nouns (not adjectives).

- Use the 6Ms to determine all high-level inputs.

    - **M**anpower
    - **M**aterials
    - **M**ethods
    - **M**easurements
    - **M**achine
    - **M**other Nature/Environment

INPUTS							
Manpower	Material	Machine	Method	Measurement	Mother Nature	Type of Input (N, C, S or X)	Quantity
Receptionist						N	1
	Instructions					S	1
		PC				S	1
			Procedure			S	1
Cashier						N	1
	Money					S	Sufficient
	Paper					S	Sufficient
		PC				S	1
		Registration				S	1
			Procedure			S	1

6. Identify suppliers for the inputs

- List the suppliers that provide the inputs to the process:

  - Can be internal or external suppliers.
  - Can be different departments.
  - Can be management.

- Respective suppliers and inputs should be aligned horizontally

  - Every input should have at least one supplier

SUPPLIER	INPUTS								
	Manpower	Material	Machine	Method	Measurement	Mother Nature	Type of Input (N, C, S or X)	Quantity	Requirements
Human Resources	Receptionist						N	1	
Process(es) Area		Instructions					S	1	
IT			PC				S	1	
Process(es) Area				Procedure			S	1	
Human Resources	Cashier						N	1	
Safe Box		Money					S	Sufficient	
Supplies		Paper					S	Sufficient	
IT			PC				S	1	
IT			Registration				S	1	
Process(es) Area				Procedure			S	1	

7. Identify input requirements

- List the process requirements for each input.

- The requirements should be:
  - Numerical
  - Specific
  - Quantitative

- Highlight a requirement when:
  - It is not being met
  - It doesn't exist

INPUTS								
Manpower	Material	Machine	Method	Measurement	Mother Nature	Type of Input (N, C, S or X)	Quantity	Requirements
Receptionist						N	1	2+ years of experience
	Instructions					S	1	Updated
		PC				S	1	Brand: HP
			Procedure			S	1	Updated
Cashier						N	1	2+ years of experience
	Money					S	Sufficient	Continuous replenishment
	Paper					S	Sufficient	Continuous replenishment
		PC				S	1	Brand: HP
		Registration				S	1	Brand: HP
			Procedure			S	1	Updated

8. SIPOC analysis

Identify the weaknesses in the SIPOC Diagram

- Missing input and/or output *requirements*
- Missing *customers*
- Missing *suppliers*
- *Unfulfilled* input and/or output requirements:
  - This includes requirements that aren't currently measured.
- Missing *inputs and/or outputs.*
- *Unclear connection* between:
  - Inputs and outputs
  - *Outputs and customers*
  - Suppliers and inputs

Highlight all weaknesses in the same SIPOC Diagram.

Determine the focus and objective:

- State which *weaknesses* the improvement opportunity will address.
- State which weaknesses will *not* be addressed and why.
- State the success *metric* of the improvement opportunity.

Determine:

- Process *owners*
- *Suppliers* affected
- *Customers* affected

SIPOC example

- SIPOC Diagram – Customer care at bank branch:

SUPPLIER	INPUTS						Type of Input (N, C, S or X)	Quantity	Requirements	PROCESS	OUTPUTS	OUTPUT REQUIREMENTS	CUSTOMER
	Manpower	Material	Machine	Method	Measurement	Mother Nature							
Human Resources	Receptionist						N	1	2+ years of experience				
Process(es) Area		Instructions					S	1	Updated	Customer welcome	Instructions on where to request service	Detailed instructions Less than 2 minutes	External customer
IT			PC				S	1	Brand: HP				
Process(es) Area				Procedure			S	1	Updated				
Human Resources	Cashier						N	1	2+ years of experience				
Safe Box		Money					S	Sufficient	Continuous replenishment				
Supplies		Paper					S	Sufficient	Continuous replenishment	Customer care	Service provided	Less than 6 minutes	External customer
IT			PC				S	1	Brand: HP				
IT			Registration				S	1	Brand: HP				
Process(es) Area				Procedure			S	1	Updated				

C. Cross-functional flowchart

Provides a graphical representation of the steps in a process, with an emphasis on interdepartmental relationships and responsibilities.

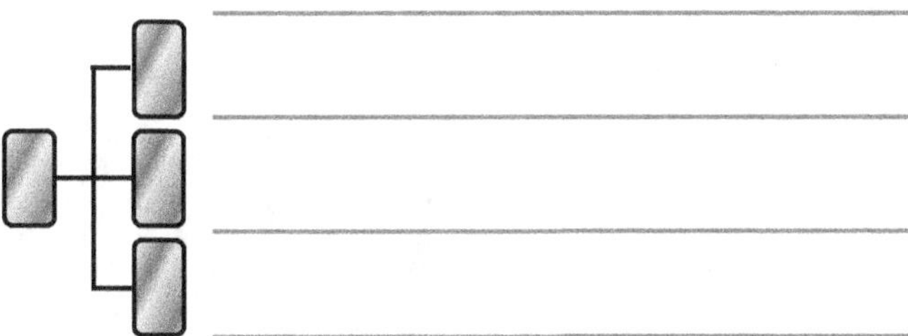

When is a cross-functional flowchart used?

- When you want to know the existing *relationships and responsibilities* between departments in a process.

- When you want to identify the *possible causes* of an existing problem between departments or individuals.

- When you want to *delineate and delegate* responsibilities to the areas involved in a process.

Cross-functional flowchart procedure

1. Identify the steps or activities in a process.

2. Define the person/people and/or department(s) responsible for the process.

3. Arrange the sequence of process activities according to the person/people and/or department(s) responsible with respect to time.

4. Validate the cross-functional flowchart.

LSSI
LEAN SIX SIGMA INSTITUTE

Cross-functional flowchart

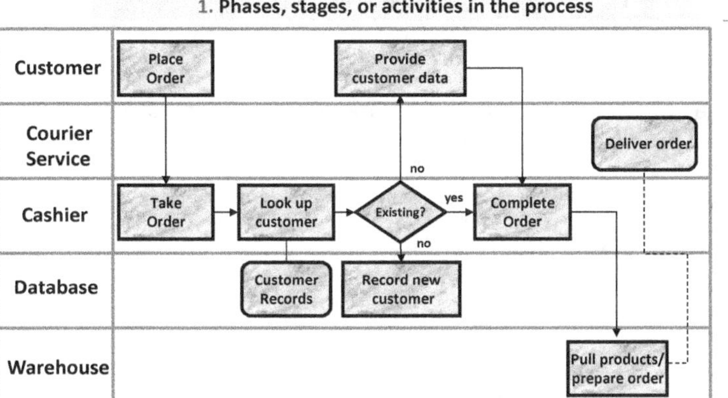

Common mistakes during process mapping

- Sources of variation were *not captured completely.*
  - Walk the process multiple times, during different shifts.
  - Consider all input variables.
  - What you think it is may be very different from what it actually is.

- Unidentified *hidden workplace.*
  - Undocumented process steps can be key variation entry points.

- Expected process *step outputs* that are *not clearly defined.*

Additional information

You may include the following to improve the Process Map, as well as your understanding of the process:

- Process observations:
  - The team's – as well as your own – observations of the process.
  - Operators' and process owners' observations.

- Pictures or diagrams to illustrate process steps
- Output data
- Input data
- Process data

If a process step needs to be described in more detail...

- Break it down and develop a detailed process map of that process step.

> **Exercise**

- Form teams.

- Each team should have a flipchart sheet and markers. As a team, build the type of process map indicated by the instructor for a specific process.

- Present your diagrams to the group.

Measurement System Analysis (MSA)

Data is only as good as the system that measures it

Objectives

1. Understand the terms and concepts of measurement systems.
2. Interpret the basic coefficients from an MSA study.
3. Develop an MSA study.

Content

> Background
> What is MSA?
> When is it used?
> Key concepts
> Procedure
> Examples
> Exercise

Background

"I often say that when you can measure what you are speaking about, and express it in numbers, you know something about it..." Lord Kelvin

- Lord Kelvin emphasized that, without precise measurements, there would be little progress in the various fields of science.

- Increases in knowledge are intrinsically related to increases in the precision of measurements.

Measurement System Evaluation

How good is our measurement system?

Can you detect these defects?

- Missed call from a customer.
- Lost paperwork.
- Error in an invoice form.
- Unplanned absences.
- Defective part/assembly.

- Accident at work.
- Data typing error.
- Wrong price list sent to customers.
- Missed or incomplete delivery to the customer.

Defect: A failure or nonconformity that causes a product or service to fail to meet customers' expectations or CTQs.

Inspection exercise

- A thorough inspection is not always 100% effective. To demonstrate the effectiveness of a visual inspection, determine the number of times the letter **f** appears in the following paragraph.

- Read the entire paragraph one time and simultaneously count the number of "fs."

> **Black holes stand at the very edge of scientific theory. Most scientists believe they exist, although many of their theories break down under the extreme conditions within. But Professor Cornelius Van Bockstein of the University of Ushuaia says he knows what you would find inside, and challenges the traditional idea that gravity would cause you death by "spaghettification."**

- Try again...

> **Black holes stand at the very edge of scientific theory. Most scientists believe they exist, although many of their theories break down under the extreme conditions within. But Professor Cornelius Van Bockstein of the University of Ushuaia says he knows what you would find inside, and challenges the traditional idea that gravity would cause you death by "spaghettification."**

Effectiveness of our system

What would be an acceptable degree of effectiveness for this exercise?
90%, 95%, 99% or more?

$$\% \text{ Effectiveness} = \frac{\text{Number of correct answers on an exam}}{\text{Total number of participants}}$$

Is this group an adequate measurement system?

What is MSA?

- Measurement system: Comprises the operations, procedures, gauges, instruments, equipment, software, and personnel required to obtain a measurement.

- Gauge: Device used to obtain a measurement.

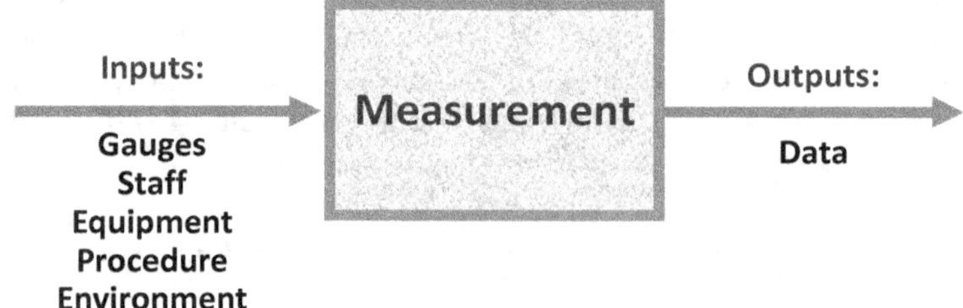

What is Measurement System Analysis (MSA)?

Measurement System Analysis (MSA) allows us to:

- **Identify and quantify** how much the different sources of variation contribute to the overall measurement system variability.

- **Identify the measurement error:** Measurement variation can be attributed to variation in what is being measured or the measurement system itself. Variation in the measurement system is considered a measurement error.

$$\sigma_T^2 = \sigma_P^2 + \sigma_M^2 + \varepsilon$$

Product Measurement Process
system Error

$$\sigma_M^2 = \sigma_O^2 + \sigma_E^2$$

Operator Equipment

Statistical properties

All measurement systems must possess the following statistical properties:

- Be in a state of statistical control (statistical stability).

- Its variability should be small relative to the specifications and process variation.

- Measurement increments should not be greater than 1/10 of the total tolerance (discrimination or resolution).

- Little bias.

When is it used?

- **When do we use measurement systems?**

  - When accepting new equipment.

  - When comparing equipment to each other.

  - When evaluating a suspicious caliper.

  - When evaluating a caliper before and after repairing it.

  - When starting to use control charts.

  - When process variation decreases.

  - Regularly, according to the frequency of measurements recommended by the study.

Key concepts

Components of a measurement system

- Accuracy

- Precision

- Discrimination (resolution)

- Stability (consistency)

- Repeatability and reproducibility

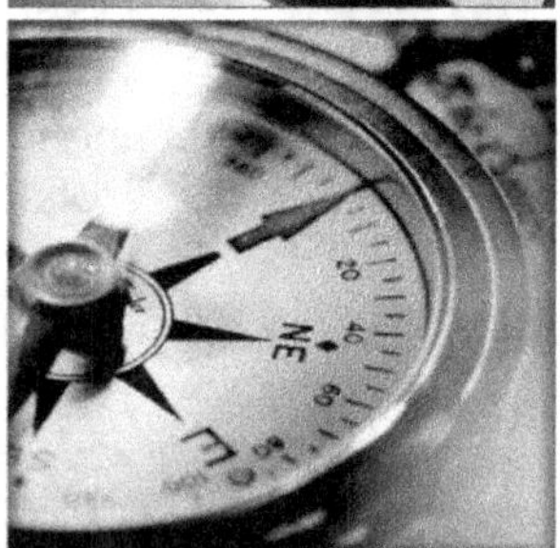

LSSI
LEAN SIX SIGMA INSTITUTE

Precision and accuracy

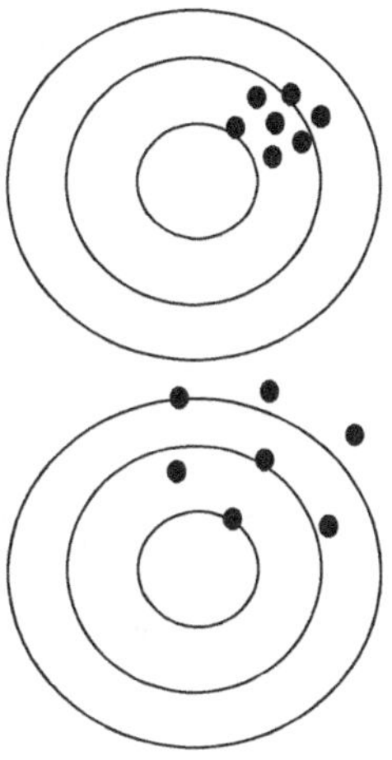

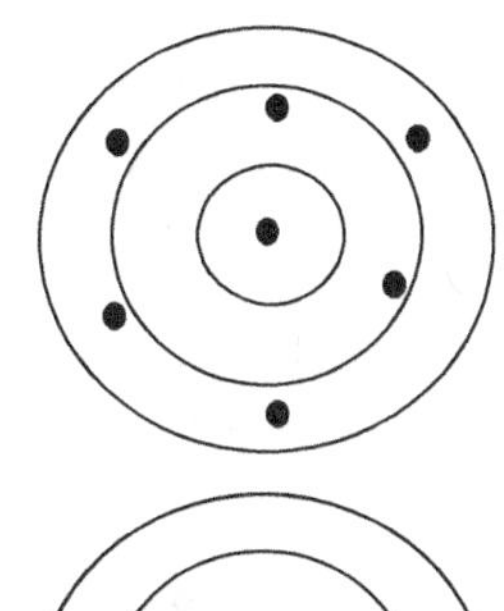

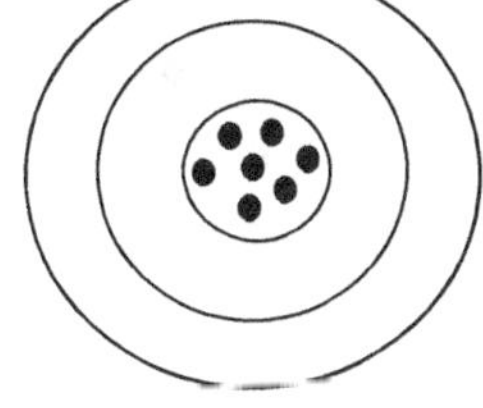

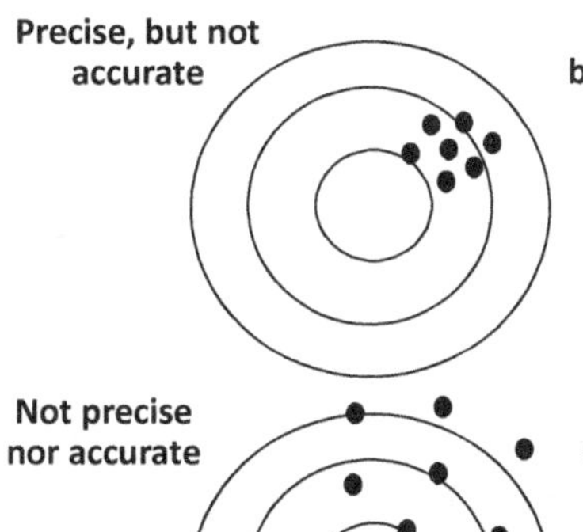

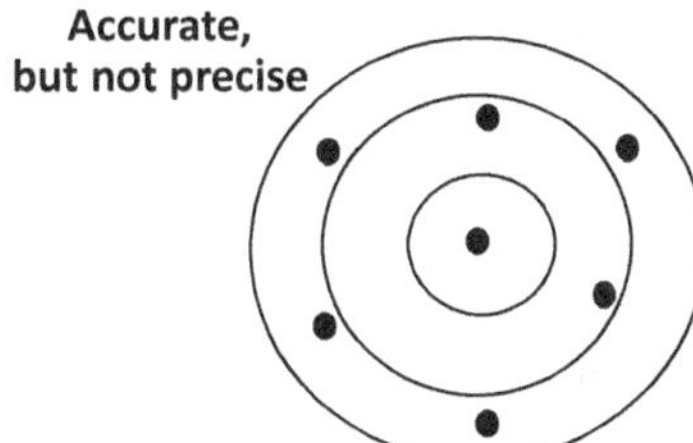

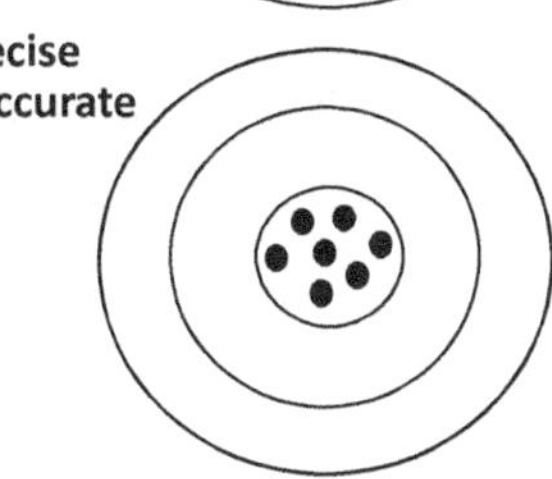

Accuracy

- Defined with respect to the closeness (bias) to the objective. The closer to the objective, the higher the degree of accuracy.

- It is the difference between the observed average of measurements and the reference or standard value.

- The reference value is known as a measurement standard.

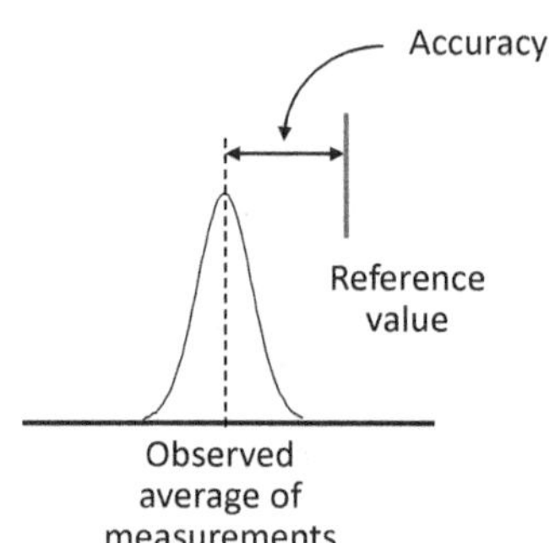

Precision

- The ability to obtain the same measurement results from different measurement systems when measuring a part.

- Precision is expressed in terms of standard deviations.

- Variation or dispersion of the measurements or events.

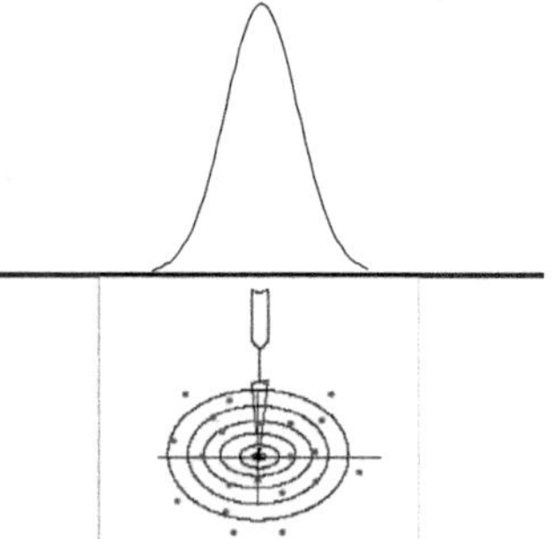

LSSI
LEAN SIX SIGMA INSTITUTE

Discrimination (resolution)

The ability of a measurement system to detect small changes in the characteristics being measured.

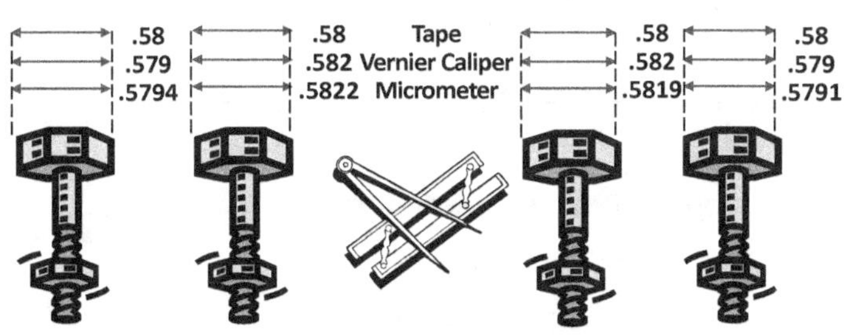

The resolution should be 1/10 the tolerance limits.
Example: If you want to measure up to ± 1 cm, then the instrument should be capable of measuring at least ± 0.1 cm.

Stability

Consistency of measurements over an extended period of time.

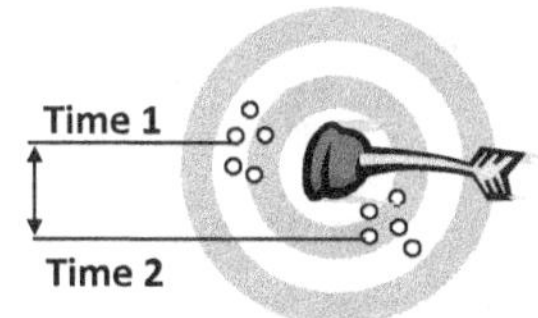

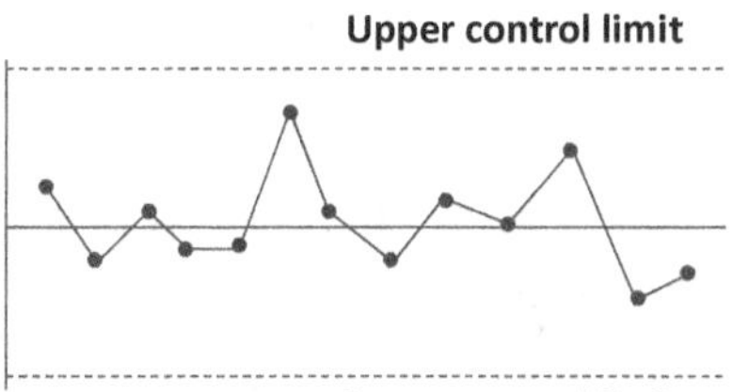

Process variance components

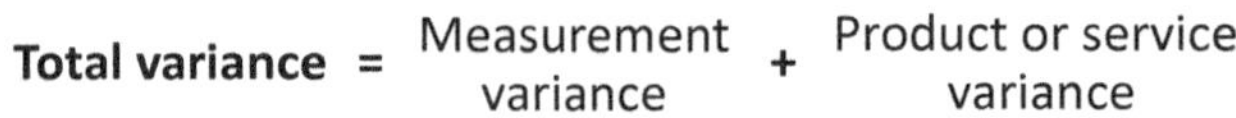

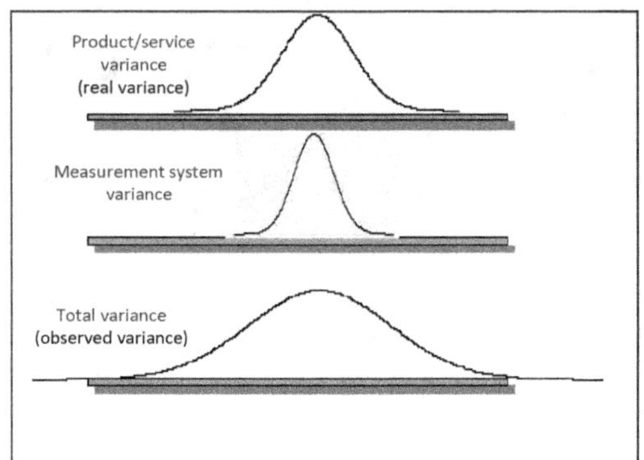

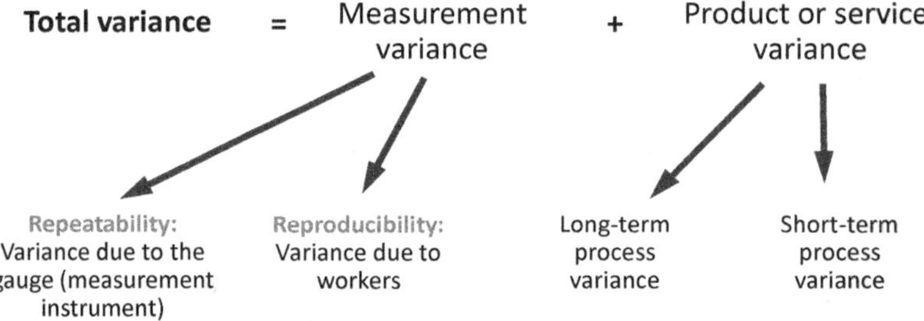

Repeatability and reproducibility

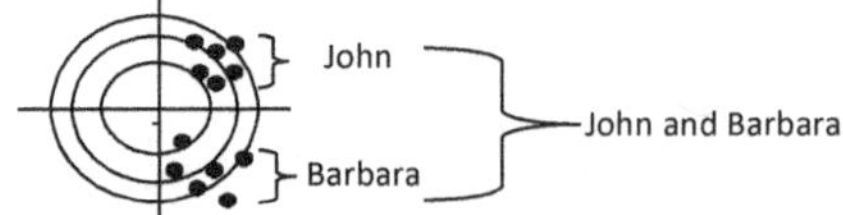

Gauge R&R (repeatability and reproducibility) study

- It is a statistical methodology to evaluate a measurement system.

- Basically, a measurement system is composed of:
  - The parts or items that will be measured
  - The measurement instrument
  - The individuals(s) who will perform the measurement

- Causes of variability are due to:
  - Variability between parts (process)
  - Variability between individuals
  - Variability of the measurement instrument

Repeatability

Repeatability is the variability obtained when one individual uses *one gauge* multiple times on the same characteristic of *one process or part*.

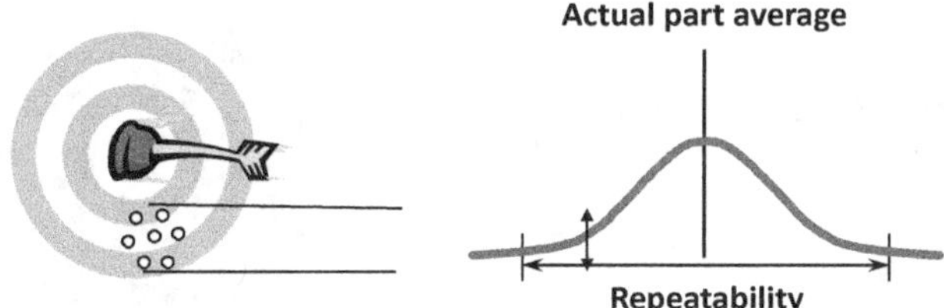

Reproducibility

Reproducibility is the variability in the average measurements due to *different individuals (e.g., employees)*, when using the *same gauge* on the same process or part.

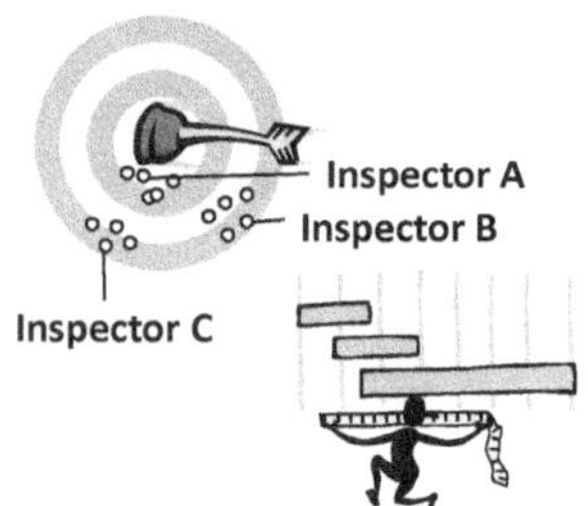

The difference between the average of the measurements

Types of MSA (R&R study)

- **Variable MSA (R&R study) for quantitative data**
  It is used to determine if the measurement instrument, the operators using it, and the process are adequate when measuring the same parts.

  - Numbers
  - Units

- **Attribute MSA (R&R study) for qualitative data**
  It is used to determine if the criteria of different operators is the same while inspecting or measuring a part, product, service, or document.

  - Subjective (cosmetic defects)
  - Inspection
  - Visual and tactile

LSSI
LEAN SIX SIGMA INSTITUTE

R&R study procedure (variable MSA – quantitative)

1. Calibrate the measurement instrument.

2. Select 10 items, parts, or services from the process that represent the specification's range of variation and number them from 1 to 10.

3. Select 2 to 3 appraisers to measure the parts at least twice in a random order.

4. Record results in the R&R spreadsheet and/or use statistical software.

5. Determine if the measurement system is capable.

R&R study interpretation (variable MSA – quantitative)

- **Less than or equal to 10% variation:** The measurement system is acceptable. The contribution of variation is small enough to make good decisions based on the measurements.

- **Between 10% and 30% variation:** The measurement system is marginal and may be acceptable, but the contribution of variation is starting to obscure the results. There is a significant risk in making a decision based on the measurements. Improve the system by training employees, standardizing procedures, or recalibrating or replacing the measurement instrument/equipment.

- **Over 30% variation:** The measurement system is unacceptable. You cannot make important decisions based on the measurements. Consider improving or replacing the system. Investigate the causes of inconsistencies.

R&R study procedure (attribute MSA – qualitative)

1. Select 5 to 10 **marginal** services or parts (that have been approved and rejected) and number them from 1 to 10.

2. Select another 5 to 10 services or parts that are evidently out of the specification range or defective.

3. Select the rest of the parts or services that are in good standing until gathering between 30 and 50 in total.

4. Select 2 to 3 appraisers to take measurements at least twice in a random order.

5. Record results in the R&R spreadsheet and/or use statistical software.

6. Determine if the measurement system is capable.

R&R study interpretation (attribute MSA – qualitative)

- The values of the degree of variation range from −1 to +1. The higher the result obtained, the stronger the consistency will be. When the result is consistently equal to 1, there is perfect achievement.

- The Minitab® support manual, based on AIAG,[1] suggests that a value of at least 0.75 indicates an appropriate match. However, values greater than 0.90 are ideally preferred.

[1] Automotive Industry Action Group (AIAG) (2010). *Measurement Systems Analysis Reference Manual*, 4th edition. Chrysler, Ford, General Motors Supplier Quality Requirements Task Force.

Example 1

Variable MSA (R&R) for quantitative data

- Juliana Wilson is conducting an R&R study in at **Chemical Manufacturing** in order to determine the reliability of the measurement system used for weighing the empty containers after the products have been packaged. For this task, she selected 10 containers with varied weights (within the specifications and slightly outside) and numbered them on the bottom. The specified range is between 0.600 and 1.000 kilograms.

- Juliana then provided the three inspectors who normally perform measurements (Sarah, Michael, and Edward) with the containers – in random order – on three different instances (at the beginning, middle and end of the work shift). She then recorded the weights obtained by each one of them on the following table:

Sample	Sarah			Michael			Edward		
	Test 1	Test 2	Test 3	Test 1	Test 2	Test 3	Test 1	Test 2	Test 3
1	0.650	0.600	0.650	0.650	0.600	0.650	0.650	0.600	0.650
2	1.000	1.000	0.950	1.050	0.950	1.000	1.050	1.000	0.950
3	0.850	0.800	0.850	0.800	0.750	0.800	0.800	0.800	0.850
4	0.850	0.950	0.900	0.850	0.950	0.900	0.850	0.950	0.900
5	0.550	0.450	0.500	0.550	0.450	0.500	0.550	0.450	0.500
6	1.000	1.000	0.950	1.000	1.050	1.000	1.000	1.000	1.050
7	0.950	0.950	0.950	0.950	0.900	0.900	0.950	0.950	0.900
8	0.850	0.800	0.850	0.850	0.800	0.850	0.850	0.800	0.900
9	1.000	1.000	1.000	1.000	0.950	1.000	1.000	1.000	0.950
10	0.600	0.700	0.650	0.600	0.650	0.550	0.700	0.700	0.650

- Lastly, Juliana used an Excel format (and verified her calculations using the Minitab software) to determine the values for repeatability, reproducibility, and total R&R, obtaining the following results:

	AVERAGE & RANGE	ANOVA
Repeatability	**23.52%**	**20.66%**
Reproducibility	2.16%	2.92%
Total R&R	**23.62%**	**20.87%**

Conclusion: Example 1

Variable MSA (R&R) for quantitative data

With this data, Juliana arrived at the following conclusions:

1. The measurement system is marginal: Total R&R = 20.87% (total R&R between 10% and 30%).

2. The operational process is acceptable, and operators are properly trained: Reproducibility is less than 10%.

Juliana then programmed the calibration of the instrument (scale), since repeatability is in the marginal category (between 10% and 30%). This means that it can continue to be used, but it requires revision. Once the scale was calibrated, she repeated the analysis and obtained acceptable values (less than 10%) for all three factors.

Example 2

Attribute MSA (R&R) for qualitative data

- Emily Walker from **Chelsea Footwear** recently began performing an R&R study to determine whether the criteria used by inspectors Ben and Cynthia is accurate in approving or rejecting shoes at the final step of the production process. For this study, Emily selected 10 samples graded by Richard, his supervisor and a certified inspector, and numbered each shoe sole. Four of these samples have no defects, and the remaining six do have marginal defects (e.g., a small glue stain, a loose thread, etc.).

- The study was carried out under normal operating conditions (inspection time, lighting, noise level, etc.). Emily provided both Ben and Cynthia with each sample twice (the first at the start of the workday, and the second near the end of the work shift) and recorded the results obtained by each.

- Emily then recorded the results of the study and analyzed them on an Excel file – as shown on the following table:

Study results:

Known Population		Ben		Cynthia	
Sample #	Criteria	Test #1	Test #2	Test #1	Test #2
1	Approved	Rejected	Rejected	Approved	Approved
2	Approved	Approved	Approved	Approved	Approved
3	Approved	Approved	Approved	Approved	Approved
4	Approved	Approved	Approved	Approved	Approved
5	Rejected	Rejected	Rejected	Rejected	Rejected
6	Rejected	Approved	Approved	Rejected	Rejected
7	Rejected	Rejected	Rejected	Rejected	Rejected
8	Rejected	Rejected	Rejected	Rejected	Rejected
9	Rejected	Rejected	Approved	Rejected	Rejected
10	Rejected	Rejected	Rejected	Rejected	Rejected

Note: For the purposes of this exercise, only 10 samples were taken – and not between 30 to 50, as is normally recommended for attribute or qualitative studies.

Analysis of results:

Source	% Appraiser[1]		%Score vs Attribute[2]	
	Ben	Cynthia	Ben	Cynthia
Total Inspected	10	10	10	10
# Matched	9	10	7	10
False Negative (operator biased toward rejection)			1	0
False Positive (operator biased toward acceptance)			1	0
Mixed			1	0
95% UCL	99.7%	100.0%	93.3%	100.0%
Calculated Score	**90.0%**	**100.0%**	**70.0%**	**100.0%**
95% LCL	55.5%	69.2%	34.8%	69.2%

	Screen % Effective Score[3]	Screen % Effective Score vs Attribute[4]
Total Inspected	10	10
# in Agreement	7	7
95% UCL	93.3%	93.3%
Calculated Score	**70.0%**	**70.0%**
95% LCL	34.8%	34.8%

Notes
(1) Operator agrees with him/herself on both trials
(2) Operator agrees on both trials with the known standard
(3) All operators agreed within and between themselves
(4) All operators agreed within & between themselves AND agreed with the known standard

Conclusion: Example 2

Attribute MSA (R&R) for qualitative data

- This analysis shows that Ben had a score of 90% (9 correct out of 10): On sample #9, he labeled the shoes as "Rejected" on the first inspection, but then as "Approved" on the second one. Moreover, Ben accumulated 3 inconsistencies, or "disagreements" with the known standard (score set by Richard the certified inspector) – hence a score of 70%.

- Sample #1 was graded by Richard as "Approved." Ben, however, rejected this sample in both inspections (false negative).

- Sample #6 was rated by Richard as "Rejected," whereas Ben approved it in both instances (false positive).

- Sample #9 reflects Ben having an inconsistency with his own inspection: he rejected the sample at first, but then eventually approved it.

- Cynthia, on the other hand, demonstrated acceptable inspection criteria – both with herself and the known standard. She attained a score of 100% on both inspections (10 correct out of 10).

- Based on these results, Emily and her team provided training for Ben until he acquired the skills needed to demonstrate acceptable inspection criteria. An additional R&R study was eventually performed, in which he obtained a score of 100%.

Exercise

Exercise

- **Form teams.**
- **Conduct a variable MSA (R&R study) for quantitative data.**
- **Conduct an attribute MSA (R&R study) for qualitative data.**

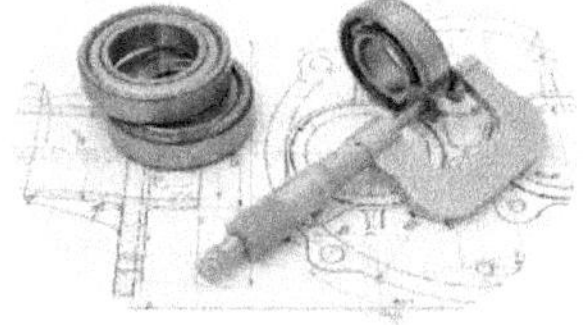

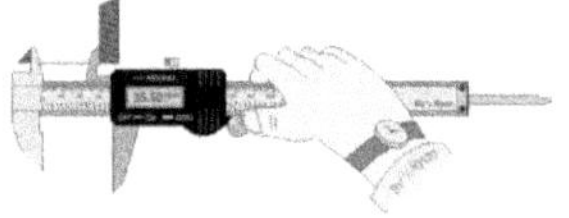

LSSI
LEAN SIX SIGMA INSTITUTE

Basic statistics

Listen to what data has to say

Objectives

1. Know the basic concepts of statistics.
2. Apply statistics to the development of Six Sigma projects.

Content

> Background
> What is statistics?
> Reasons to apply statistics
> Branches of statistics
> Properties of data
> Procedure
> Exercise

- Around the year 3000 B.C., the Babylonians used small clay tablets to collect data on agricultural production and these would later be sold or traded.

- In the 11th century B.C., the Egyptians analyzed their nation's income and population data long before they began to construct the pyramids.

- Around 594 B.C., the classical Greeks conducted censuses and used the information to collect taxes.

- The word "statistics" comes from the Latin words *statisticum collegium* (State Council) and its Italian derivative *statista* (man of the state or politician).

- The German term *Statistik* was first introduced by the German economist Gottfried Achenwall (1749), and referred to the analysis of the state's data.

- In the 19th century the term "statistics" acquired the meaning to collect and classify data and this concept was first introduced by the English economist and politician John Sinclair.

What is statistics?

- **Statistics** is the branch of mathematics that involves the collection, analysis, and interpretation of data.

- Some fields of application:
  - Physics
  - Social Sciences
  - Business
  - Quality
  - Government

Importance of statistics

Listen...

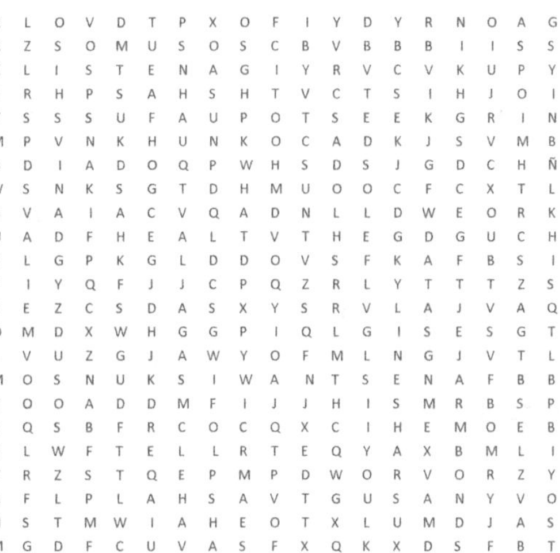

```
K L O V D T P X O F I Y D Y R N O A G
R Z S O M U S O S C B V B B B I I S S
K L I S T E N A G I Y R V C V K U P Y
S R H P S A H S H T V C T S I H J O I
T S S U F A U P O T S E E K G R I N
M P V N K H U N K O C A D K J S V M B
B D I A D O Q P W H S D S J G D C H Ñ
W S N K S G T D H M U O O C F C X T L
B V A I A C V Q A D N L L D W E O R K
U A D F H E A L T V T H E G D G U C H
Z L G P K G L D D O V S F K A F B S I
F I Y Q F J J C P Q Z R L Y T T T Z S
S E Z C S D A S X Y S R V L A J V A Q
O M D X W H G G P I Q L G I S E S G T
L V U Z G J A W Y O F M L N G J V T L
M O S N U K S I W A N T S E N A F B B
T O O A D D M F I J J H I S M R B S P
S Q S B F R C O C Q X C I H E M O E B
K L W F T E L L R T E Q Y A X B M L I
V R Z S T Q E P M P D W O R V O R Z Y
A F L P L A H S A V T G U S A N Y V O
H S T M W I A H E O T X L U M D J A S
M G D F C U V A S F X Q K X D S F B T
```

Learn to listen data

Listen...

K	L	O	V	D	T	P	X	O	F	I	Y	D	Y	R	N	O	A	G
R	Z	S	O	M	U	S	O	S	C	B	V	B	B	B	I	I	S	S
K	L	I	S	T	E	N	A	G	I	Y	R	V	C	V	K	U	P	Y
S	R	H	P	S	A	H	S	H	T	V	C	T	S	I	H	J	O	I
T	S	S	U	F	A	U	P	O	T	S	E	E	K	G	R	I	N
M	P	V	N	K	H	U	N	K	O	C	A	D	K	J	S	V	M	B
B	D	I	A	D	O	Q	P	W	H	S	D	S	J	G	D	C	H	Ñ
W	S	N	K	S	G	T	D	H	M	U	O	O	C	F	C	X	T	L
B	V	A	I	A	C	V	Q	A	D	N	L	L	D	W	E	O	R	K
U	A	D	F	H	E	A	L	T	V	T	H	E	G	D	G	U	C	H
Z	L	G	P	K	G	L	D	D	O	V	S	F	K	A	F	B	S	I
F	I	Y	Q	F	J	J	C	P	Q	Z	R	L	Y	T	T	T	Z	S
S	E	Z	C	S	D	A	S	X	Y	S	R	V	L	A	J	V	A	Q
O	M	D	X	W	H	G	G	P	I	Q	L	G	I	S	E	S	G	T
L	V	U	Z	G	J	A	W	Y	O	F	M	L	N	G	J	V	T	L
M	O	S	N	U	K	S	I	W	A	N	T	S	E	N	A	F	B	B
T	O	O	A	D	D	M	F	I	J	J	H	I	S	M	R	B	S	P
S	Q	S	B	F	R	C	O	C	Q	X	C	I	H	E	M	O	E	B
K	L	W	F	T	E	L	L	R	T	E	Q	Y	A	X	B	M	L	I
V	R	Z	S	T	Q	E	P	M	P	D	W	O	R	V	O	R	Z	Y
A	F	L	P	L	A	H	S	A	V	T	G	U	S	A	N	Y	V	O
H	S	T	M	W	I	A	H	E	O	T	X	L	U	M	D	J	A	S
M	G	D	F	C	U	V	A	S	F	X	Q	K	X	D	S	F	B	T

- To develop improvement projects.

- To better *understand* data and use it as information to *make impactful decisions*.

- To know when to perform actions to adjust a process that has gone out of control.

- To analyze and summarize a process in order to understand it in detail.

- To understand the amount of variation in any process.

LSSI
LEAN SIX SIGMA INSTITUTE

Statistics today

- Today, the use of statistics has been extended beyond its original use for government applications.

- People and organizations apply statistics to understand data and make informed decisions in various areas such as natural sciences, social sciences, medicine and business.

The role of statistics in Six Sigma

We use the science of statistics to understand variation

- Stated in more accurate terms, we use statistical methods and tools to effectively determine $Y = f(x)$ and the amount of expected variation around that Y.

- We will transform the data from a random and diverse state to an organized state:

  - Quantify the Ys.

- Quantify the cause-effect relationships:

  - Quantify the effect of the Xs on the Ys.

- Inferential measurement tools.

- Confidence in the influence of the Xs over time.

Branches of statistics

Descriptive statistics:

- Data collection
- Description
- Visualization
- Data summary (numerical or graphical)

Inferential statistics:

- Statistical models
- Inferences
- Predictions / Forecasts

Properties of data

Two important properties of data

Any group of data collected has two important properties:

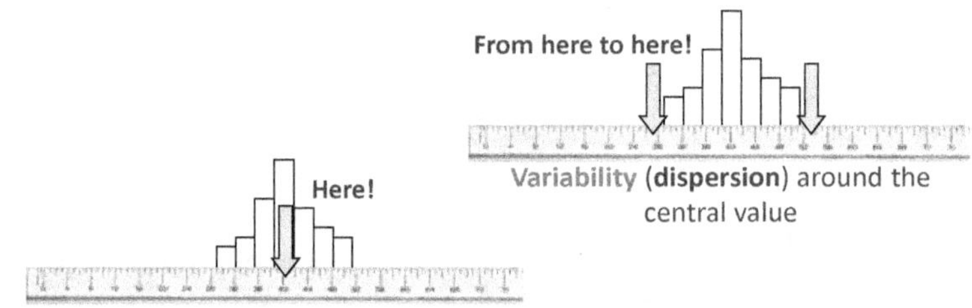

Measures of central tendency

If you want to describe a population or sample with one number, which one would you use?

- Mean: Arithmetic average
- Mode: Most frequent data value
- Median: Center point of the data set

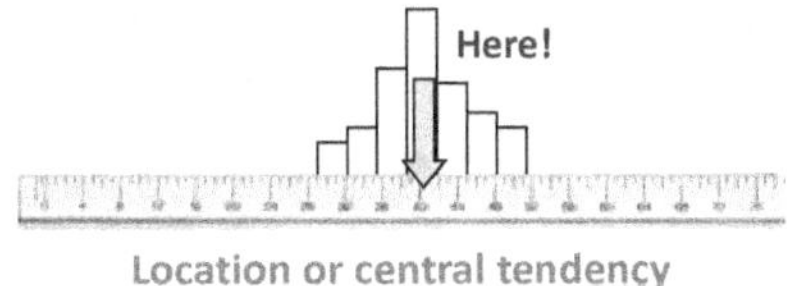

Location or central tendency

Example: The data represents students' grades in a statistics course are 64, 88, 66, 82, 68, 68, 70, 78, 76, 80, 90. Calculate:

Mean (average):

$$\overline{X} = \frac{\sum_{i=1}^{n} X_i}{n} = \frac{(64+88+66+82+68+68+70+78+76+80+90)}{11} = 75.5$$

Median:

64 66 68 68 70 (76) 78 80 82 88 90

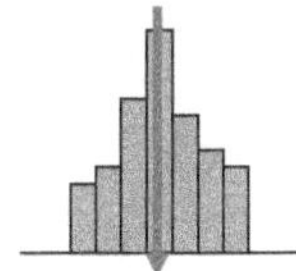

Mode:

68 is the most frequently occurring data point.

Measures of variability

- **Range:** Measure of variability of a data set, calculated by subtracting the lowest data value from the highest data value.

- **Standard deviation:** The most common variability measurement that indicates how scattered the data is with respect to its mean.

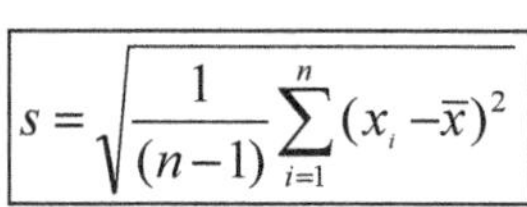

$$s = \sqrt{\frac{1}{(n-1)}\sum_{i=1}^{n}(x_i - \bar{x})^2}$$

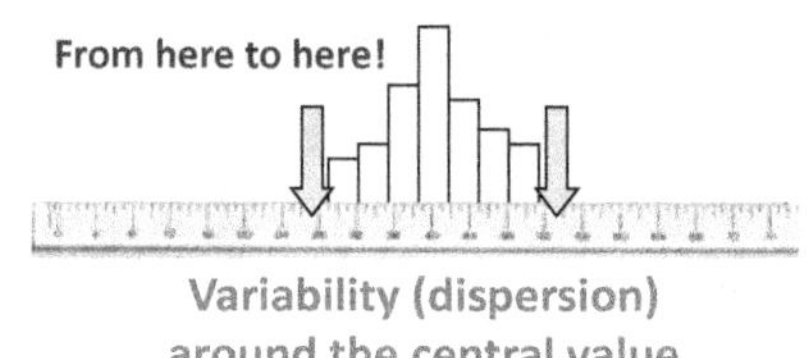

Variability (dispersion)
around the central value

- **Variance:** Standard deviation squared.

Example: The data represents students' grades in a statistics course are 64, 88, 66, 82, 68, 68, 70, 78, 76, 80, 90. Calculate:

Range: R = (90 - 64) = **26**

Standard deviation:

$$S = \sqrt{\frac{\sum_{i=1}^{n}(x_i - \bar{x})^2}{n-1}} = \sqrt{\frac{(64-75.5)^2 + (88-75.5)^2 + \ldots + (90-75.5)^2}{11-1}} = \textbf{8.94}$$

Variance:

$$s^2 = \frac{\sum_{i=1}^{n}(x_i - \bar{x})^2}{n-1} = \textbf{80.07}$$

LSSI
LEAN SIX SIGMA INSTITUTE

Statistics: applicable fields

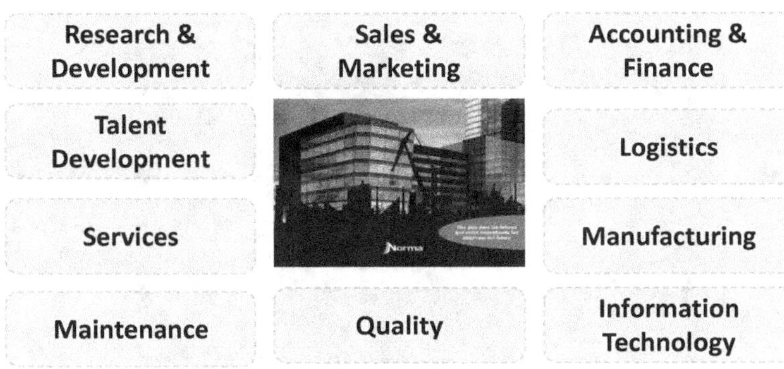

Research & Development

Sales & Marketing

Accounting & Finance

Talent Development

Logistics

Services

Manufacturing

Maintenance

Quality

Information Technology

Wherever there is a process, there is data.
The secret is to transform data into information to make better decisions.

Concepts of variation

Principle 1: No object is identical to another.

Variation is *everywhere!!!* And *in everything!!!*

Principle 2: Variations exists in two states of control:

In control: Known as common cause. It is a pattern of stable or consistent variation throughout time (predictable).

Out of control: Known as special cause. It is a pattern that changes over time (unpredictable).

> To control and reduce variation in a process, you should first understand, quantify, and interpret the variation.

Types of variation

The usual, historical, and quantifiable variation in a system.

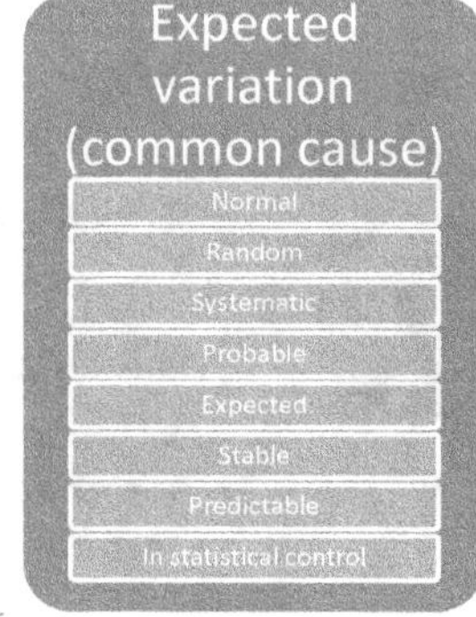

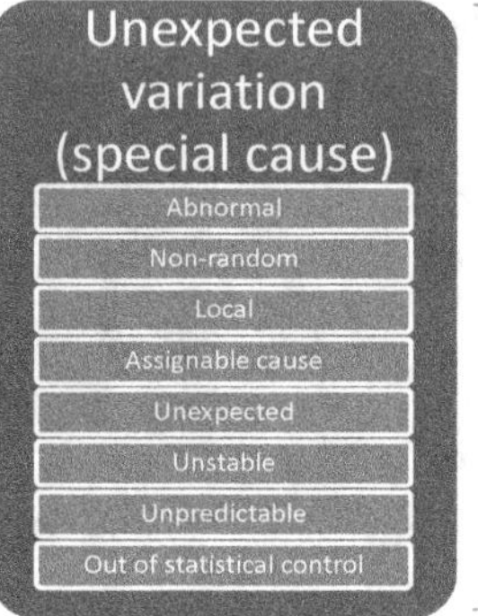

The unusual, non-quantifiable, and previously not observed variation.

Immediate goal: Eliminate the unexpected variation.
Long-term goal: Continuously reduce variation.

Our goal is to reduce variation

- The first step towards making better decisions is to understand that all systems and processes have common cause variation.

- We must also understand that most systems and processes have special cause variation and the effects caused by adjustments or attempts made to decrease it.

- How should we approach variation and reduce it to improve our processes?

  - Measure and analyze sources of variation.
  - Make appropriate improvements to systems/processes.
  - Control and maintain process improvements at the source.

Tree ways to reduce variation

- **Stratification:** Classifying and analyzing data according to the distinct sources where they come from (e.g., equipment, batches, suppliers, shifts, customer segments, etc.)

- **Experimentation:** Deliberate and carefully planned changes are made, and the results are recorded. This process is done until the optimal point or level is reached.

- **Sub-grouping:** Dividing a process into its sub-processes to conduct a more in-depth and detailed analysis, as well as analyzing the systemic relationship between the different sub-processes.

Sources of variation

- Remember, variation exists EVERYWHERE!!!
- What are the causes for variation? To find them, we use the 6Ms – a simple acronym that reminds us where to look for sources of variation.

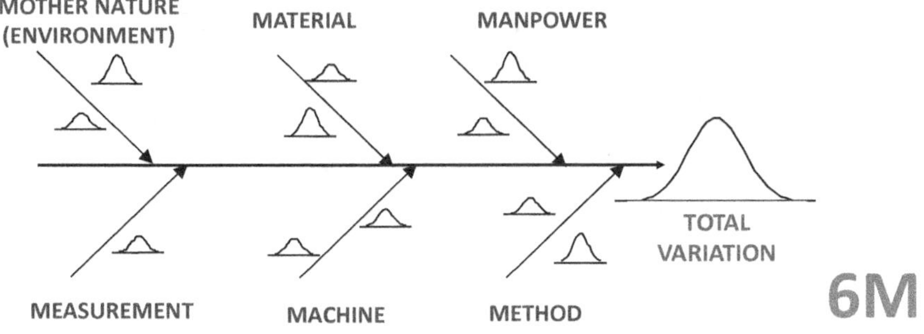

Normal distribution

- Processes produce results that have distributions.
- A distribution has three distinct properties:

    1. Shape
    2. **Central location**
    3. Variation or dispersion

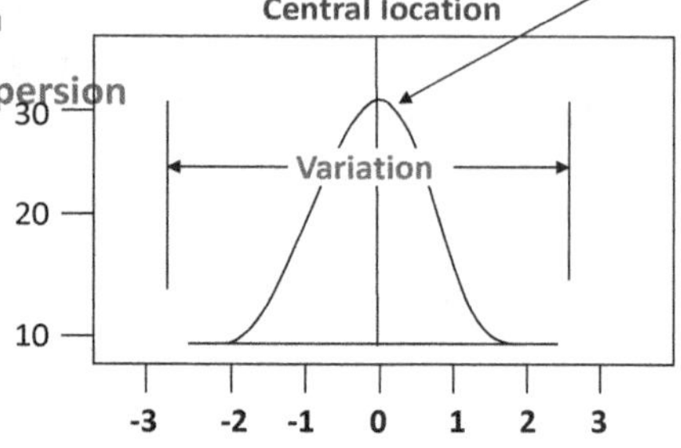

Normal distribution is common in nature, business, and industry.

Many statistical tools used are based on the assumption that data follows a normal distribution.

- Most data sets tend to follow a normal distribution, or bell-shaped curve.

    - One of the key properties of the normal distribution is the relationship between the shape of the curve and the standard deviation.

- 99.7% of the area under the normal distribution is within -3 sigma and +3 sigma measured from the mean.

    - The 3 sigma limits define the limits of the expected behavior of the process.

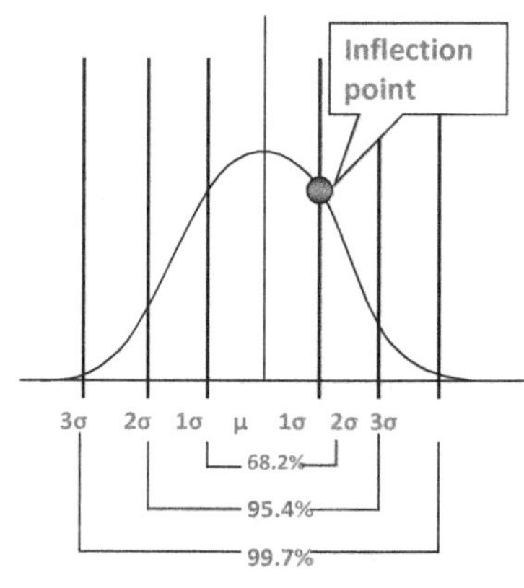

What do we mean by a 3σ process?

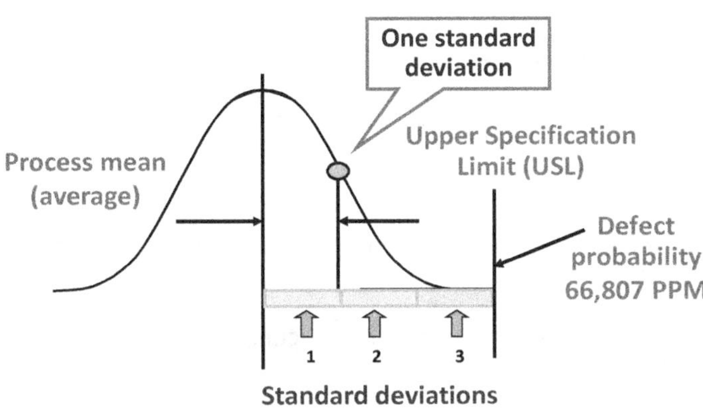

What do we mean by a 6σ process?

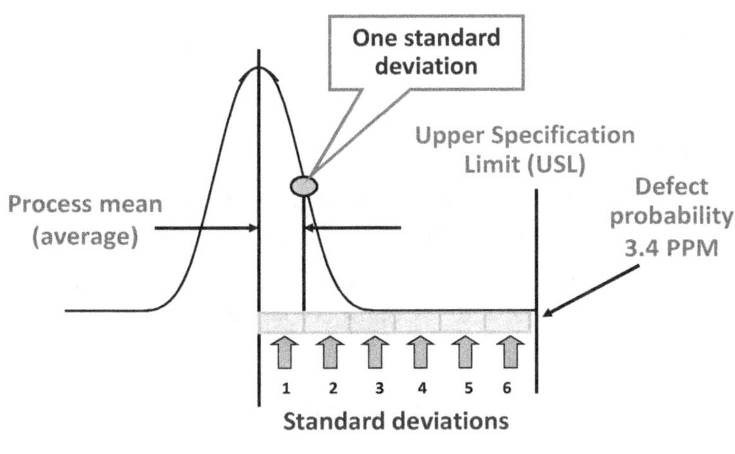

Procedure

1. Decide what event or problem will be observed.

2. Decide when the data will be collected and for how long.

3. Design the form. Set it up so that the data can be recorded simply by making checkmarks ☑ or **"X"** symbols so the data does not have to be collected for analysis.

4. Label all the spaces in the form.

5. Test the control sheet for a short trial period to make sure it collects the appropriate data and is easy to use.

6. Each time the event or objective problem occurs, record the data on the verification sheet.

Exercise

LSSI airplane production:

1. Form two to four teams with an equal or similar number of members for each.

2. Each team must design an airplane model; make sure that each model is different from rest.

3. Once the instructor has approved all models, each team will build ten airplanes of its own model.

   Note: It is very important for each model to have its own unique name, and for each airplane to portray the number and color that represents its team.

4. Select participants from each team to randomly throw an equal number of airplanes in the air, and measure the distance traveled.

5. Capture data and obtain the:

   * Maximum, minimum, mean, mode, median, standard deviation, and range.

Sampling

Data is critical for all projects

Objectives

1. Understand the basic concepts of sampling.
2. Develop sampling in processes and projects.
3. Learn the procedure to perform samplings in any process of the company (sales, marketing, quality, service, human resources, etc.).

Content

> Background
> What is sampling?
> What is it used for?
> Types of sampling
> When is it used?
> Procedure
> Examples
> Exercises

Background

- In Lean Six Sigma, data is the *basis* for *decision* making.

- Data collection has to be as *clear and simple* as possible to prevent errors.

- The following are common areas for mistakes during data collection:

Measurement: Procedure, instrument, calibration.

Operational: Failure to follow instructions, including missing data and deliberate errors.

Influence by interaction: The act of measuring something can impact the performance of the operation.

Perception: The person who records the data tends to see what they want to see.

Sampling: The data collected does not represent the entire process.

Concepts

- **Variable:** Characteristic that has a different value for each element of the population.

Types:

Qualitative data:

- Category: e.g., colors
- Hierarchy: e.g., size

Quantitative data:

- Discrete: count, proportion, or percentage (1, 2, 3...)

- Continuous: any variable measures on a scale (5 inches, 100°F, 5.80 lbs)

- **Population:** Total number of elements with a common characteristic from which we seek to obtain information.

- **Unit:** An individual member of a population.

- **Sample:** Representative portion of a population used to obtain information about the same population.

- **Sample size:** List of units from which the sample is taken.

- **Parameters:** Characteristics expressed as numerical values that help to describe a set of elements or individuals.

- **Statistic:** Measurement or calculation obtained from a set of data in order to understand Its most relevant characteristics.

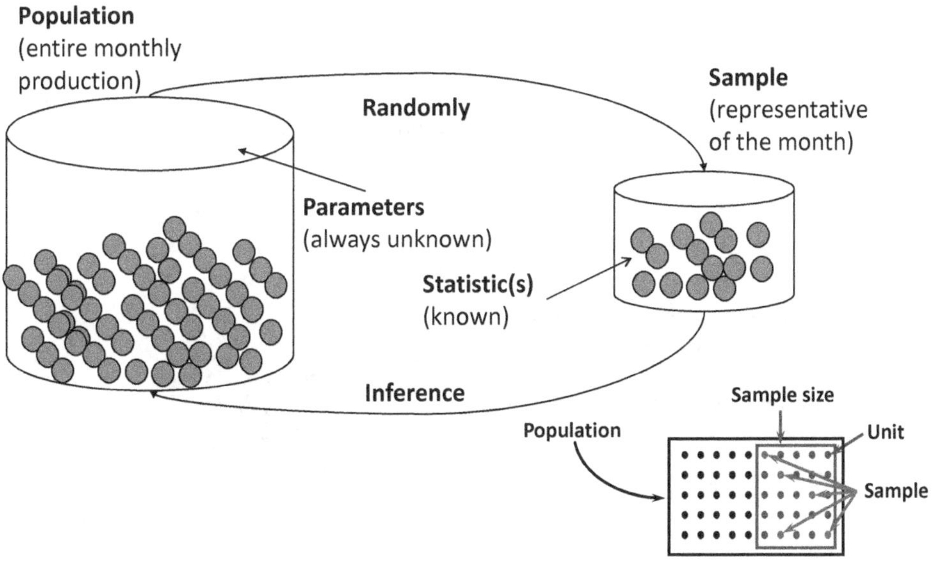

Sampling

What is sampling?

It is a technique used to select a sample from a statistical population.

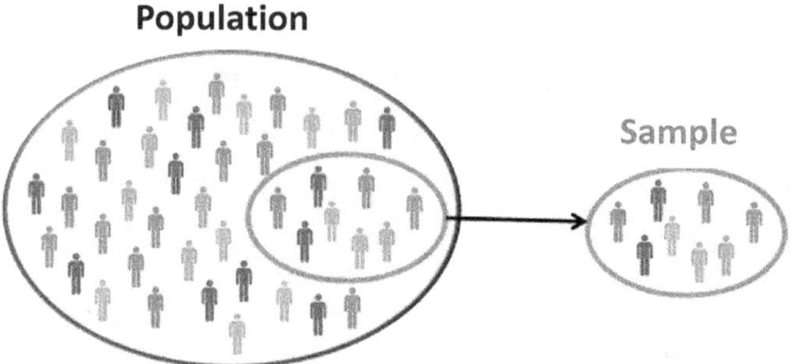

What is it used for?

- It allows a considerable reduction of the cost and the time when analyzing only a part of the data and with it being able to make improvements in the process.

- It helps us to understand the behavior of a population or data universe with only a fraction of them.

  - **100% testing is very expensive and time-consuming.**

  - **Sampling saves time and money.**

Types of sampling

1
- Random
- Systematic

2
- Stratified
- Subgroup

Random sampling

- Used when the variation is equal across all samples of **n** experimental units.

- Characteristics:

  - *Random: Each unit has the same chance of being selected.*

  - *Independent: The selection of an experimental unit is not dependent on the selection of any other unit.*

Example: Selecting a number of bottles randomly from a case.

Systematic sampling

- Systematic sampling starts with the random selection of a unit and then a sample is taken every *n* units.

  Example: The beverage company has only one final packaging line. A bottle is selected at random at the beginning of the shift and from that point on a bottle is taken every 50 bottles.

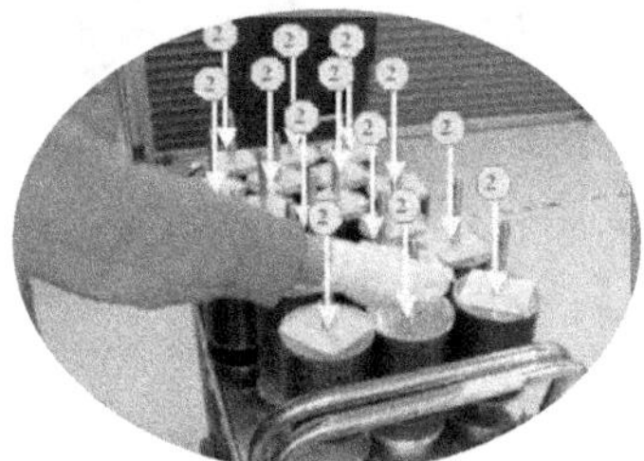

Stratified sampling

- Divide the population into homogenous strata or groups and randomly sample a proportionate number of units from each group.
- There is more variation between groups than within a group.

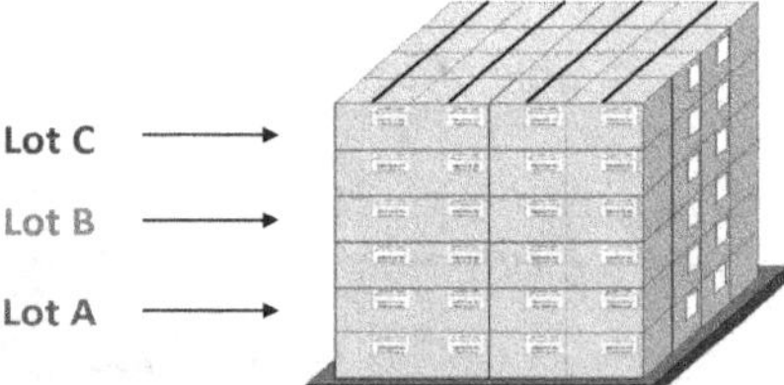

Example: The beverage company only has two packaging lines for the same product.

- Randomly select samples from each line.
- Helps estimate the effects of each packaging line on the variability of the packaged bottles.

LSSI
LEAN SIX SIGMA INSTITUTE

Subgroup sampling

- Subgroups that are very similar to each other.

- There is more variation within the subgroup than between the subgroups, i.e. the variability within the subgroup is very similar to the population's.

- It is recommended to take a subgroup and sample all or randomly select elements of the subgroup.

Census

- When the task of collecting data from the sample universe is beyond the scope of the team.

- When there is limited and resources to collect data.

Procedure

1. Determine what to measure.

2. Identify the sources of information.

3. Prepare the sampling plan and data collection sheet(s).

1. Determine what to measure

- Identify a defect (related to the customer) and its process output.

- Write a list of questions related to the defect.

- Identify stratification factors (what patterns or trends can we see?).

- Define specific data or metrics that will be collected (similar to a CTQ Tree).

- Evaluate what data should be collected.

- Select the most significant data (Measurement Assessment Tree).

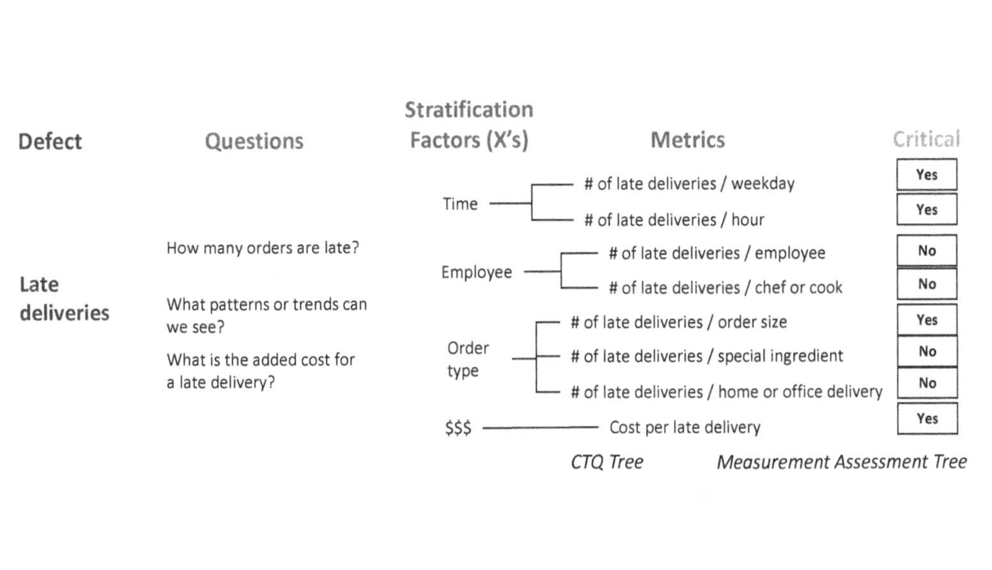

2. Identify the sources of information

- Existing sources (historical data)

- New sources of information

Validation

3. Prepare sampling plan and collection data sheet(s)

- Determine:
  - Sample size
  - Sampling frequency

Discrete data

Continuous data

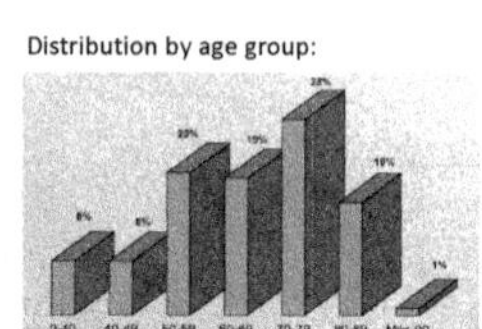

Discrete data

Discrete Data Sampling Plan

1.- Initial information

a) What is going to be counted?   Units = ______________________

b) What is the population size?   N = __________

c) What is the measurement characteristic (e.g., defects)?   Characteristic = ______________________

d) What proportion of the population do you estimate has this characteristic (e.g., defect)?   p = __________

e) What is the precision of this estimate (proportion in decimals)?   +/- d = __________

f) Select the confidence level:
(z = 1.64 for a 90% confidence level)
(z = 1.96 for a 95% confidence level)   z = __________

2.- Select the sampling method

☐ Random   ☐ Systematic

3.- Determine the sample size

$$n = p(1-p) / (d/z)^2$$

n = __________

4.- Determine the sampling frequency

Frequency = __________

5.- Adjust for a finite population

a) Determine the proportion of the sample with respect to the population   n / N = __________

b) If n/N is greater than 0.05, adjust the answer using the following formula: n / (1+ n/N) = __________

Continuous data

Continuous Data Sampling Plan

1.- Initial Information

a) What is being measured?   Units = ___________________________

b) What is the size of the population?   N = __________

c) What is the measurement characteristic?   Characteristic = ___________________________

d) What is the standard deviation of the estimated population?   s = __________

e) What is the precision of the estimate (same units)?   +/- d = __________

f) Select the confidence level:
(z = 1.64 for a 90% confidence level)
(z = 1.96 for a 95% confidence level)   z = __________

2.- Select the sampling method

☐ Random   ☐ Systematic

3.- Determine the sample size

$$n = (zs/d)^2$$

n = __________

4.- Determine the sampling frequency

Frequency = __________

5.- Adjust for a finite population

a) Determine the proportion of the sample with respect to the population   n / N = __________

b) If n/N is greater than 0.05, adjust the answer using the following formula: n / (1+ n/N) = __________

Data collection sheet

- A data collection sheet, in its different forms, is a tool to manage the collection of information in a reliable way so that the data can later be used with more sophisticated tools to define actions that need to be taken.

Types:

1. Data collection sheet
2. Location check sheet

- General information input on all data sheets:

  - Date data was collected
  - Person responsible for collecting the data
  - Measurement equipment/tool used

1. Data collection sheet

Continuous or measurable data

Used to record elements such as operating times, diameters, lengths, temperatures, etc.

Date: February 5th, 2020
Branch: 2035 San Diego   Responsible: James Roberts

Hour	Window	No. of Transactions	Customer Care Time (min)
08:30	1	1	3.45
08:32	5	1	2.17
08:34	3	3	10.50
08:36	5	5	17.10
08:38	1	1	7.55
08:40	7	5	15.00

Discrete data

It is used in cases where the information that you want to register is data that does not have a measurement scale and therefore, a count needs to be established. For example: add record of customer complaints, absenteeism, etc.

Date: February 24th, 2020
Branch: Emergency Department   Responsible: Diana Fletcher

Patient Category	Count	Frequency	Total Accumulated
A			
B	I	1	1
C	II	2	3
D	IIII	4	7
E	卌 II	7	14
F	卌 卌	10	24

2. Location check sheet

The Location Check Sheet or Defect Concentration Diagram includes graphical elements such as planes, diagrams, drawings and even illustrations to indicate the specific location of defects, errors or problem areas.

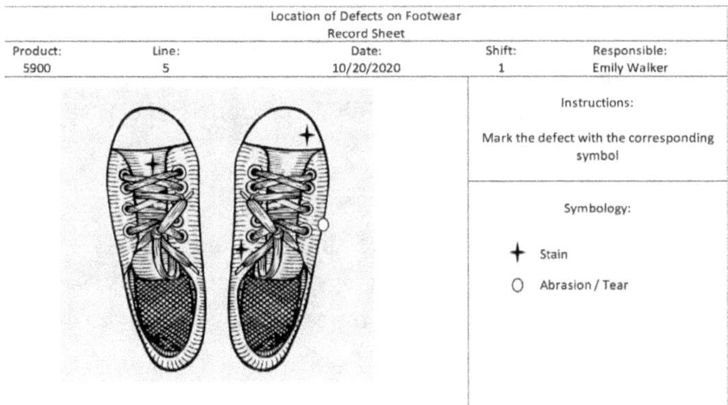

Location of Defects on Footwear Record Sheet				
Product:	Line:	Date:	Shift:	Responsible:
5900	5	10/20/2020	1	Emily Walker

Instructions:

Mark the defect with the corresponding symbol

Symbology:

+   Stain

O   Abrasion / Tear

Sampling plan

Example	Measurement	Stratification Factors	Operational Definition	Sample Size	Source of Information	Collection Method	Who Collects the Data
A - Bank of the Pacific	Customer care time at bank teller window	Only between 1 and 5 transactions	Customer care time in minutes	1 customer for each 25 that enter the branch (235 in total per week)	Chronometer	Data collection sheet	Continuous improvement engineer
B - Logistics Company	Fulfilled and timely order	Only standard orders	Fulfilled and timely order	15 orders per day (339 per month)	Delivery sheet	Data collection sheet	Billing employee
C - Chemical Manufacturing	Net packaged weight	None	Weight of each package in kilograms	1 package every 6 minutes (81 samples per lot)	Weighing machine (in grams)	Data collection sheet	Package inspector
D - Chelsea Footwear	Designs that are timely and within budget	Only designs for adults	Designs that are timely and within budget	35 designs per season	Management	Data collection sheet	General manager

Example 1

Discrete sample

Paul Evans's team at **Logistics Company** wants to define the number of deliveries to sample in one month in order to determine whether each was late or incomplete. Based on historical data, it is estimated that approximately 400 orders are delivered in a month, and around 9% of these are delivered late (accuracy of ± 1%). A 90% confidence level is selected for the measurement.

- We can observe that – since the proportion of late deliveries is very small – the sample size is high. Even the initial calculation is larger than the population. The adjusted calculation indicates that 339 of the 400 orders must be sampled.

<table>
<tr><td colspan="2" align="center">Discrete Data Sampling Plan</td></tr>
<tr><td colspan="2">1.- Initial Information</td></tr>
<tr><td>a) What is going to be counted?</td><td>Units = <u>Orders</u></td></tr>
<tr><td>b) What is the population size?</td><td>N = <u>400</u></td></tr>
<tr><td>c) What is the measurement characteristic (e.g., defects)?</td><td>Characteristic = <u>Late deliveries</u></td></tr>
<tr><td>d) What proportion of the population do you estimate has this characteristic (e.g., defect)?</td><td>p = <u>0.09</u></td></tr>
<tr><td>e) What is the precision of this estimate (proportion in decimals)?</td><td>+/- d = <u>0.01</u></td></tr>
<tr><td>f) Select the confidence level:
(z = 1.64 for a 90% confidence level)
(z = 1.96 for a 95% confidence level)</td><td>z = <u>1.64</u></td></tr>
<tr><td colspan="2">2.- Select the sampling method

☐ Random   ☐ Systematic</td></tr>
<tr><td colspan="2">3.- Determine the sample size

$n = p(1-p) / (d/z)^2$ n = <u>2203</u>   Use value from section 5</td></tr>
<tr><td colspan="2">4.- Determine the sampling frequency

Frequency = <u>   </u></td></tr>
<tr><td colspan="2">5.- Adjust for a finite population

a) Determine the proportion of the sample with respect to the population   n / N = <u>5.506956</u>
b) If n/N is greater than 0.05, adjust the answer using the following formula: n / (1+ n/N) = <u>339</u>   This is the correct value</td></tr>
</table>

Example 2

Continuous sample

Juliana Wilson's improvement team at **Chemical Manufacturing** wants to define the number of packages to sample in one lot order to determine if the packages meet weight specifications and root causes (if they do not). Based on historical data, it is estimated that approximately 3,200 products are packaged in one lot. The standard deviation is 0.458 ± 0.100. The team selected a 95% confidence level for the measurement.

- The improvement team has to sample 81 packages per lot in order to determine the real standard deviation as a basis for defining its root causes (in the **analysis phase)** and subsequent corrective actions (during the **improve phase).**

- Once the sample size has been determined, the team can define the sampling frequency. This can be done with simple calculations. For example, the lot containing 3,200 packages at Chemical Manufacturing is processed in 8 hours (480 minutes). Samples will be taken every 5 min 55 s. (480 min./81 packages = 5.926, which is approximately 6 min.) until all 81 samples are completed.

Continuous Data Sampling Plan	
1.- Initial Information	
a) What is being measured?	Units = **Packages**
b) What is the size of the population?	N = **3200**
c) What is the measurement characteristic?	Characteristic = **Package weight**
d) What is the standard deviation of the estimated population?	s = **0.458**
e) What is the precision of the estimate (same units)?	+/- d = **0.1**
f) Select the confidence level: (z = 1.64 for a 90% confidence level) (z = 1.96 for a 95% confidence level)	z = **1.96**
2.- Select the sampling method	
☐ Random ☐ Systematic	
3.- Determine the sample size	
$n = (zs/d)^2$	n = **81**
4.- Determine the sampling frequency	
	Frequency = _______
5.- Adjust for a finite population	
a) Determine the proportion of the sample with respect to the population	n / N = **0.02518217**
b) If n/N is greater than 0.05, adjust the answer using the following formula:	n / (1+ n/N) = **79**

Exercise 1

- The engineering department plans to conduct a study to determine mean time to repair (MTTR) for injection molding machines.

- The sample will be taken from a population of 100 machines and based on previous data from a pilot study the standard deviation is known to be 0.5 hours.

- It is required that the result is within ± 0.25 hours at a 95% confidence level.

- What is the required sample size?

Exercise 2

- As a continuation of the study, let's suppose that we are trying to estimate the proportion of machines that are running 10 or more hours without stopping.

- As a result of a pilot study it is estimated that the probability of this occurring is 30% (P = 0.30). We set the confidence level at 0.95 and the level of precision to 0.25 hours.

- What is the minimum sample size required to be able to estimate the proportion of machines with the required precision?

Histograms

A simple tool for complex problems

Objectives

1. Learn the basic concepts of histograms.
2. Build histograms to better understand how data is distributed for any process.
3. Interpret histograms to make decisions on improvement or problem-solving projects.

Content

> Background
> What is a histogram?
> What is it used for?
> Components
> When is it used?
> Procedure
> Examples
> Exercise

Histograms

- The histograms were developed by Karl Pearson (1857 - 1936)

- He was an influential English mathematician and biostatistician.

- He founded the first Department of University Statistics in the world at the University College of London in 1911, and contributed significantly to the field of biometrics, meteorology, and the theories of social Darwinism.

What is a histogram?

A histogram is a graphical representation (bar chart) of the frequency distribution of a data set in which the following three properties can be observed:

1. Distribution shape
2. Central tendency
3. Variability

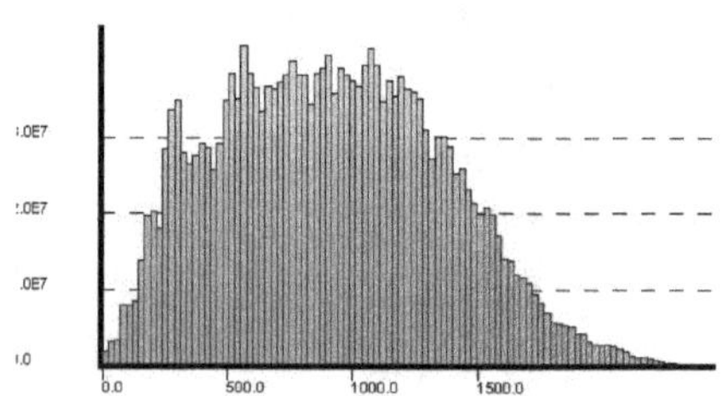

What is it used for?

Histograms are frequently used for the following purposes:

- To obtain a clear and effective communication of the variability of the system.

- To show the result of a change in the system.

- To identify abnormalities by examining its shape.

- To compare the variability with specification limits.

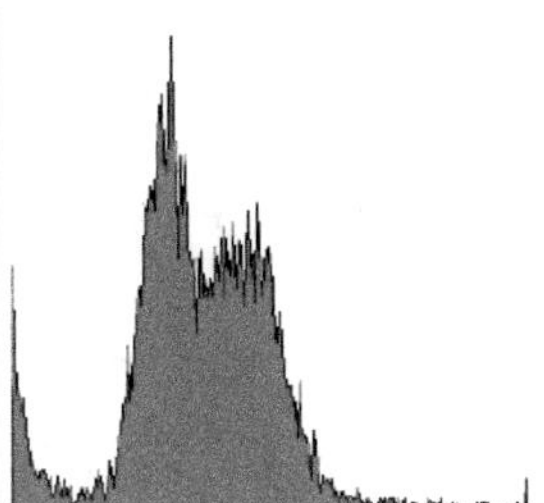

Components

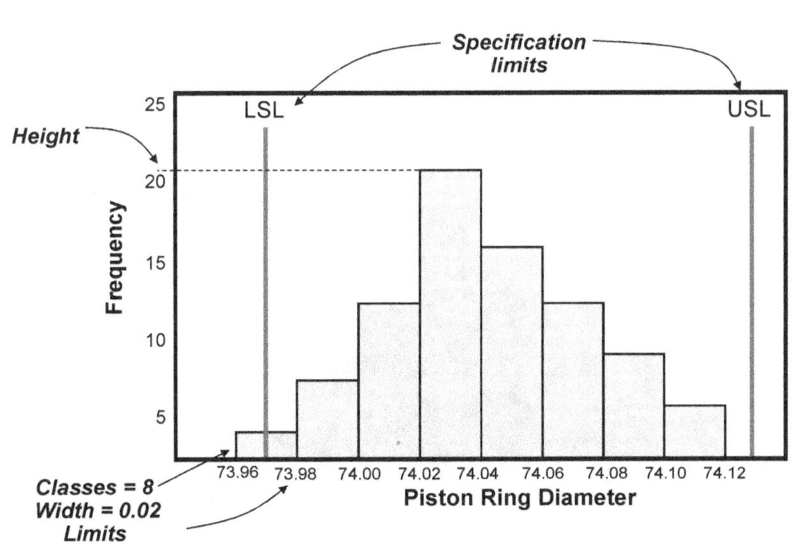

When is it used?

Measure and analyze phase

- When you want to display data graphically to help determine the distribution of the data set or to visually detect the presence of multiple distributions.

- When you want to better understand a variable.

  For example:

  - Current process performance and data distribution

  - Comparison against specifications

  - Basic probability calculations

Improve phase

- To validate an improvement to the product, service or process.

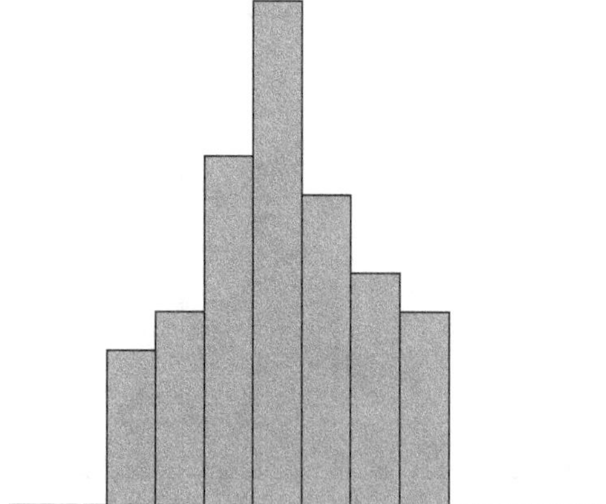

Procedure

1. Collect and arrange data.

2. Calculate the range of the data.

3. Determine the number of classes.

4. Determine the width of each class.

5. Calculate the intervals for each class.

6. Create a frequency table.

7. Graph.

Examples

Example 1: Delivery service

A logistics company wants to examine the distance travelled by its trucks during the month of August in order to optimize its routes and reduce costs, given that each kilometer travelled costs \$2. The upper and lower limits for travel distances are 152 and 176 km, respectively. Moreover, the company incurs an additional cost of \$0.80 for every kilometer driven above or below the upper or lower limit.

The additional cost incurred for distance driven below the lower limit exists due to the driving charging a minimum fee for 152 km, regardless if fewer are driven. The additional cost incurred for exceeding the upper limit exists because the driver charges an extra fee as soon as he or she drives more than 176 kilometers.

Step 1: Data collection and arrangement

Collect at least 50 data points and divide them into groups or columns in order to find the highest and lowest value in the data set.

161	165	168	164	163	170	162	166	177	173
170	164	165	167	174	167	167	167	167	169
165	164	164	159	169	164	168	164	164	176
164	168	163	163	173	167	165	167	167	161
170	161	171	170	163	166	166	167	166	170
178	158	172	171	168	155	154	174	155	161
170	167	174	158	165	167	168	170	157	167
160	168	159	164	159	163	160	166	163	166
163	170	170	169	175	170	164	177	170	164
164	164	161	159	179	158	179	165	158	166
168	173	164	168	171	177	165	164	177	169
173	163	170	150	170	153	167	171	153	172
158	177	169	156	167	162	166	164	162	170
161	165	163	159	156	170	163	170	170	157
164	169	166	160	163	163	169	166	163	160
159	170	157	164	165	175	163	165	175	165
161	168	167	166	169	166	171	159	166	164
153	161	157	163	160	163	165	158	163	157
155	174	170	169	167	179	157	166	179	159
164	163	174	168	165	160	173	164	160	159

Highest value

Lowest value

Step 2: Calculate the range of the data set

The range (R) is the difference between the highest and lowest value in a data set.

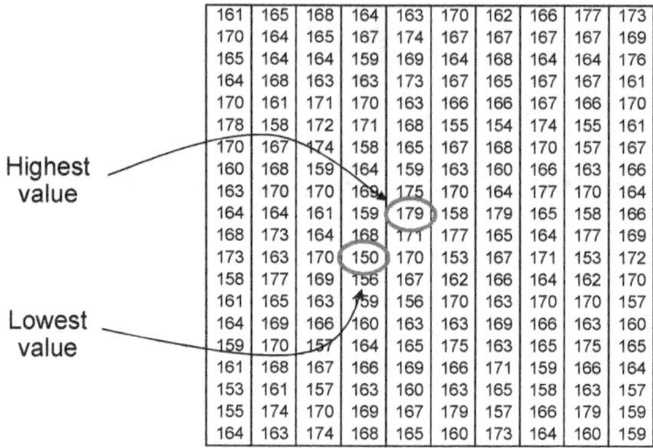

Highest value = 179

Lowest value = 150

Range = Highest value – Lowest value

Range = 179 – 150

Range = 29

Step 3: Determine the number of classes

To determine the number of classes to use for a histogram it is recommended to group the data and use the following table:

Number of data points (N)	Number of classes (K)
< 50	5 to 7
Between 50 and 100	6 to 10
Between 101 and 250	7 to 12
> 250	10 to 20

This can be calculated by using the following formula:

$$K = \sqrt{N}$$

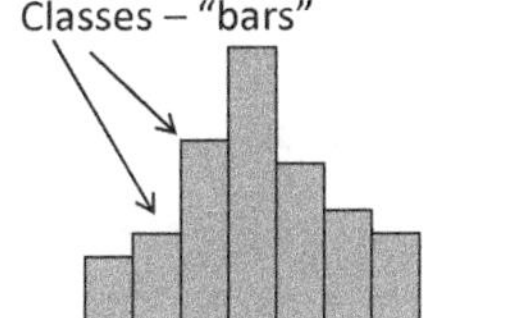

Using the table,
N = 200 so we pick K = 10

Step 4: Determine the width of each class

To determine the width of each class, add one unit of measurement (U) to the range (R) of the data and divide the outcome by the total number of classes (K):

Width = (Range + unit of measurement) / # of classes

$$W = (R + U) / K$$

$$W = (29 + 1) / 10$$

$$W = 3$$

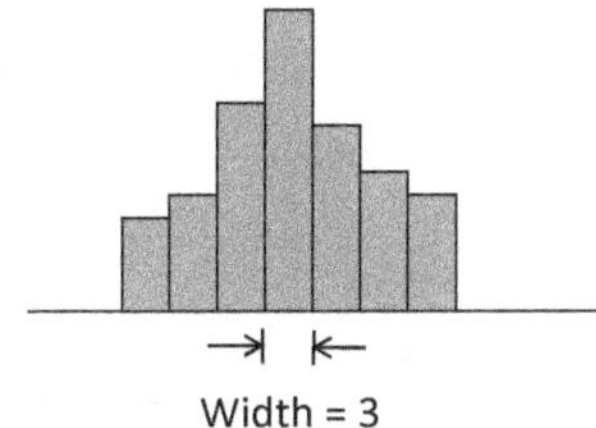

Step 5: Calculate intervals for classes

To calculate the interval for the first class, subtract one half the unit of measurement from the lowest value of the data set. To calculate the upper limit, add the lower limit to the class width.

First class interval

Lower limit = lowest value − (U)/2

Lower limit = 150 − ½

Lower limit = 149.5

Upper limit = lower limit + class width

Upper limit = 149.5 + 3

Upper limit = 152.5

Class	Interval
1	149.5 – 152.5
2	152.5 – 155.5
3	155.5 – 158.5
4	158.5 – 161.5
5	161.5 – 164.5
6	164.5 – 167.5
7	167.5 – 170.5
8	170.5 – 173.5
9	173.5 – 176.5
10	176.5 – 179.5

Step 6: Create a frequency table

- Frequency is the number of data points in each class.

Class	Interval	Frequency
1	149.5 – 152.5	1

- Relative frequency is equal to the frequency of each class divided by the total number of data points (N).

Class	Interval	Frequency	Relative frequency
1	149.5 – 152.5	1	1 / 200 = .005

Class	Interval	Frequency	Relative frequency	Relative cumulative frequency
1	149.5 – 152.5	1	0.005	0.005
2	152.5 – 155.5	7	0.035	0.040
3	155.5 – 158.5	14	0.070	0.110
4	158.5 – 161.5	24	0.120	0.230
5	161.5 – 164.5	42	0.210	0.440
6	164.5 – 167.5	43	0.215	0.655
7	167.5 – 170.5	38	0.190	0.845
8	170.5 – 173.5	12	0.060	0.905
9	173.5 – 176.5	9	0.045	0.950
10	176.5 – 179.5	10	0.050	1.000

Step 7: Graph

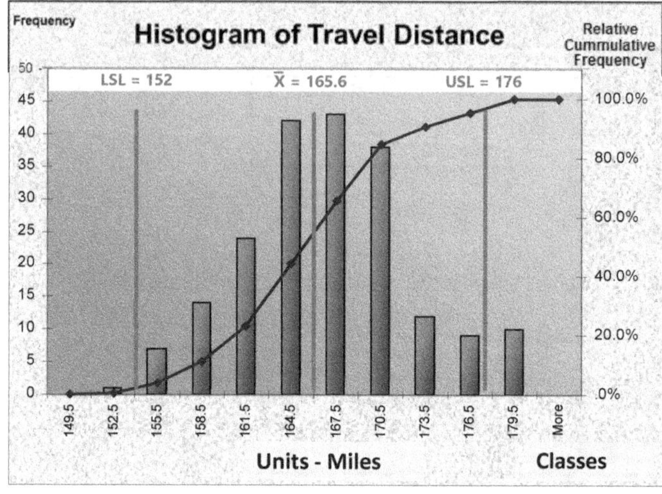

Central tendency
Mean = 165.6
Median = 165
Mode = 164

Variability
Range = 29
Variance = 32.5
Standard Dev = 5.7

Interpretation

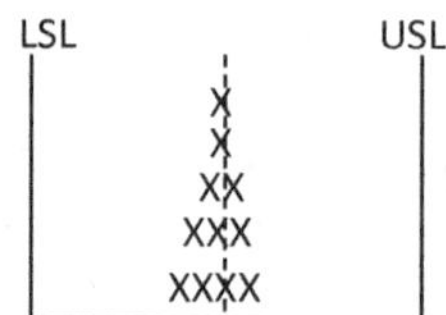

Case 1: Process is centered and with low variability

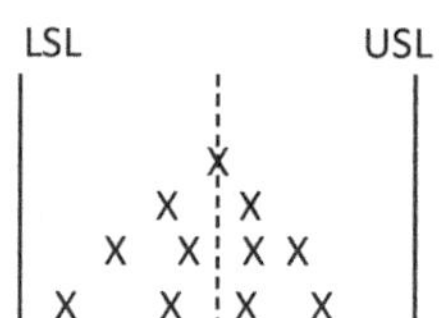

Case 2: Process is centered and with high variability

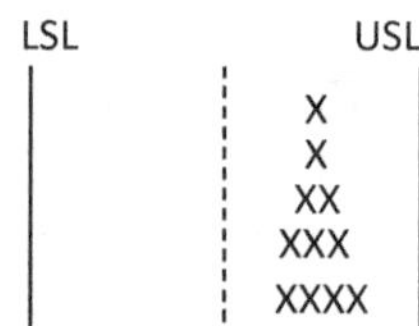

Case 3: Process is not centered and with little variability

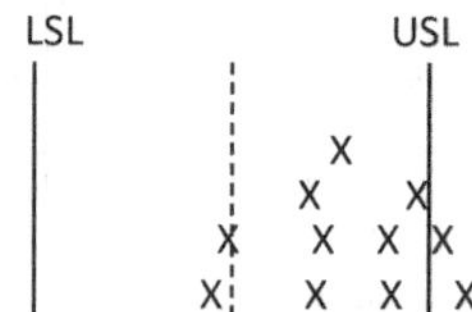

Case 4: Process is not centered and with high variability

LSSI
LEAN SIX SIGMA INSTITUTE

Interpretation: types of distributions

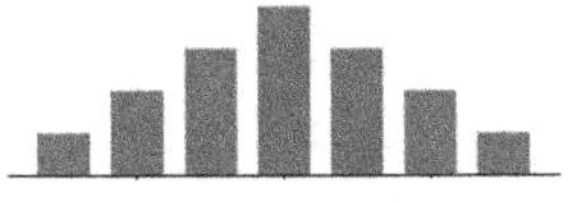

Normal distribution: Symmetric data gathered around the mean. Values closer to the mean have a higher frequency, while those farther away from the mean have a lower frequency. Bell-shaped.

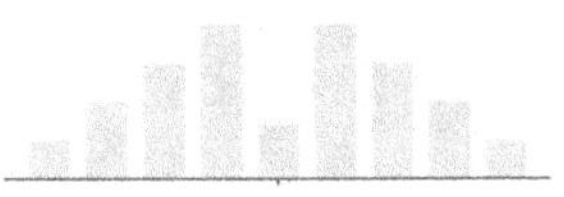

Bimodal distribution: Double-peak histogram. Usually indicates that there are two populations in the process.

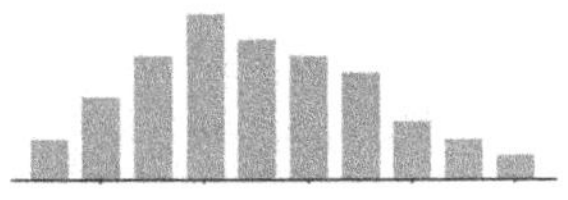

Skewed distribution: Data is concentrated on the higher values (positive skewness) or the lower values (negative skewness). Values are not symmetrically distributed.

Exercise

Build a histogram for the following information.

- LSL = 73.9
- USL = 74.05

1	74.030	74.002	74.019	73.992	74.008
2	73.995	73.992	74.001	74.011	74.004
3	73.988	74.024	74.021	74.005	74.002
4	74.002	73.996	73.993	74.015	74.009
5	73.992	74.007	74.015	73.989	74.014
6	74.009	73.994	73.997	73.985	73.993
7	73.995	74.006	73.994	74.000	74.005
8	73.985	74.003	73.993	74.015	73.988
9	74.008	73.995	74.009	74.005	74.004
10	73.998	74.000	73.990	74.007	73.995
11	73.994	73.998	73.994	73.995	73.990
12	74.004	74.000	74.007	74.000	73.996
13	73.983	74.002	73.998	73.997	74.012
14	74.006	73.967	73.994	74.000	73.984
15	74.012	74.014	73.998	73.999	74.007
16	74.000	73.984	74.005	73.998	73.996
17	73.994	74.012	73.986	74.005	74.007
18	74.006	74.010	74.018	74.003	74.000
19	73.984	74.002	74.003	74.005	73.997
20	74.000	74.010	74.013	74.020	74.003
21	73.988	74.001	74.009	74.005	73.996
22	74.004	73.999	73.990	74.006	74.009
23	74.010	73.989	73.990	74.009	74.014
24	74.015	74.008	73.993	74.000	74.010
25	73.982	73.984	73.995	74.017	74.013

Process capability

Quality depends on the ability to deliver products and services that are within customers' specifications

Objectives

1. Understand the general concepts of process capability studies.
2. Analyze the capability of any process.
3. Document process capability for your Six Sigma projects.

Content

> Introduction
> What is process capability?
> Why measure it?
> Capability measurement
> When do you measure it?
> Procedure
> Examples
> Exercises

Introduction

- When analyzing data, it is very important to understand if the results fall within the limits defined by the customer.

- A process capability study will help us to identify the level of variability in a process as well as how likely it is that it will meet customer specifications.

What is process capability?

- The potential process capability index, Cp, is a comparison between natural tolerance limits and specification limits without taking into consideration the location of the process mean.

- The real process capability index, Cpk, does take into consideration the location of the process mean in comparison to specification limits.

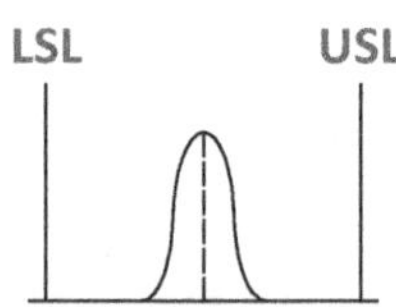

Measures the capability of a process to meet required specifications.

LSSI
LEAN SIX SIGMA INSTITUTE

Process variation vs. customer specifications

- The Voice of the Process (VoP) is represented by the natural process variation.

- Customer specifications represent customer needs or requirements, or the Voice of the Customer (VoC).

- It is important to compare natural process variation to customer requirements. This is called process capability.

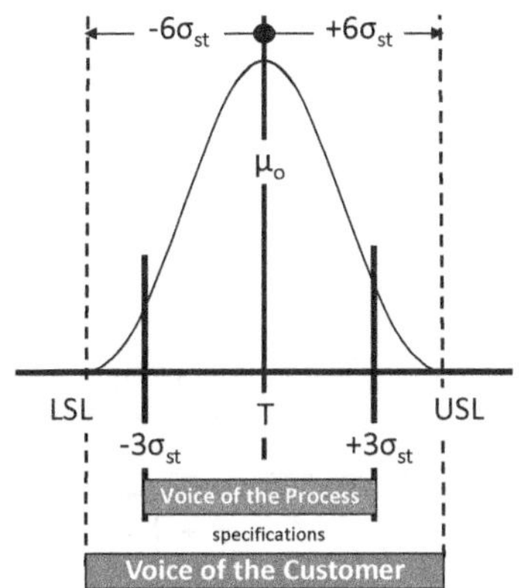

1. It allows us to quantify the problem we want to focus on. Examples:

   - Are the *specifications* correct for the process output or performance variable (Y) we are interested in?

   - Is the central tendency location of the Y parameter centered between the *specifications?*

   - Is the process variation of the parameter greater than that allowed by the *specifications?*

2. It helps the organization predict defect levels that will result from the process.

3. It justifies the change and modification of a process if the product is not meeting customer specifications.

- A way of measuring process capability is to compare the specification width to the process width.

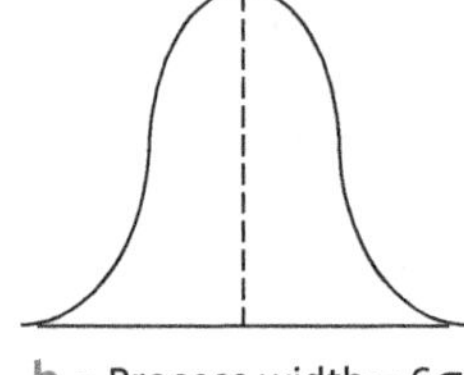

Potential capability index (Cp)

We can define and calculate Cp as:

$$Cp = \frac{a}{b} = \frac{USL - LSL}{6s} \qquad s = \hat{\sigma}$$

- **Cp** represents a comparison of the widths, *without* taking into consideration the *location* of the process mean. It indicates the number of times the process "fits" within the specification limits.

- In order to account for fluctuations in the process mean, consider a ± 1.5 operating "window" – given that Shewhart's Control Charts are not fit to detect long-term changes.

Real capability index (Cpk)

Given that **Cp** does not take into consideration the location *(centeredness)* of the process mean, it is necessary to define another index that will.

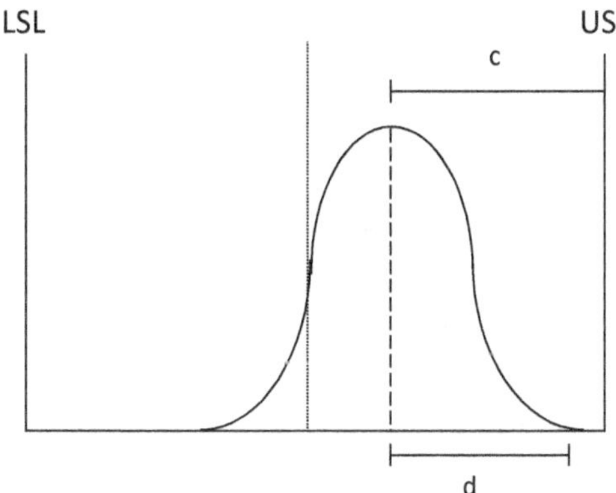

Both **Cp** and **Cpk** assume normality, even though there are other types of distributions that will also work (Wheeler & Chambers, 1992).

One can think of Cpk as the tolerance available when a process needs 100%.

Gunter (1989)

- By comparing **c/d,** you can see the process *centeredness* in relation to half the process *variation*.

  - **c** = Distance between the center of the process (mean) and the closest specification limit.
  - **d** = Half the width of the process.

- The **real capability index** is then calculated and defined as follows:

$$Cpk = \frac{\bar{x} - LSL}{3s}$$

$$Cpk = \frac{USL - \bar{x}}{3s}$$

Choose the lower Cpk calculation (including negative values)

- In the case of **unilateral tolerance**:

$$Cpk = \frac{|SL - \bar{x}|}{3s}$$

SL = Specification limit (whether upper or lower)

- The **Cp** index is used to **measure** the process. It separates variation from the process center.

- The **Cpk** index is used for **monitoring** the process with respect to time. It measures the variation and process center.

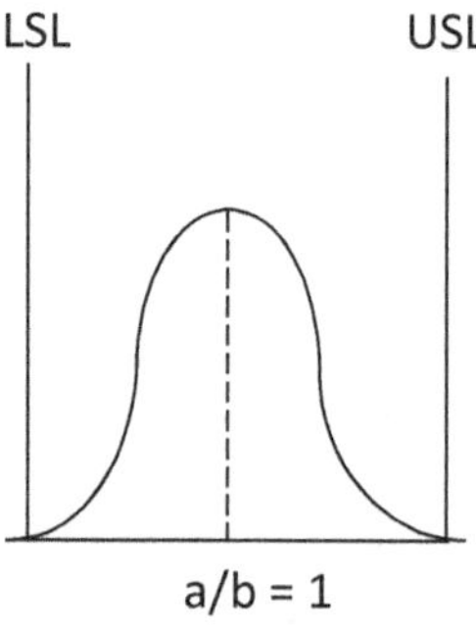

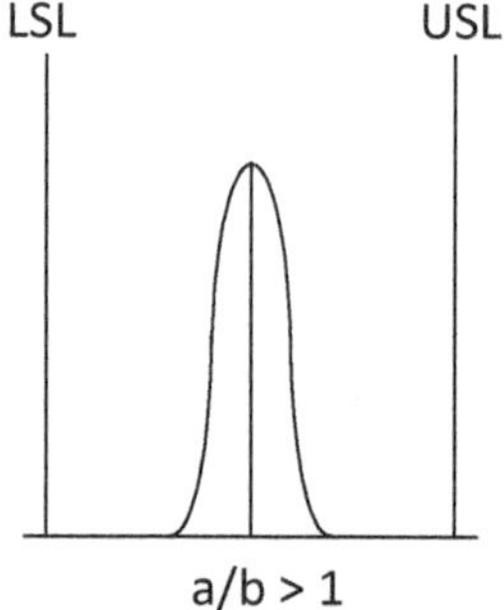

By comparing both processes, we can see that the process for which a/b is > 1 performs better.

Examples of graphical evaluation of Cp and Cpk

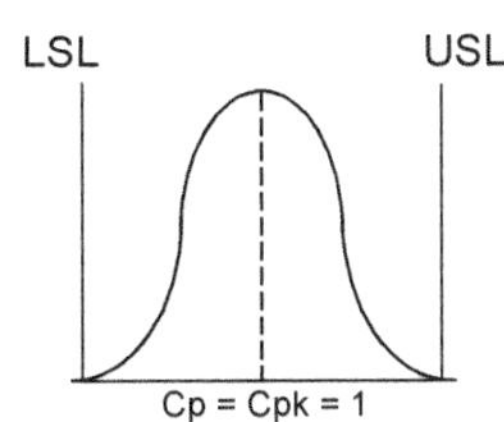

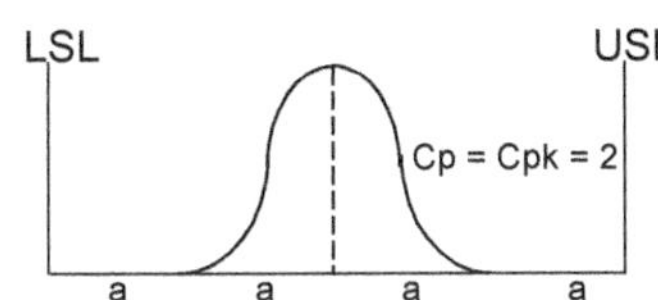

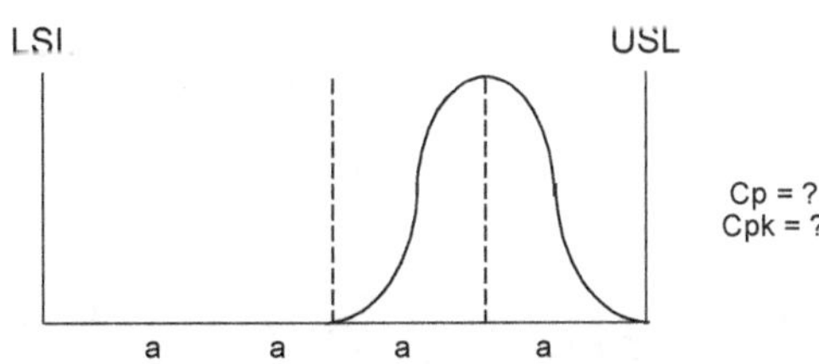

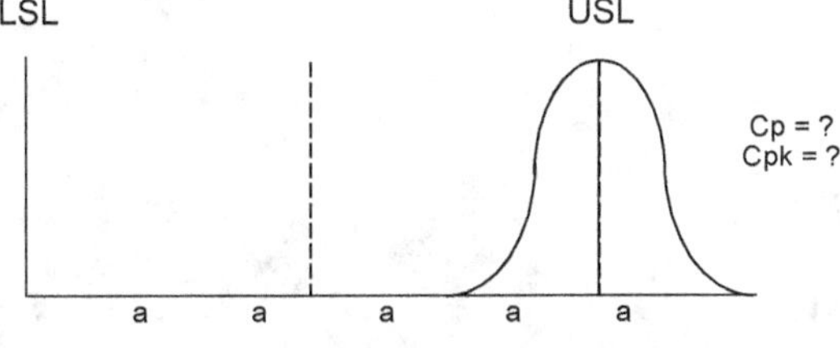

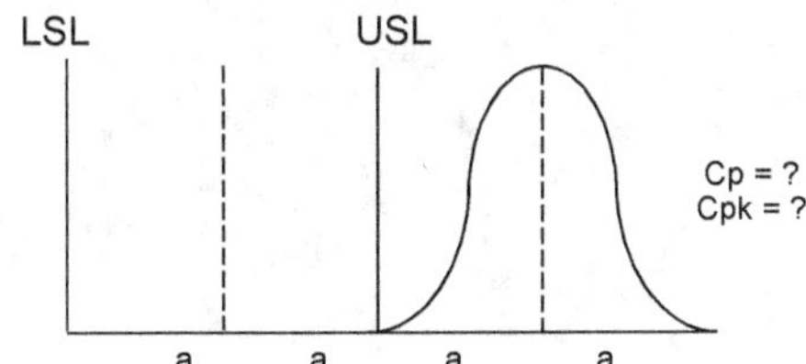

Relationship between Cp and Cpk

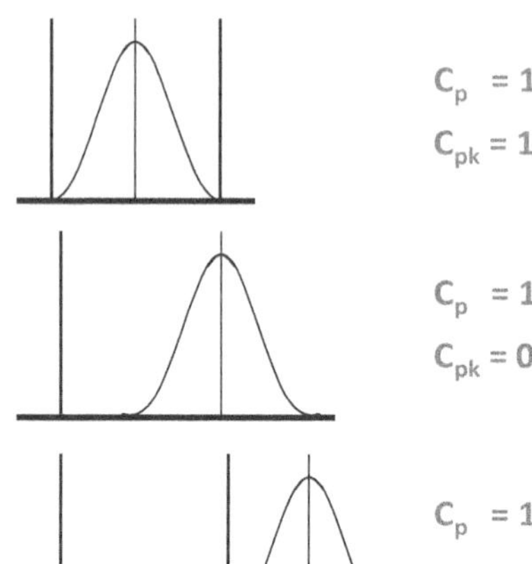

Some details...

- Cp is positive; it is the ratio of two positive numbers.

- Cpk can be positive, zero, or negative.

- When Cpk is zero, the output (yield) is 50%.

- When Cpk is negative, the output (yield) is less than 50%.

- Cpk is at its maximum value when it is equal to Cp; the process is centered when this happens.

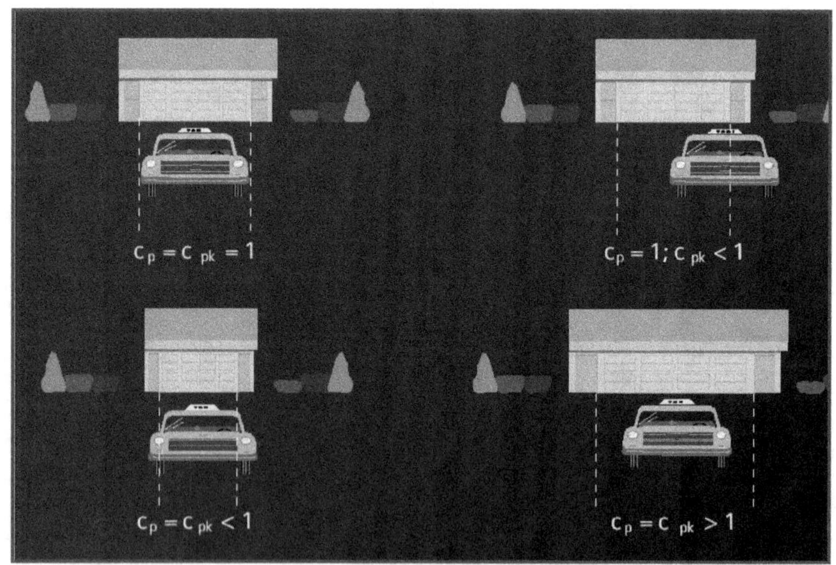

Interpretation of Cp and Cpk

- If Cp > Cpk, then the process is not centered at the target value.

- If Cp or Cpk < 1, then the process is incapable.

- If Cp or Cpk is between 1 and 1.33, then the process is barely capable.

- If Cp or Cpk > 1.33, then the process is capable.

- Cpk is a better representation of the real process.

Long- vs. short-term capability

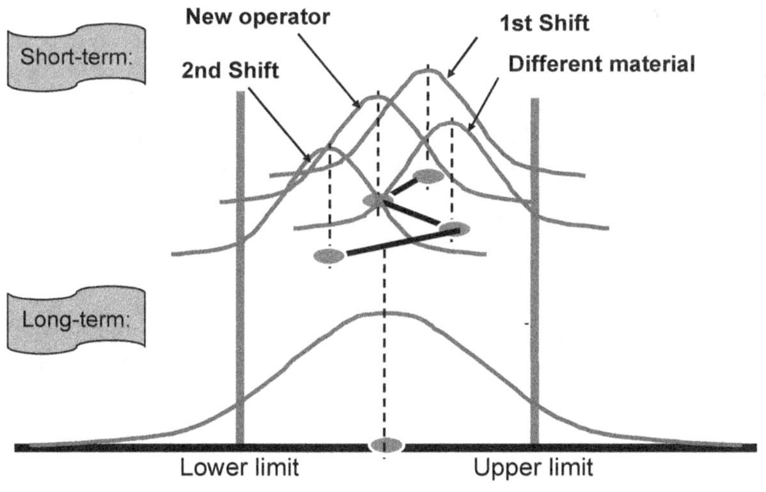

Long- and short-term capability studies

- The difference between Cp and Pp (or Cpk and Ppk) is that Cp and Cpk are indices calculated from data obtained in short-term studies, while Pp and Ppk are calculated from data obtained in long-term studies.

- Long-term studies are generally preferred, since these include all sources of variation in the process (different lots, employees, etc.). This does not necessarily imply that these studies should be conducted over extremely long periods of time.

- Instead of calculating internal standard deviation (subgroups), data is combined into one single group and a new standard deviation is calculated. This standard deviation estimates internal variation (subgroups) due to fluctuations between subgroups.

- The advantage of short-term studies is that they are simpler and faster to perform compared to long-term studies.

- To conduct a short-term evaluation, you usually consider 20 subgroups of five samples each and estimate the internal standard deviation.

"Short-term is like looking at the photo. Long-term is watching the movie."

Luis Socconini

LSSI
LEAN SIX SIGMA INSTITUTE

Capability and sigma level

- The Sigma level is the number of standard deviations that fit between the center of the process (process mean) and the closest customer specification limit.

- Usually, this is used as a measurement of quality.

- Sigma level can be derived from Cpk or Ppk.

Short-term sigma level = Cpk × 3

Long-term sigma level = Ppk × 3

Process performance report

- An important consideration is that since short-term studies do not consider variation between subgroups directly, they use the "window" of ±1.5σ. This window was obtained from the analysis of a large sum of data of a very diverse nature, and – based on the following table – it allows us to simplify the presentation of results:

	Period of Study	
Report	Short-term	Long-term
Short-term	Leave as is	Add 1.5
Long-term	Subtract 1.5	Leave as is

Dr. E. Escalante

- Reporting the short-term sigma level is an international best practice.

What do these results mean?

$DPMO_{LT}$	$Sigma_{ST}$	Cpk_{ST}	
66,807	3.0	1.00	Poor
22,750	3.5	1.17	Poor
6,210	4.0	1.33	Good
1,350	4.5	1.50	Good
233	5.0	1.67	Excellent
32	5.5	1.83	Excellent
3.4	6.0	2.0	At 6 Sigma!

What do these results mean?

	Short-term quality		Long-term quality (1.5σ)	
Cp	Quality in Z sigmas	PPM out of specification	Quality in Z sigmas	PPM out of specification
0.33	1	317,300	-0.5	697,700
0.67	2	45,500	0.5	308,700
1.00	3	2,700	1.5	66,807
1.33	4	63	2.5	6,210
1.67	5	0.57	3.5	233
2.00	6	0.002	4.5	3.4

When do you measure it?

- Measure phase

  - To establish an estimated baseline for a controlled process.

- Analyze phase

  - To confirm process capability and determine the level of variation.

- Improve phase

  - To verify process improvements.

- Control phase

  - To regularly verify the capability of the improved process and how it is being sustained.

Procedure

1. Collect the required data.

2. Calculate Pp or Cp.

3. Calculate Ppk or Cpk.

4. Interpret the data.

5. Make improvement decisions.

Example 1

Emily Walker and her improvement team (at **Chelsea Footwear**) want to determine the potential and real process capability indices for the production of molded shoe soles. The following data was obtained from a long-term capability study:

- Mean: 165.2 g
- Standard deviation: 5.484 g
- Lower Specification Limit (LSL):   155 g
- Upper Specification Limit (USL):   180 g

Potential capability index (Pp)

Emily Walker evaluated the potential capability to produce molded shoe soles that are within specification limits, obtaining the following result:

$$\textbf{Pp} = (180 - 155) / (6 \times 5.484) = 0.76$$

Real capability index (Ppk)

Emily's team then calculates the real process capability:

- $\textbf{Ppk}_1 = (165.2 - 155) / (3 \times 5.484) = 0.62$

- $\textbf{Ppk}_2 = (180 - 165.2) / (3 \times 5.484) = 0.90$

The resulting Ppk value is 0.62 (the lower value of the two).

Emily's team at **Chelsea Footwear** uses the calculated indices to interpret the process capability (Pp = 0.76, Ppk = 0.62):

- The process is incapable of meeting the specifications, since both the Pp and Ppk values are less than 1, and there are existing values out of the specification limits.

- The process is slightly off-center, since the Pp value is slightly greater than the Ppk value.

- The approximate long-term sigma level is: (0.62 × 3) = 1.86.

- The approximate short-term sigma level is: 1.86 + 1.50 = 3.36.

Graph for the sole molding process at Chelsea Footwear:

- We can see that the Pp value is 0.76 and the Ppk value is 0.62 (we can also observe the calculated Ppk values for each specification limit).

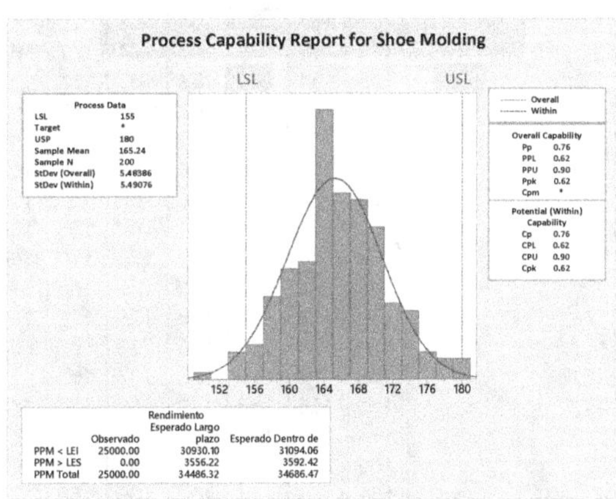

	Observado	Rendimiento Esperado Largo plazo	Esperado Dentro de
PPM < LEI	25000.00	30930.10	31094.06
PPM > LES	0.00	3556.22	3592.42
PPM Total	25000.00	34486.32	34686.47

Example 2: Delivery service

A delivery company wants to calculate its process capability by using data collected over the long term. Its specification limits are as follows:

- Lower Specification Limit (LSL): 152 km

- Upper Specification Limit (USL): 176 km

Data for delivery trips – collected over the long term – is summarized below:

161	165	168	164	163	170	162	166	177	173
170	164	165	167	174	167	167	167	167	169
165	164	164	159	169	164	168	164	164	176
164	168	163	163	173	167	165	167	167	161
170	161	171	170	163	166	166	167	166	170
178	158	172	171	168	155	154	174	155	161
170	167	174	158	165	167	168	170	157	167
160	168	159	164	159	163	160	166	163	166
163	170	170	169	175	170	164	177	170	164
164	164	161	159	179	158	179	165	158	166
168	173	164	168	171	177	165	164	177	169
173	163	170	150	170	153	167	171	153	172
158	177	169	156	167	162	166	164	162	170
161	165	163	159	156	170	163	170	170	157
164	169	166	160	163	163	169	166	163	160
159	170	157	164	165	175	163	165	175	165
161	168	167	166	169	166	171	159	166	164
153	161	157	163	160	163	165	158	163	157
155	174	170	169	167	179	157	166	179	159
164	163	174	168	165	160	173	164	160	159

Resulting graph for the process

Results:

- Mean   165.595
- Standard deviation   5.71276
- Pp   0.70
- Ppk   0.61

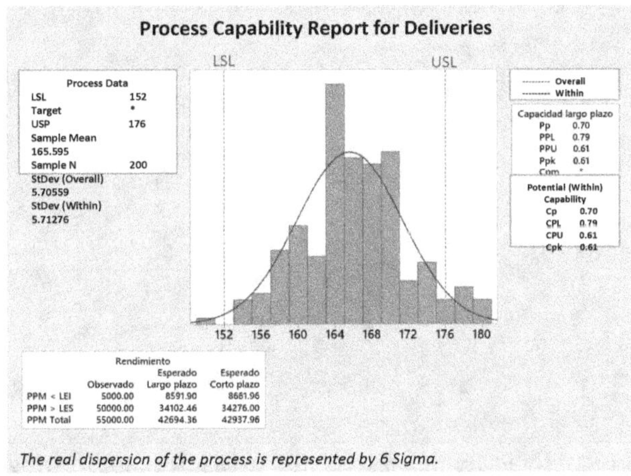

The real dispersion of the process is represented by 6 Sigma.

The team at the delivery company used the calculated indices to interpret the process capability (Pp = 0.70, Ppk = 0.61):

- The process is incapable of meeting the specification, since both the Pp and Ppk values are less than 1, and there are existing values out of the specification limits.

- The process is slightly off-center, since the Pp value is slightly greater than the Ppk value.

- The approximate long-term sigma level is: (0.61 × 3) = 1.83.

- The approximate short-term sigma level is: 1.83 + 1.50 = 3.33.

Conclusions

The calculations for capability and sigma level of a process are highly important as they enable us to compare these values before and after improvements are implemented. They also serve as a guide to determine if the process remains under control once a Lean Six Sigma project is finalized.

Exercise 1

A team at a production facility performed 150 measurements during a long-term study, obtaining the following results:

* Mean = 1.03

* Standard deviation = 0.0573

* Specification limits:

  LSL = 0.90
  USL = 1.10

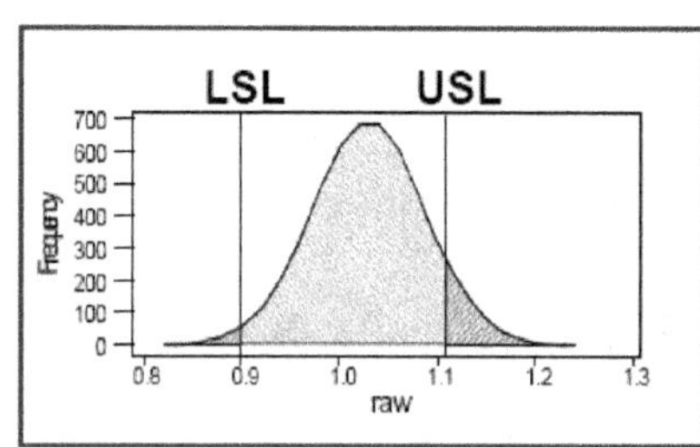

Calculate the capability indices.

Exercise 2

Calculate the process capability for the length of car doors whose specification is 100 $\pm$ 5 cm if the following results were obtained from a long-term study:

- Mean = 102.3

- Standard deviation = 1.2

Calculate the capability indices.

Exercise 3

A team at a production facility performed a long-term study and collected data for a piston cylinder manufacturing process. Calculate and interpret the capability indexes for the following specification limits:

- LSL = 73.90
- USL = 74.05

74.030	74.002	74.019	73.992	74.008
73.995	73.992	74.001	74.011	74.004
73.988	74.024	74.021	74.005	74.002
74.002	73.996	73.993	74.015	74.009
73.992	74.007	74.015	73.989	74.014
74.009	73.994	73.997	73.985	73.993
73.995	74.006	73.994	74.000	74.005
73.985	74.003	73.993	74.015	73.988
74.008	73.995	74.009	74.005	74.004
73.998	74.000	73.990	74.007	73.995
73.994	73.998	73.994	73.995	73.990
74.004	74.000	74.007	74.000	73.996
73.983	74.002	73.998	73.997	74.012
74.006	73.967	73.994	74.000	73.984
74.012	74.014	73.998	73.999	74.007
74.000	73.984	74.005	73.998	73.996
73.994	74.012	73.986	74.005	74.007
74.006	74.010	74.018	74.003	74.000
73.984	74.002	74.003	74.005	73.997
74.000	74.010	74.013	74.020	74.003
73.988	74.001	74.009	74.005	73.996
74.004	73.999	73.990	74.006	74.009
74.010	73.989	73.990	74.009	74.014
74.015	74.008	73.993	74.000	74.010
73.982	73.984	73.995	74.017	74.013

Process performance

Indicators to evaluate any type of industry

Objectives

1. Understand the importance of measuring process performance.
2. Calculate the yield.
3. Calculate defects per million opportunities.
4. Calculate the sigma level of any process.

Content

> Background
> Process performance
> Process yield
> Defects Per Million Opportunities (DPMO)
> Six Sigma metric
> Integrative example
> Exercises
> Checklist: Reviewing the measure phase

Why measure a process?

- Processes are *critical* to executing operations, strategies, and plans to achieve business objectives.

- Processes have to be measured, controlled and improved in order to:

  - Understand the past.

  - Control the present.

  - Predict the future.

Effectiveness indicators

- They allow us to evaluate the *degree to which the purpose is being met.*

- The purpose of the process should have importance for the organization relative to either customer satisfaction or its contribution to achieve strategic objectives.

- Effectiveness indicators are determined by answering the following questions:

  - How well are customer *requirements* being met?

  - How well does the process contribute to the *strategic objectives* of the organization?

Efficiency indicators

- A process is efficient when it creates products and/or services with the *optimal utilization of resources.*

- The focus of efficiency indicators should be on how resources are utilized during transformation or when value is added.

- Efficiency indicators are established by asking the following questions:

  - How well does the process *perform?* i.e., How many errors/defects, rework and/or waste does the process generate?
  - How well *are resources utilized* to satisfy customer requirements?, i.e., How are things such as productivity, cycle time, equipment utilization and energy consumption measured?

Process performance

- Why is it important to measure process performance?

  - To understand how the process is performing and to confirm performance baseline.

- For any process, there are various indicators that are useful in understanding the functions and operations being performed.

- Some of these indicators are useful in the development of Lean Six Sigma projects.

Indicators

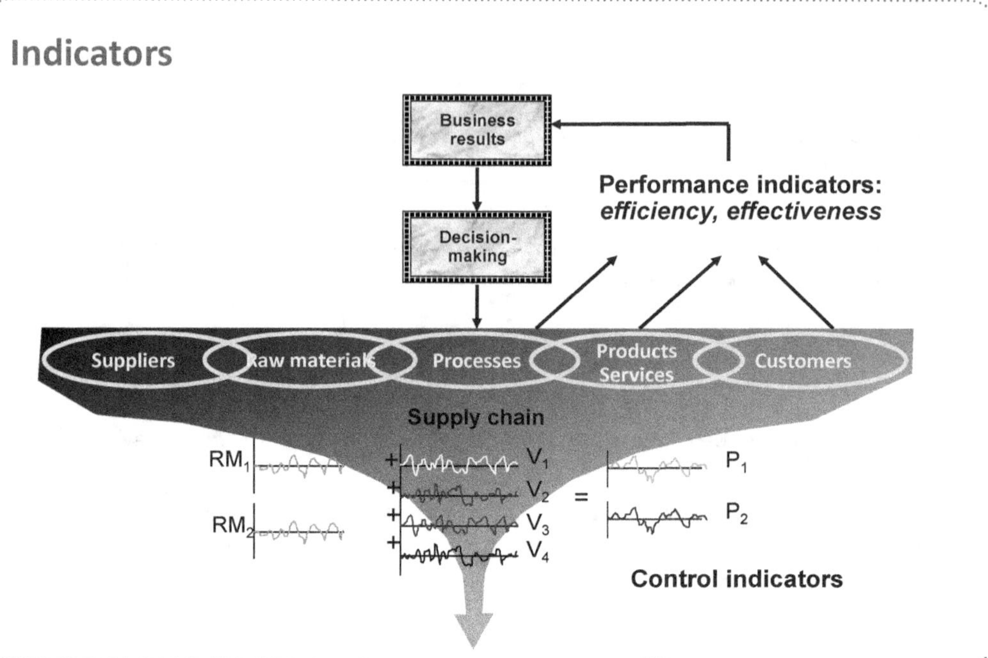

Process yield

- **Traditional yield**
  - Yield at the end of the process.
    - Excludes internal rework.
    - Probability of 0 defects is measured at the end of the process.

- **First-Time Yield (FTY)**
  - Average yield for consecutive processes or steps in a process.

- **Rolled Throughput Yield (RTY)**
  - Total process yield.
  - Includes internal rework.
  - Probability of 0 defects is measured throughout the process.

Traditional yield

Traditional yield is calculated by dividing the number of units that exit the process by the number of units that entered the process.*

Example

Calculate traditional yield for the following process:

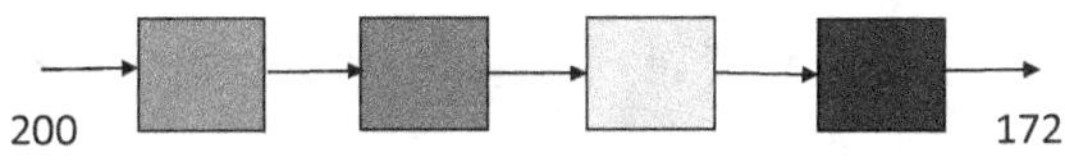

Yield = 172/200 = 0.86 = **86 %**

* Units may refer to one product or to a single instance of a service.

First-time yield (FTY)

First-Time Yield (FTY) is calculated by dividing the number of good units produced at each step of the process by the total number of units going into each step of the process.

Example

Calculate FTY for the following process:

FTY = 197/200 = **0.9850**　177/197 = **0.8985**　172/177 = **0.9718**　172/172 = **1.00**

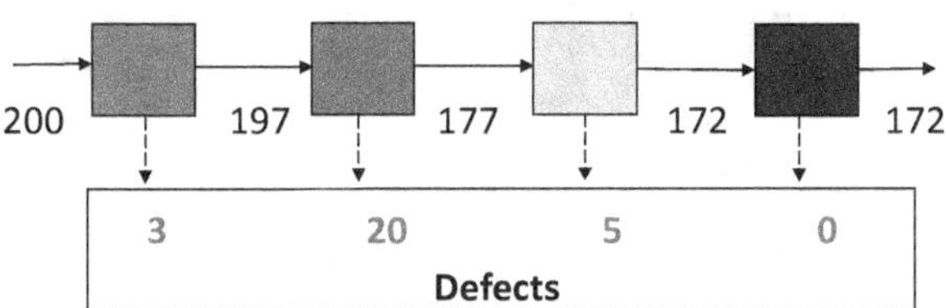

Rolled Throughput Yield (RTY)

(Not including re-work)

Rolled Throughput Yield (RTY) is calculated by multiplying the yields at each step of the process. In this case, the re-work is not included.

Example

$$RTY = (0.985)(0.8985)(0.9718)(1) = \mathbf{0.86} = FTY = 172/200$$

$$FTY = 197/200 = \mathbf{0.9850} \quad 177/197 = \mathbf{0.8985} \quad 172/177 = \mathbf{0.9718} \quad 172/172 = \mathbf{1.00}$$

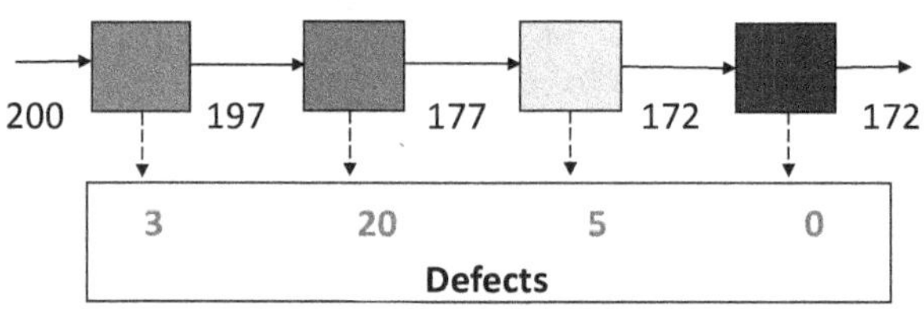

(Including re-work)

In this case, the re-work is included.

Example

$$FTY = 192/200 = \mathbf{0.96} \quad 177/197 = \mathbf{0.8985} \quad 172/177 = \mathbf{0.9718} \quad 169/172 = \mathbf{0.9826}$$

$$RTY = (0.96)(0.8985)(0.9718)(0.9826) = \mathbf{0.8237}$$

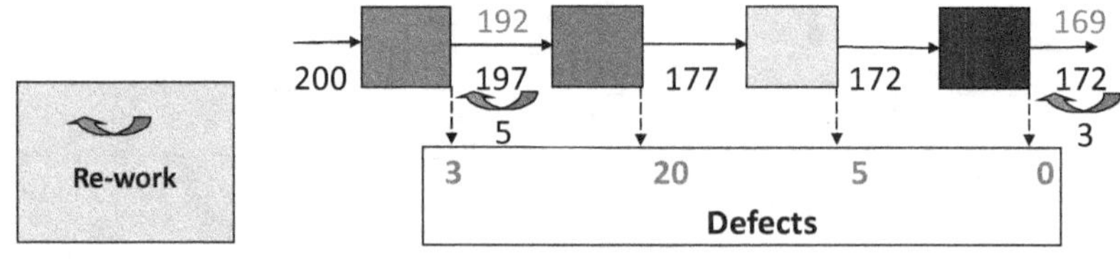

The hidden workplace

- The concept of the "hidden workplace" arises when a company is using *additional resources* because they do not provide their products or services right the first time.

- Re-work and waste is considered as the hidden workplace.

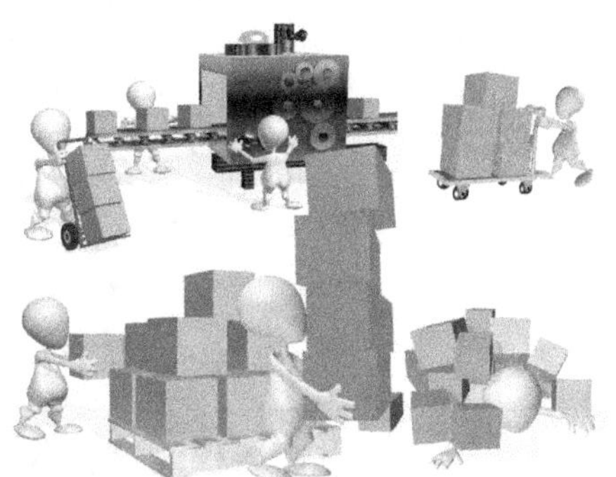

Example of hidden workplace

These "hidden" workplaces are found in steps 1 and 4, respectively, and each one represents an improvement opportunity.

FTY = 192/200 = **0.96**   177/197 = **0.8985**   172/177 = **0.9718**   169/172 = **0.9826**

RTY = (0.96)(0.8985)(0.9718)(0.9826) = **0.8237**

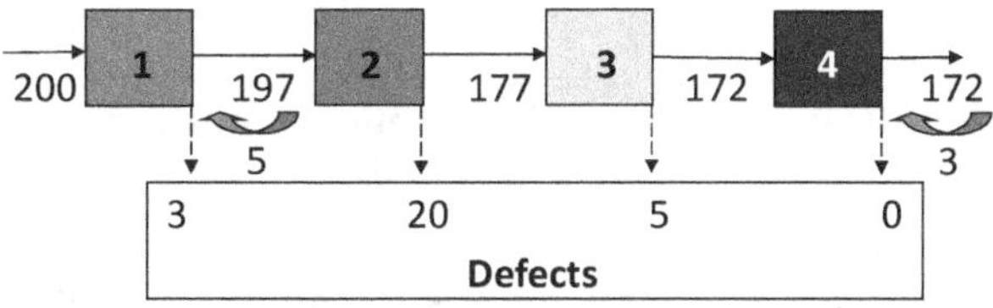

RTY = 82.37% represents the percentage of units that will be produced defect-free on the first pass.

Defects Per Million Opportunities (DPMO)

DPMO is:

- The number of defects observed per million opportunities.
- A key measurement in Six Sigma.
- A corporate standard to count defects.
- A way to quantify the impact of improvements made.
- A way to amplify the urgency of our problems identified.

$$DPMO = \frac{Defects}{Units \times Opportunities} \times 1{,}000{,}000$$

Six Sigma (6σ) = 3.4 DPMO

Sigma Level	Defect per million opportunities (DPMO)	Yield
6	3	99.9997%
5	233	99.997%
4	6,210	99.379%
3	66,807	93.32%
2	308,537	69.20%
1	690,000	31%

Important terminology

- **Defects:** Number of units that do not meet specifications.

- **Units:** Total number of units.

- **Opportunities:** Total number of opportunities per unit to make a mistake that turns into a defect.

- **Total of opportunities:** Number of units per number of opportunities for defects.

- **Defects per total of opportunities:** Defects/total numbers of opportunities.

- **Defects per million opportunities:** Defects/total numbers of opportunities per one million.

LSSI
LEAN SIX SIGMA INSTITUTE

How to calculate DPMO

1. Assess the number of opportunities.

2. Count # of defects in a sample.

3. Calculate the number of defects per million opportunities.

$$DPMO = \frac{Defects}{Units \times Opportunities} \times 1{,}000\,000$$

Example 1

Call center

Rita makes a mistake once every 100 calls.

90% of the calls are international (11 digits).
10% of the calls are local (8 digits).

Rita
935 DPMO's

Martha makes a mistake once every 100 calls.

10% of the calls are international (11 digits).
90% of the calls are local (8 digits).

Martha
1,205 DPMO's

The great advantage of talking in terms of DPMO is that it helps us compare different type of processes.

Example 2

- The following defect opportunities (failure to meet specifications) were found in a food delivery process:

Delivery order unit of measurement	One delivery	50 deliveries
Late or too early	1	13
Wrong quantity	1	3
Food is not fresh	1	0
Opportunities	**3**	**16**

- A total of 16 defects were found for a sample of 50 deliveries.

- Calculate DPMO.

Example 2 (solution)

Defects D	Units U	Opportunities OP	TOP Total opportunities U X OP	DPO Defects per total opportunity. D / TOP	DPMO DPO X 1 million	PPM
16	50	3	150	0.106666667	106,666.7	0.10666667

Delivery order unit of measurement	One delivery	50 deliveries
Late or too early	1	13
Wrong quantity	1	3
Food is not fresh	1	0
Opportunities	**3**	**16**

$$\frac{16}{50 \times 3} = \frac{16}{150} \quad 0.106667$$

DPMO = 0.10666667 x 1 million = **106,666.67**

Six Sigma metric

- From a quality perspective, Six Sigma is defined as 3.4 defects per million opportunities. This is called the "Six Sigma Quality Level."

- **Z-Value:** Measures the capability of a process by calculating the distance between specifications and the mean, μ, of a process in units of standard deviation, σ.

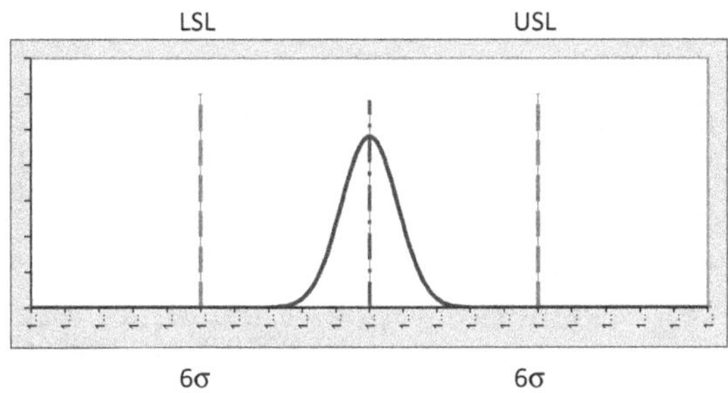

How many standard deviations fit?

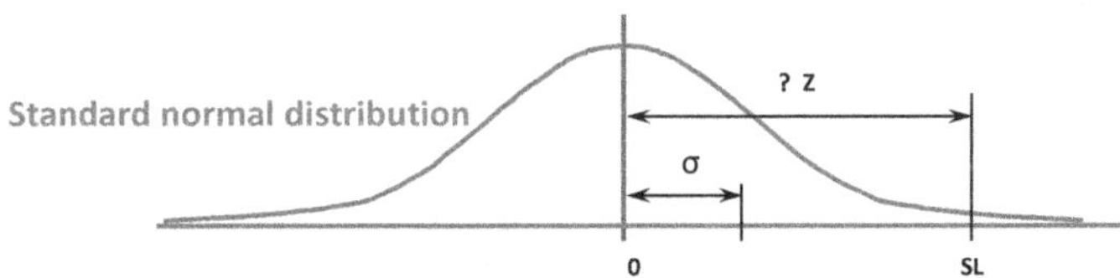

- In a normal distribution, the central tendency is defined by its *mean*.

- The amount of variation in performance or the width of the distribution is defined by its *standard deviation*.

- If we ask ourselves how many standard deviations can fit between the mean and the specification limits (SL), we can use the following equation:

$$Z = \frac{SL - Mean}{Standard\ deviation}$$

Normal distribution: Width of a process

The following general rules apply for a distribution to be considered normal:

- Approximately 68% of the data falls within ±1σ from the mean.

- Approximately 95% of the data falls within ±2 σ from the mean.

- Approximately 99.7% of the data falls within ±3 σ from the mean.

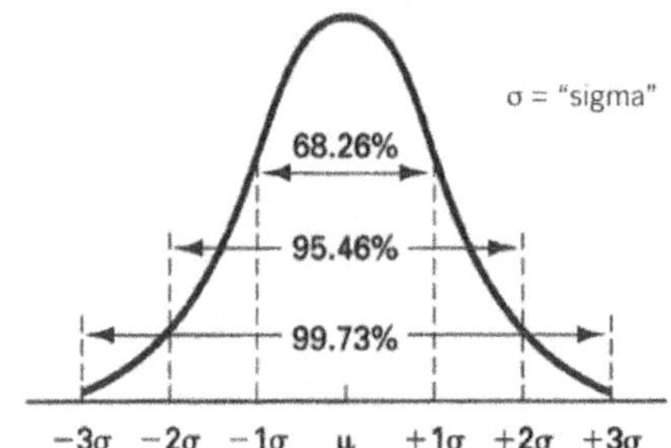

- In the figure below, we can observe that 4 standard deviations can fit between the mean and the specification limit.

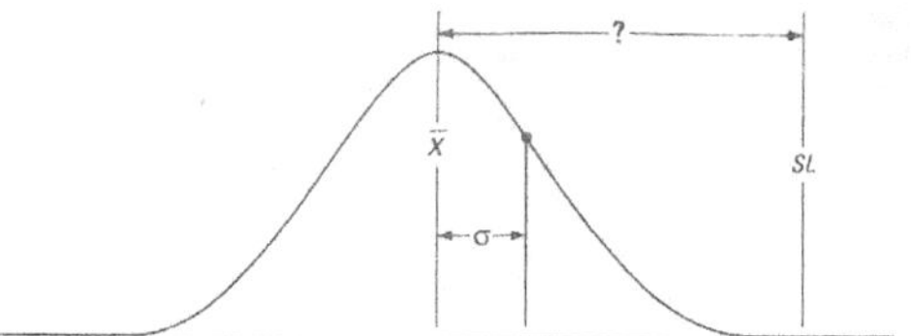

- **There are three ways in which the sigma value (Z) can change:**

  - The distribution's *central tendency*, the mean, deviates closer to or farther away from the specification limit.

  - The *width* of the distribution, defined in standard deviations, gets wider or narrower.

  - The *specification limit* moves closer to or farther away from the mean.

LSSI
LEAN SIX SIGMA INSTITUTE

Methods to calculate sigma level

Sigma level can be calculated using two different methods:

1. **Attribute data**
   Determine the number of defects (by using DPMO, previously explained) and calculate sigma level based on this number.

2. **Variable data**
   Determine the degree to which a variable (e.g., net weight of packages) meets customers' specifications and calculate sigma level based on this number.

Sigma level: Procedure for attribute data

1. Count the number of opportunities.

2. Obtain number of defects in a sample.

3. Calculate the number of defects per million opportunities.

4. Calculate the long-term sigma level (with Excel, using the inverse standard normal distribution of the DPOs).

5. Add 1.5 to obtain the short-term sigma level.

Long-term sigma level

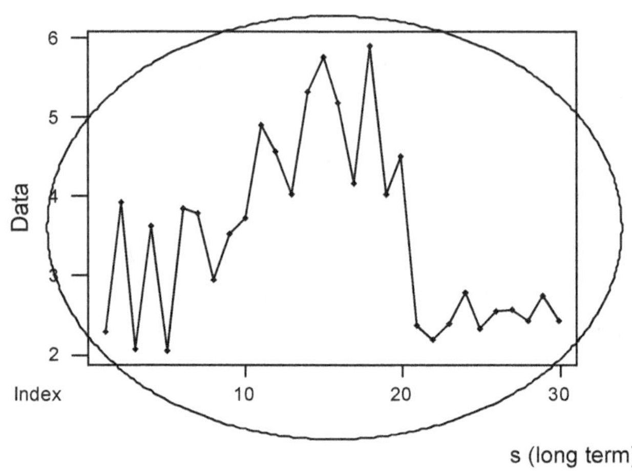

Short-term sigma level

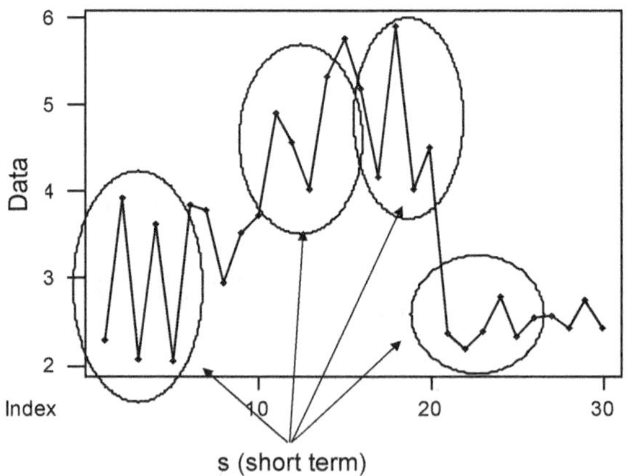

Example 1

Sigma level for attribute data

The food delivery company from the earlier example now wants to calculate the (short-term and long-term) sigma levels. Use the data in the following spreadsheet to calculate the levels:

Defects D	Units U	Opportunities OP	TOP Total Opportunities U X OP	DPO Defects per total opportunity D / TOP	DPMO DPO X 1 million	Long-term Sigma Level	Short-term Sigma Level
16	50	3	150	0.106666667	106,666.67	1.24445	**2.7445**

Unidad de orden de pedido	One delivery	50 deliveries
Late or too early	1	13
Wrong quantity	1	3
Food is not fresh	1	0
Opportunities	**3**	**16**

Example 2

Sigma level for attribute data

- The following defect opportunities are found in the assembly of printed circuit boards:

  - Wrong components — 100
  - Poorly welded components — 20
  - Poorly inserted components — 10
  - Lack of welding — 120
  - **Total defect opportunities** — **250**

- A total of 85 defects were found in a sample of 3,000 boards.

- Calculate DPMO and [short- and long-term] sigma levels.

Example 2

Sigma level for attribute data

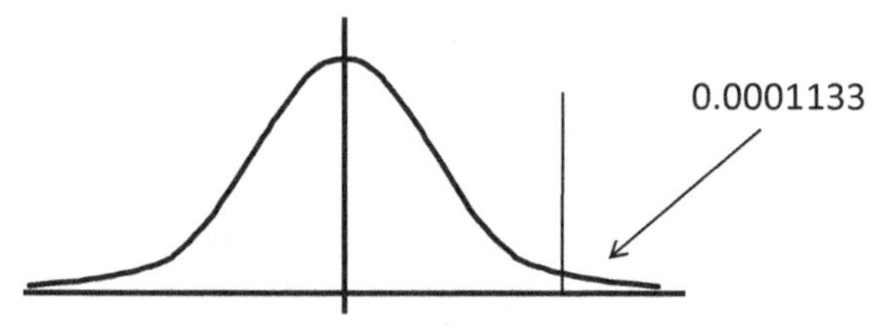

Defects D	Units U	opportunities OP	TOP Total opportunities U X OP	Defects per Total opportunities D / TOP	DPMO	Long-term Sigma level	Short-term sigma level
85	3000	250	750000	0.00011333	113.333333	3.6872769	5.1872769

Sigma level: Procedure for variable data

1. Calculate the Z-Value for each specification limit.

$$Z = \frac{SL - Mean}{Standard\ deviation}$$

2. Select the corresponding percentage for each Z-value (or use Excel functions).

3. Add the two percentage values and obtain the long-term sigma level (or use Excel functions).

4. Add 1.5 to obtain the short-term sigma level.

Example: Sigma level for variable data

- 150 data points were collected with the following results:

  Mean = 1.03

  $\sigma = 0.0573$

- Specification limits:

  LSL = 0.90

  USL = 1.10

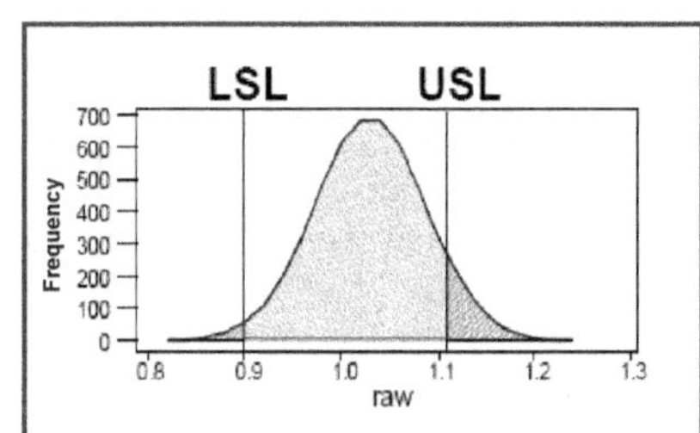

- Calculate sigma level.

The task is to calculate the portion of the normal curve that is outside the lower and upper specification limits.

1. Calculate the Z-value for each specification limit.

$$Z_L = \frac{\left(LSL - \mu \right)}{S}$$

$$= \frac{0.9 - 1.03}{0.0573}$$

$$= -2.27$$

$$Z_L = \frac{\left(USL - \mu \right)}{S}$$

$$= \frac{1.1 - 1.03}{0.0573}$$

$$= 1.22$$

2. Identify the corresponding percentage for each Z-value (in Excel, use the standard normal distribution).

- Standard normal distribution (-2.27) = 0.0116 = **1.16%**

- 1 – Standard normal distribution (1.22) = 0.1109 = **11.09%**

3. Add the two percentage values and obtain the long-term sigma level (in Excel, use the inverse standard normal distribution)

- 0.0116 + 0.1109 = **0.1226**

- Inverse standard normal distribution (1-0.1226) = **1.1623**

4. Add 1.5 to obtain the short-term sigma level = **2.6623.**

Exercise: Sigma level for variable data

Determine the % of products that are out of specification and the sigma level for the following case:

Mean = 5.2

$\sigma = 0.8$

LSL = 4.00

USL = 6.00

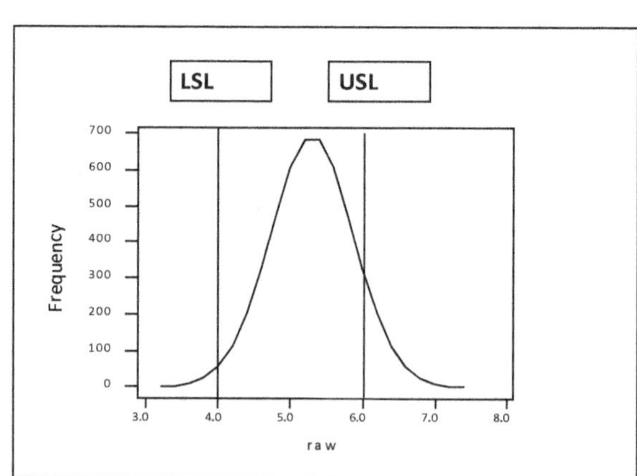

We will now analyze the process of making and serving a cup of coffee:

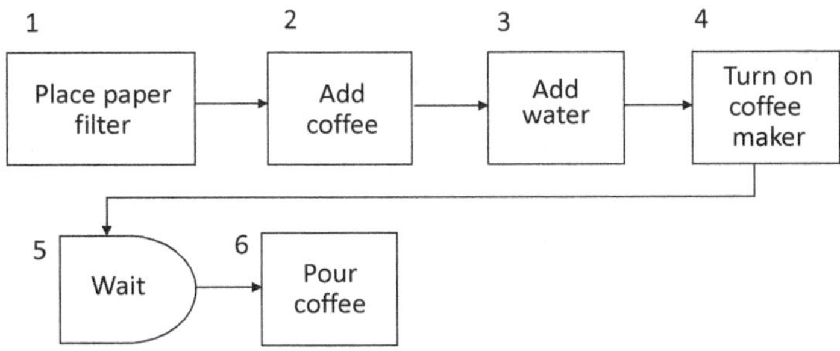

A sample of 100 preparations was collected over the long term (i.e., all possible sources of variation in the process were taken into account).

1. **Identify CTQs**

   Temperature of the coffee and fill height.

2. **Define defect opportunities**

Step	Description	Opp. for error
1	Place paper filter	2
2	Add coffee	1
3	Add water	1
4	Turn on coffee maker	1
5	Wait	2
6	Pour coffee	2
Total		**9**

3. Find defects/errors in the product or service

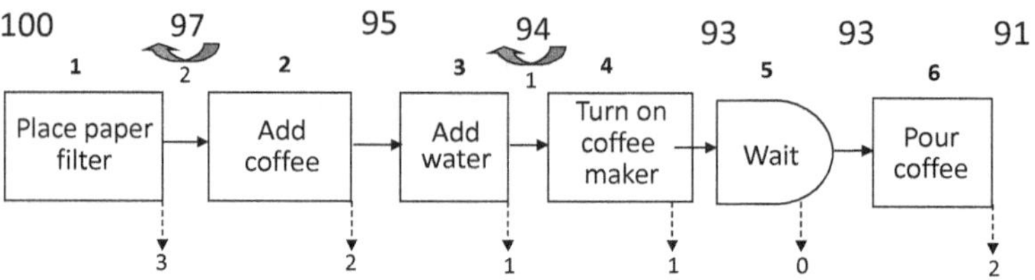

4. and 5. Calculate each step's DPMO and convert to sigma level

Individually:

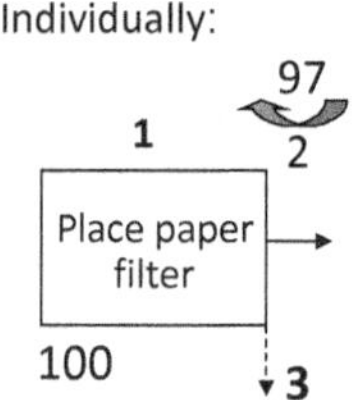

FTY = 95/100 = 0.95   DPU = (5/100) = 0.05

DPO = 5 / (100*2) = 0.025

DPMO = (0.025)(10^6) = **25,000**

LTSG = **1.96**   STSG = **3.46**

FTY = 95/97 = 0.9794   DPU = (2/97) = 0.0206

DPO = 2 / (97*1) = 0.020619

DPMO = (0.020619)(10^6) = **20,619**

LTSG = **2.04**   STSG = **3.54**

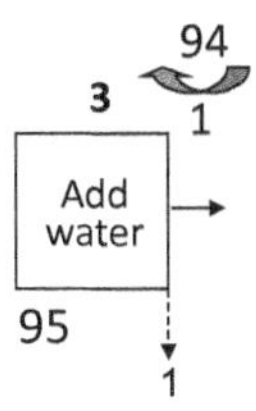

FTY = 93/95=0.9789 DPU = (2/95)=0.02105

DPO = 2 / (95*1) = 0.021053

DPMO=(0.021053)(10^6) = **21,053**

LTSG = **2.03**   STSG = **3.53**

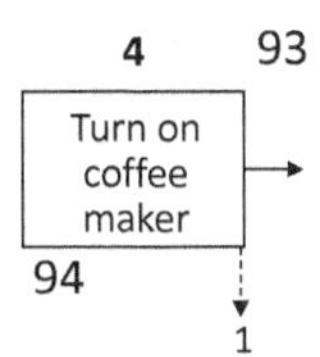

FTY = 93/94 = 0.9894   DPU = (1/94) = 0.010638

DPMO = (0.010638/1)(10^6) = **10,638**

LTSG = **2.30**   STSG = **3.80**

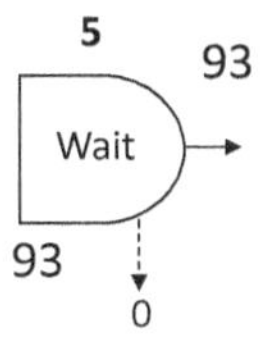

FTY = 93/93=1.0   DPU = 0

DPMO = **0**

LTSG (Z goes to infinity) = **4.50**   STSG = **6.00**

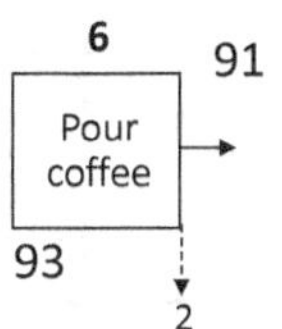

FTY = 91/93 = 0.9785   DPU = (2/93) = 0.021505

DPO= 2 / (93*2) = 0.010753

DPMO = (0.010753)(10^6) = **10,753**

LTSG = **2.30**   STSG = **3.80**

Analysis summary (Z is the long-term sigma level and Z-shift is the short-term sigma level).

Step	Defects	Units	Units w/o defect	FTY	Opp.	Total Opp.	DPU	DPO	DPMO	Long term-sigma level	Short-term sigma level
1	5	100	95	0.95	2	200	0.05000	0.025000	25000.00	1.96	3.46
2	2	97	95	0.98	1	97	0.02062	0.020619	20618.56	2.04	3.54
3	2	95	93	0.98	1	95	0.02105	0.021053	21052.63	2.03	3.53
4	1	94	93	0.99	1	94	0.01064	0.010638	10638.30	2.30	3.80
5	0	93	93	1.00	2	186	0.00000	0.000000	0.00	4.50	6.00
6	2	93	91	0.98	2	186	0.02151	0.010753	10752.69	2.30	3.80
Total	12				9	858		0.013986	13986	2.20	3.70

The number of defects per million opportunities **(DPMO)** of the **entire** process is **(Total DPO)(10^6) = 13,986** and corresponds to a **2.20** long-term sigma level (and a **3.70** short-term sigma level).

Identifying areas of opportunity

Process sequence

Step	DPMO	Sigma
Place filter	25000	3.46
Add coffee	20619	3.54
Add water	21053	3.53
Turn on	10638	3.80
Wait	0	6.00
Pour	10753	3.80

Process sequence based on sigma level

Step	DPMO	Sigma
Place filter	25000	3.46
Add water	21053	3.53
Add coffee	20619	3.54
Pour	10753	3.80
Turn on	10638	3.80
Wait	0	6.00

Exercise 1

Bank of the Atlantic identified five potential defects for every instance in which a customer requests a service on a bank teller window:

- Slow process (e.g., transaction)
- Transaction type error
- Wrong quantity
- Account number error
- Poor customer service

During the week of February 2nd to 8th, 6,956 customers visited branch #2035 in San Diego, CA. A total of 13,738 defects were identified during these instances.

Calculate DPMO and the short-term sigma level for the process.

Exercise 2

The following data for a process was collected over the long term:

- Mean   102.3
- Standard deviation   1.2
- Lower Specification Limit (LSL)   95
- Upper Specification Limit (USL)   105

Calculate Pp, Ppk, the probability of the data being out of specification, and short-term sigma level for the process.

Checklist: Reviewing the measure phase

Once the activities for the measure phase have been completed – and before moving into the analyze phase – the improvement team must verify if the objectives were met. The following checklist can be used to do so:

Review: Measure Phase

Project: ____   Date: __________

	Yes	No
1.- The team has confirmed its willingness to learn about the problem at hand, and the part of the process in which answers can be found has been identified.	☐	☐
2.- The team has identified the indicators that will be used, as well as feasibility in terms of gathering data.	☐	☐
3.- The team has developed operational definitions for the characteristics that it wants to measure.	☐	☐
4.- The operational definitions have been tested and used among team members in order to ensure that there is a common language being spoken.	☐	☐
5.- The team has confirmed that the data it needs must be new and currently do not exist in the organization.	☐	☐
6.- The team has confirmed if stratification factors are required in order to facilitate data analysis.	☐	☐
7.- The team has confirmed that data collection sheets, templates, capturing system, etc., are easy to use and these provide the necessary data.	☐	☐
8.- An appropriate sampling type, size, and frequency has been determined in order to ensure that data collected will be representative of the product, service, or process being measured.	☐	☐
9.- The measurement system has been approved and validated (R&R, stability, etc.).	☐	☐
10.- The data collected has been used to determine the baseline for the project.	☐	☐
11.- The team has confirmed (and has stated on the Project Charter) that all elements are still valid.	☐	☐

Box plots

A tool to display the full range of variation

Objectives

1. Understand the basic elements of a box plot.
2. Build box plots to visualize variation and compare data sets.

Content

> Background
> What is a box plot?
> What is it used for?
> Procedure
> Example
> Exercise

What does a box and whiskers have to do with statistics?

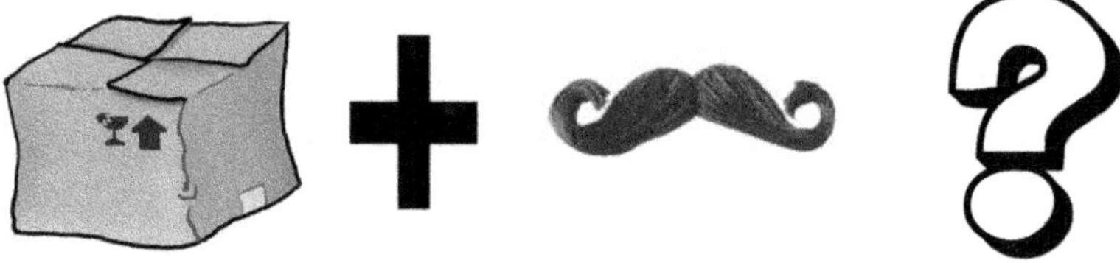

What is a box plot?

- It is a graph that displays the variation and distribution of a data set.

- In this graph, multiple sets of data can be compared side by side, making it possible to evaluate the variation of independent data samples.

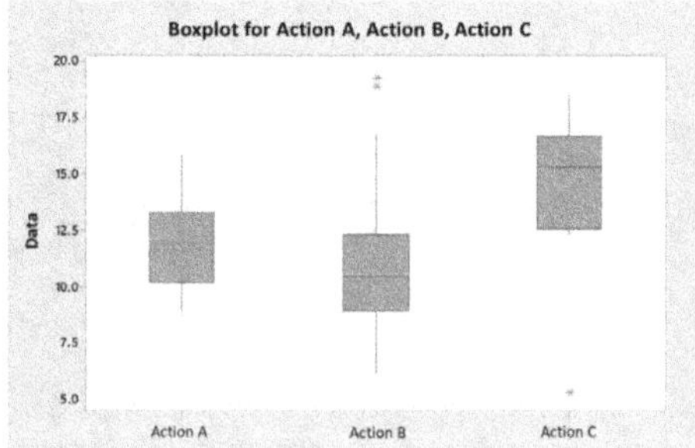

What is it used for?

- Box plots are used to quickly compare variation between two or more data sets with the same characteristics.

- It is like having two people standing back-to-back to compare their height.

- In this case, the questions that we should answer are:

  - **Which distribution has the largest *dispersion*?**
  - **Which distribution has the highest *central tendency* measurements?**

Procedure

1. Sort the data in ascending order.

2. Calculate the values to plot:

   a. Minimum value
   b. 1er Quartile (Q1)
   c. 2do Quartile (median)
   d. 3er Quartile (Q3)
   e. Maximum value

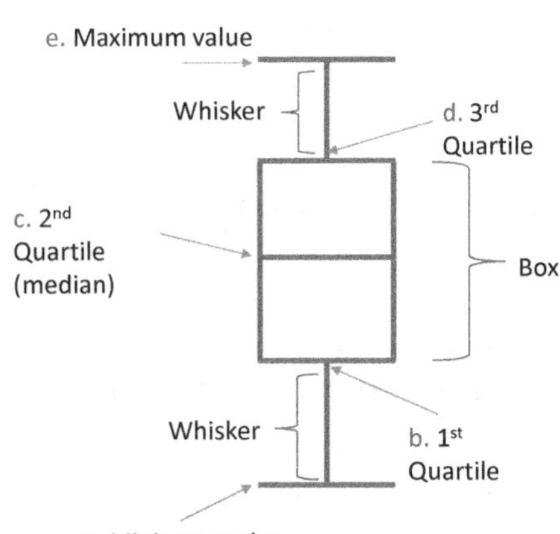

Note the following:

1. The distance between Q1 and Q3 is known as interquartile range.

2. The maximum length of each whisker is 1.5 times the interquartile range.

3. Remaining points found beyond the whiskers (if this is limited by the maximum length) are known as outliers.

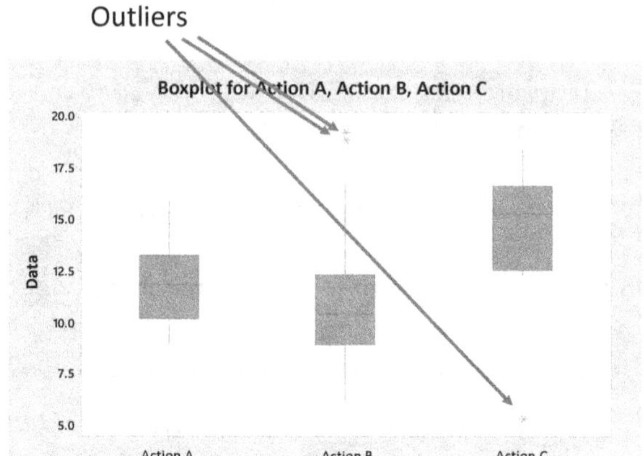

Interpret the plot as follows:

1. Variability is depicted by the dimension of the graph (taking both the box and whiskers into account). In other words, observe the amplitude between the maximum and the minimum values: the wider the graph, the greater the variability of the data.

2. The measure of central tendency (point where most of the data accumulates) is represented by the center line of the box (which is the median).

3. If outliers are observed, then their root cause should be analyzed.

The improvement team at Bank of the Atlantic wants to determine if training for bank tellers is a significant factor affecting *customer care time.* In order to do this, the team measures times for employees with different levels of experience in the process. Results are recorded in minutes as follows:

Emily	James	Elijah	Aubrey	Ava	Pete
3.2	1.5	8.4	2.2	3.1	1.2
1.7	9.2	6.3	1.4	10.2	3.2
5.8	3.2	9.1	3.2	5.6	2.2
5.2	6.7	6.8	5.8	8.8	10.0
5.4	4.5	7.3	3.3	4.3	1.1
5.6	5.3	10.4	4.5	1.1	1.0
1.9	2.1	8.3	4.5	3.3	2.1
3.1	3.3	7.5	3.3	4.5	2.8
2.2	2.3	3.2	1.8	6.5	9.2
4.3	3.2	8.5	2.1	3.2	3.2
5.0		7.3	2.2	3.1	4.3
5.3			5.5		2.1
3.5			3.2		1.8
3.0					2.0

The resulting box plot diagram (using Minitab) is:

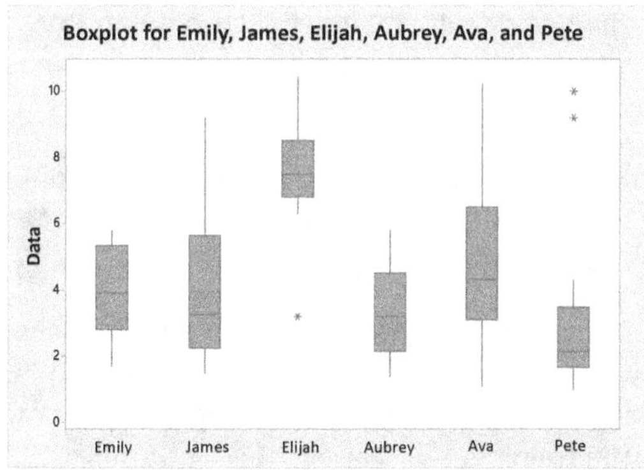

- Use the box plot diagram to draw conclusions for the following factors:

  - *Dispersion* of distributions.

  - Which process has the highest *central tendency measurements*?

  - Which process has the *least variability*?

  - To which *side* does the dispersion lean?

  - Which employee performs the *shortest customer care time*?

These conclusions are an example of the usefulness of box plots – also known as box-and-whisker charts.

The improvement team at **Bank of the Atlantic** formed the following conclusions:

- Pete is the bank teller who has received the most training at the Bank. His work reflects very low variability and the lowest measure of central tendency. His diagram shows two outliers of approximately 10 minutes each. After analyzing the root cause for these, it was discovered that the computer system failed during both instances, causing data loss and processing errors.

- Aubrey and Emily have both received an adequate amount of training. Their work reflects moderate variability and similar measures of central tendency (between 3 and 4 minutes).

- Ava and James have not received training on some modules of the system. Their work reflects high variability mainly because when they perform a certain type of transaction, they have to ask other bank tellers for help, especially since there is no instruction manual.

- Elijah is a new bank teller, and he has not received any training at all. His work so far reflects low variability, but his measure of central tendency (around 8 minutes) is higher than the target range.

The improvement team discovered that more than 80% of the work at the bank teller windows falls within the responsibility of Ava, James, and Elijah. In other words, 80% of the bank teller transactions are performed by employees who have received very little training.

Use box plots to compare the length of roads produced by three different processes and draw conclusions on the data:

Process 1	Process 2	Process 3
30.23	24.21	30.03
47.32	42.29	29.99
44.76	31.21	38.56
20.34	25.87	30.55
54.54	37.50	29.55
25.56	29.66	33.00
42.99	27.66	29.50
45.54	54.40	31.01
50.05	30.55	30.12
36.89	33.02	29.44
48.43	36.02	31.33
48.51	40.88	50.78
50.67	39.22	32.43
47.87	46.99	32.00
49.87	53.08	29.98
49.54	43.05	30.89
48.36	45.55	59.30
49.77	51.70	32.09
50.05	48.01	29.40
55.50	49.66	32.67
53.21	22.76	31.88
54.43	21.10	36.00
54.89	34.90	43.45
54.66		39.72
		33.67

Multi-vari analysis

*Obtain information about variables that affect
a process, without interrupting it*

Objectives

1. Understand the basic concepts of multi-vari charts.
2. Develop multi-vari charts to perform continuous
   improvement projects.

Content

> Background
> What are multi-vari charts?
> What are multi-vari charts used for?
> Sources of variation
> When are multi-vari charts used?
> Procedure
> Example
> Exercise

Multi-vari analysis

Background

- Multi-vari charts were developed by Leonard Seder in 1950.

Leonard Seder

- Dorian Shainin is credited with *perfecting* and promoting this tool in manufacturing applications and processes.

Dorian Shainin

What are multi-vari charts?

- A graphical procedure to break down sources of variation.

- Their objective is to identify/show the most important sources of variation in any given process.

- A graphical tool that, together with a logical sub-grouping, analyzes the effects/impact of inputs on the outputs.

- Identifies inherent capabilities and limitations within a process.

- The goal is to reduce the many immaterial **X** variables to the few vital ones.

- The few vital variables will determine the approach/path to the experimental design.

LSSI
LEAN SIX SIGMA INSTITUTE

What are multi-vari charts used for?

- To observe the variation that occurs within a part or event – as well as between different parts of a batch or events in a set of activities – for any type of process, simultaneously and in relation to time.

- Graphically analyzes the relationships between independent variables against one or more dependent variables.

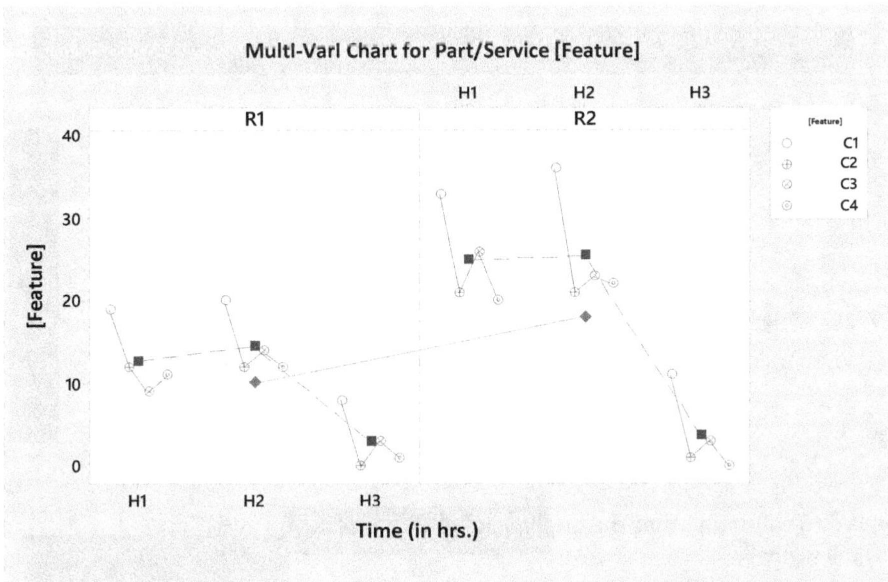

Multi-vari analysis

- **Internal (position):** Occurs when there is variation in a certain quality characteristic along the part (e.g., eccentricity, flatness, thickness, etc.). This is applicable to services indicators such as NPS (Net Promoter Score). The objective value of said quality characteristics is zero.

- **Between parts or events (cyclical):** The variation between parts produced or services provided in a relatively short amount of time.

- **Time variation:** The variation between parts or among services in a longer period of time (such as a quarter or a year). It represents variation in staff, raw material, machinery, etc.

- **Source variation:** Variation caused by different sources that manufacture the same product or provide the same service (e.g., different stations, logistics solutions, etc.).

When are multi-vari charts used?

- Analyze phase
  - When identifying the root cause(s) of variation in a process.

- Improve phase
  - When validating that the applied solution has reduced variation in a process.

Procedure

1. Define sample size.

   - It is recommended that the sample size (Kasmiersky, 1995) is between three and five units, at least.

   - Time between samples must be long enough to observe the variation between them.

   - At least 15 measurements should be taken for the study.

2. Separate samples into groups of data to identify the variation between the groups.

3. Build the graph.

4. Interpret the results.

Example

The improvement team at **Bank of the Atlantic** plans to use multi-vari charts to analyze customer wait time at bank teller windows (measured in minutes) for:

- Three employees with different levels of training
- Number of transactions (from 1 to 5 transactions, or more than 5 transactions)
- Time of day (beginning of, halfway through, or at the end of a work shift)

	Emily		Anthony		Laura	
Work Shift	1-5 transactions	>5	1-5 transactions	>5	1-5 transactions	>5
Beginning (9:00-11:30)	3.21	10.09	7.05	15.11	12.09	23.12
Mid 11:30-14:00)	4.05	9.32	6.15	17.03	11.10	21.09
End (14:00-16:30)	2.89	11.01	5.98	15.15	11.99	22.07

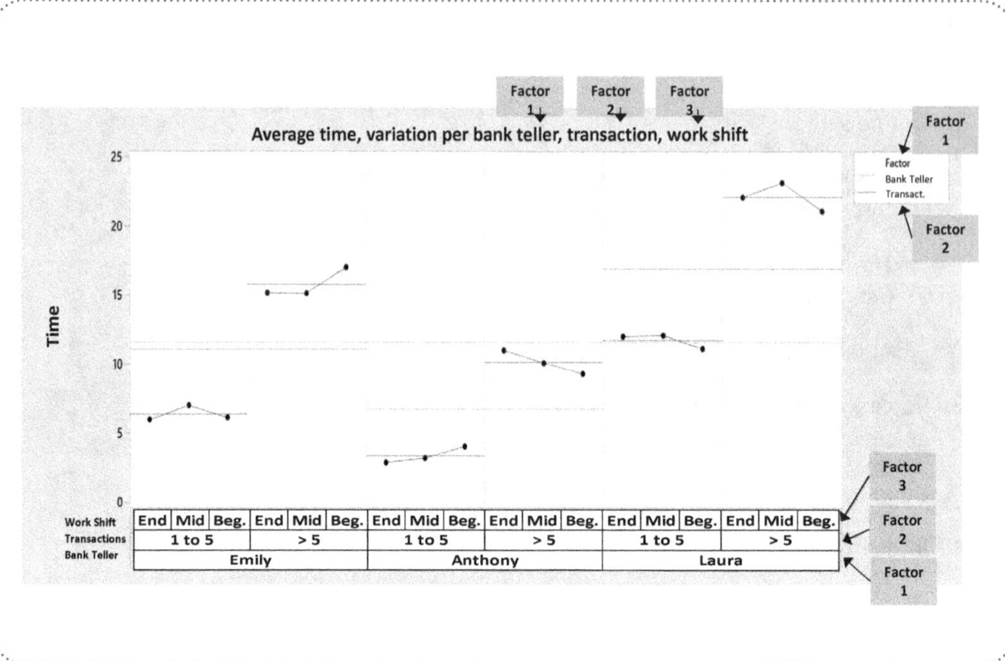

Example - Conclusions

1. Training level (yellow lines) impacts customer wait time: Emily's performance, which represents the bank teller with the most training, reflects the lowest average customer wait time, while this number is higher for Anthony, whose training level is 'medium'. Average customer wait time is even lower for Laura, who is new to the Bank and has not been trained as extensively.

2. The number of transactions (red lines) also impacts customer wait time: For all bank tellers, a higher average customer wait time is reflected when more than five transactions are performed.

3. Significant, differing levels of customer wait time are not shown among the three work shifts (blue lines), since little variation is observed in all cases. This may indicate that the number of hours in the work shift does not affect performance.

Multi-vari analysis

The improvement team at **Logistics Company** intends to identify the root cause(s) for *product shortages* by using multi-vari analysis, measuring the number of rejected products, and taking the following three factors into consideration:

- Type of customer: Small retailer or corporate retailer
- Distribution center: New York City, Boston or Philadelphia
- Season: Spring, summer, autumn or winter

Season	Small Retailer			Corporate Retailer		
	NYC	Boston	Philadelphia	NYC	Boston	Philadelphia
Spring	15	9	7	25	15	15
Summer	23	7	5	31	10	13
Autumn	17	5	11	29	13	9
Winter	37	17	19	55	27	31

Hypothesis testing and confidence intervals

Identify the most significant variables in a process

Objectives

1. Understand the basic concepts of hypothesis testing and confidence intervals.
2. Develop hypothesis testing and confidence intervals for improvement projects and/or problem solving.

Content

> Background
> What is hypothesis testing?
> Elements of hypothesis testing
> Confidence levels
> What are confidence intervals?
> What are confidence intervals used for?
> When are its used?
> Procedure
> Types
> Exercise

Background

Identify the significant variables

- Use hypothesis testing and Confidence Intervals (CI) to analyze a process and identify its *significant variables*.

- Once critical factors are identified, we can *adjust* the process and *reduce* its variation.

Central Limit Theorem (CLT)

Let's assume that for the analysis, sufficiently large samples are selected, and the means for such samples are calculated.

The means distribution for such samples will be normal, regardless of the original/underlying distribution (individual units).

$$\mu_{\overline{X}} = \mu \qquad \sigma^2_{\overline{X}} = \frac{\sigma^2}{n}$$

Original/Underlying distribution (Xs)   **Means distribution ($\overline{X}$)**

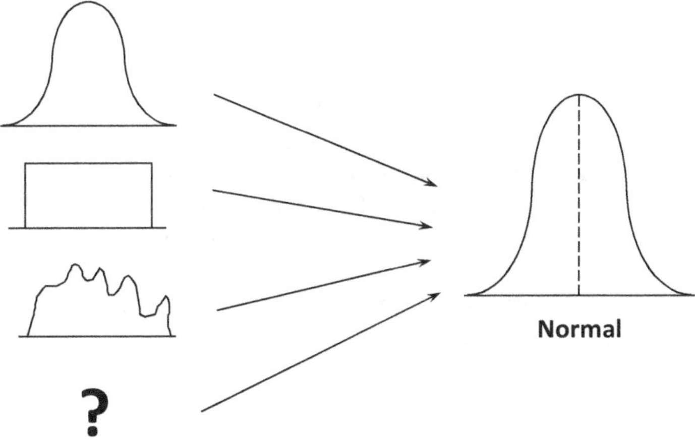

Central Limit Theorem (CLT): Definition

For populations with unknown distributions:

- The power of CLT is based on its ability to approximate x-bar not only for a normal distribution, but for ALL distributions.

- Given an unknown distribution with mean m and standard deviation σ, $n \geq 30$ observations would result in an approximation of the normal *x*-bar.

- For cases in which $n < 30$ observations, the approximation of *x*-bar is good only if the original distribution is close to the normal distribution.

Note: $n \geq 30$ is the number of subgroups pulled from a population (not the sample size). For example, if we pull 5 samples per subgroup, then we need around 30 subgroups to start seeing a normal distribution.

What is hypothesis testing?

An hypothesis testing is a statistical process that is used to infer/make a decision based on a sample of observed data: the most likely value of a parameter (mean, variance, proportion, difference between means or proportions, or ratio of two variances), or the most likely distribution of a population.

Elements of hypothesis testing

1. **Hypothesis:** Null hypothesis that you want to test (Ho) and alternative hypothesis (Ha) that you might believe to be true.

2. **Sample(s):** The data collected from a population.

3. **Test Statistics (TS):** A random variable that summarizes a data set (sample).

4. **Null hypothesis Rejection Region (RRHo):** The area in a distribution where, if the test statistic is found, then Ho is rejected.

5. **Decision:** Whether or not Ho is rejected.

6. **Test confidence level:** $(1 - \alpha)$.

Types of errors and their probabilities

By testing the hypothesis and deciding whether or not the null hypothesis (Ho) is rejected, two types of errors may occur.

1. Type I error: *Rejecting* Ho when Ho was actually *true*.
2. Type II error: *Accepting* Ho when Ho is actually false.

From these two errors, two probabilities surge:

$$\alpha = p \text{ (Type I error)}$$
$$\alpha = p \text{ (Rejecting Ho when Ho is true)}$$

$$\beta = p \text{ (Type II error)}$$
$$\beta = p \text{ (Accepting Ho when Ho is false)}$$

Confidence levels

- "Alpha" (a) represents the maximum risk or probability of concluding that the current population parameter is contained in a region (mean, standard deviation, etc.) where it actually is not, or the probability of not capturing the real parameter in the confidence interval (also known as type I error).

- This probability a is known as "significance level"; it is always greater than 0 and is usually set at 10%, 5%, or 1%.

- The value of (1 − a) is known as the "confidence level", and its commonly used values include 90%, 95%, and 99%.

What are confidence intervals?

- **Practically:**

    - A range of values (interval) from a sample population that tells us where the true population parameters are contained (considering a given confidence level).

- **Statistically:**

    - The Confidence Interval (CI) for a population, mean (μ) or sigma (σ) is a random interval that is defined as $100 (1 − \alpha)$ %, where:

        - Probability (lower CI $\leq \mu \leq$ upper CI) $= 1 − \alpha$

        - Probability (lower CI $\leq \sigma \leq$ upper CI) $= 1 − \alpha$

        - CIs commonly used include 90%, 95%, and 99%.

Confidence intervals?

For example, a 95% confidence level can be interpreted as follows:

- Approximately 95 samples out of 100 will give us a CI containing the true population parameter.

- Approximately 5 samples out of 100 will give us a CI that does not contain the true population parameter.

- We are 95% confident that the true population parameter is contained within the CI.

What are confidence intervals used for?

- Sample statistics such as the mean or standard deviation of a sample are only approximations to the true population parameters, μ and σ.

- Due to the inherent variability from sample to sample in these estimates, we quantify our uncertainty using statistically-based confidence intervals.

  - In the auto industry, a 95% CI is used for our data.

  - In the medical industry, a 99.9% CI is used for our data.

- CIs provide a way to analyze the variance among samples.

- CIs are used to calculate statistical confidence for the population parameters (mean, standard deviation, etc.).

When are its used?

- **Analyze phase:** To compare the significance of samples coming from different underlying conditions.

- **Improve phase:** To compare process means after improvements to baseline or reference means.

Procedure

1. State the problem (in practical terms).
2. Test the data for normality.
3. Determine objectives for μ, σ (or σ^2) and/or for proportion (p).
4. Define the null hypothesis (Ho).
5. Determine the appropriate test statistic to use.
6. Find the critical values using the alpha value and the distribution.

> If the calculated statistic > critical value, then **reject** Ho, or
> if p-value $\leq$ 0.05 (p-value $\leq$ alpha), then **reject** Ho.

7. Determine the Confidence Interval (CI).
8. Translate the statistical conclusion into practical process terminology.

Types

| 1. For variance(s) |
| 2. For means |
| 3. For difference of means |
| 4. For one and two proportions |
| 5. For more than two proportions |

1. Hypothesis testing and CI for variances

1.1 One-sample test

a) $n \geq 30$

Ho Rejection Region (RRHo)

$$Ho: \sigma^2 = \sigma_0^2 \qquad Ha: \sigma^2 > \sigma_0^2 \qquad Z > Z_\alpha$$

$$\sigma^2 < \sigma_0^2 \qquad Z < -Z_\alpha$$

$$\sigma^2 \neq \sigma_0^2 \qquad |Z| > Z_{\alpha/2}$$

$$Z = \frac{S - \sigma_0}{\sigma_0/\sqrt{2n}} \qquad CI: \left[\frac{S}{1 + \dfrac{Z_{\alpha/2}}{\sqrt{2n}}} \; ; \; \frac{S}{1 - \dfrac{Z_{\alpha/2}}{\sqrt{2n}}} \right]$$

1. Hypothesis testing and CI for variances

b) n < 30

Ho Rejection Region (RRHo)

$\text{Ho}: \sigma^2 = \sigma_0^2 \qquad \text{Ha}: \sigma^2 > \sigma_0^2 \qquad X^2 > X^2_{\alpha, n-1}$

$\qquad\qquad\qquad\qquad \sigma^2 < \sigma_0^2 \qquad X^2 < X^2_{1-\alpha, n-1}$

$\qquad\qquad\qquad\qquad \sigma^2 \neq \sigma_0^2 \qquad X^2 > X^2_{\alpha/2, n-1} \text{ o } X^2 < X^2_{1-\alpha/2, n-1}$

$$X^2 = \frac{(n-1)S^2}{\sigma_0^2} \qquad \text{CI}: \left[\frac{(n-1)S^2}{X^2_{\alpha/2, n-1}} ; \frac{(n-1)S^2}{X^2_{1-\alpha/2, n-1}}\right]$$

1. Hypothesis testing and CI for variances

1.2 Difference between standard deviations of normal populations

a) $(n_1, n_2) \geq 30$

Ho Rejection Region (RRHo)

$\text{Ho}: \sigma_1 = \sigma_2 \qquad\qquad \text{Ha}: \sigma_1 > \sigma_2 \qquad Z > Z_{\alpha}$

$\qquad\qquad\qquad\qquad\qquad\qquad \sigma_1 < \sigma_2 \qquad Z < -Z_{\alpha}$

$\qquad\qquad\qquad\qquad\qquad\qquad \sigma_1 \neq \sigma_2 \qquad |Z| > Z_{\alpha/2}$

$$\text{TS}: Z = \frac{S_1 - S_2}{Sp\sqrt{\dfrac{1}{2n_1} + \dfrac{1}{2n_2}}}$$

$$CI = S_1 - S_2 \pm Z_{\alpha/2} Sp\sqrt{\frac{1}{2n_1} + \frac{1}{2n_2}}$$

1. Hypothesis testing and CI for variances

1.2 Ratio of two variances for normal populations

b) $(n_1, n_2) < 30$

Ho Rejection Region (RRHo)

$\text{Ho}: \sigma_1^2 = \sigma_2^2 \qquad \text{Ha}: \sigma_1^2 > \sigma_2^2 \qquad F > F_{\alpha, n_1-1, n_2-1}$

$$\sigma_1^2 < \sigma_2^2 \qquad F < F_{1-\alpha, n_1-1, n_2-1}$$

$$\sigma_1^2 \neq \sigma_2^2 \qquad F < F_{1-\alpha/2, n_1-1, n_2-1} \text{ o } F > F_{\alpha/2, n_1-1, n_2-1}$$

$$\text{TS}: F = \frac{S_1^2}{S_2^2} \qquad \text{CI}: \left[\frac{S_1^2}{S_2^2\, F_{\alpha/2, n_1-1, n_2-1}} \; ; \; \frac{S_1^2\, F_{\alpha/2, n_2-1, n_1-1}}{S_2^2} \right]$$

Transformation of F

$$F_{1-\alpha/2, n_1-1, n_2-1} = \frac{1}{F_{\alpha/2, n_2-1, n_1-1}}$$

If value 1 is not within the confidence interval, then we reject the equality of variances.

1. Hypothesis testing and CI for variances

Example: Hypothesis testing and CI for variances

The following data for operational costs (in USD) was obtained for 20 shipments by **Logistics Company:**

2,123	1,733	1,628	1,670
1,925	2,171	1,647	1,554
2,143	1,700	2,170	1,804
1,490	1,706	1,827	1,860
2,014	1,776	2,127	2,050

We want to confirm whether the standard deviation is greater than 200. Use alpha = 5%. Assume a normal distribution and a stable process.

1. Hypothesis testing and CI for variances

Answer: Hypothesis testing and CI for variances

$$\text{Ho:}\ \sigma = 200\ \text{USD} \quad \text{vs} \quad \text{Ha:}\ \sigma > 200\ \text{USD}$$

Data:
Standard deviation of the sample = 200   n = 20

Answer:
$$X^2 = \frac{(n-1)S^2}{\sigma_0^2} = \frac{19(220)^2}{200^2} = 22.99$$

$$X^2_{\alpha,n-1} = X^2_{0.05,19} = 30.1$$

Test

Null hypothesis $H_0\!: \sigma = 200$
Alternative hypothesis $H_1\!: \sigma > 200$

Test

Method	Statistic	DF	P-Value
Bonett	—	—	0.136
Chi-Square	22.99	19	0.238

Since 22.99 < 30.1, and p-value > 0.05, Ho is not rejected. In other words, we cannot reject the hypothesis that standard deviation may be less than or equal to 200.

1. Hypothesis testing and CI for variances

Exercise: Hypothesis testing and CI for variances

Test the null hypothesis Ho using alpha = 0.05

$$\text{Ho:}\ \sigma_1 = \sigma_2 \quad \text{vs} \quad \text{Ha:}\ \sigma_1 \neq \sigma_2$$

Operational costs for January and February:

Sample 1: January	Standard deviation:	207 USD
	Sample size:	20

Sample 2: February	Standard deviation:	187 USD
	Sample size:	25

Determine the 95% confidence interval for the ratio of these two standard deviations.

1. Hypothesis testing and CI for variances

Answer: Hypothesis testing and CI for variances

Using the Excel template

Test statistic		Table statistics	
F-test		$F\,[(1 - \alpha/2),\ n1 - 1,\ n2 - 1\,]$	$F\,[\alpha/2,\ n1 - 1,\ n2 - 1\,]$
1.23		0.41	2.35

	p-value	Conclusion
Upper Limit	0.6306	Ho is accepted
Lower Limit	1.3694	Ho is accepted

Confidence Interval for the Ratio of Standard Deviations

Lower Limit	Upper Limit
0.7228	1.7335

Using Minitab

Ratio of Standard Deviations

Estimated 95% CI for Ratio

Ratio	using F
1.10695	(0.723, 1.733)

Test

Null hypothesis	$H_0:\ \sigma_1 / \sigma_2 = 1$
Alternative hypothesis	$H_1:\ \sigma_1 / \sigma_2 \neq 1$
Significance level	$\alpha = 0.05$

Test

Method	Statistic	DF1	DF2	P-Value
F	1.23	19	24	0.631

Both methods conclude that Ho is not rejected. In other words, the standard deviations for both populations are equal, so the confidence interval for the ratio contains 1 as a value (we obtain the same interval for both methods).

2. Hypothesis testing and CI for means

$$\text{Ho: } \mu_1 = \mu_0 \qquad \text{Ha: } \mu_1 > \mu_0$$

Ho Rejection Region (RRHo)

Ha	Z-test	t-test
$\mu_1 > \mu_0$	$Z > Z_\alpha$	$t > t_{\alpha,n-1}$
$\mu_1 < \mu_0$	$Z < -Z_\alpha$	$t < -t_{\alpha,n-1}$
$\mu_1 \neq \mu_0$	$|Z| > Z_{\alpha/2}$	$|t| > t_{\alpha/2,n-1}$

a) $n \geq 30$ Assume known variance, equal to the population's

$$Z = \frac{\overline{X} - \mu_0}{s/\sqrt{n}} \qquad CI = \overline{X} \pm Z_{\alpha/2}\,\frac{s}{\sqrt{n}}$$

b) $n < 30$

b1) Known variance, equal to the population's

$$Z = \frac{\overline{X} - \mu_0}{\sigma/\sqrt{n}} \qquad CI = \overline{X} \pm Z_{\alpha/2}\,\frac{\sigma}{\sqrt{n}}$$

b2) Unknown variance, may be equal to or different than the population's

$$t = \frac{\overline{X} - \mu_0}{S/\sqrt{n}} \qquad CI = \overline{X} \pm t_{\alpha/2,n-1}\,\frac{S}{\sqrt{n}}$$

Example: Hypothesis testing and CI for means

- A sample size (n) of 50 data points for operational costs (for shipping, specifically) at **Logistics Company** were obtained.

$\overline{X}$ = 890 USD   S = 220 USD

- Is this data sufficient evidence to suggest that the average operational cost for shipping is less than 1,000 USD?

- Use a 95% confidence interval.

Ho: $\mu = 1000$ **Ha: $\mu < 1000$**

$$Z = \frac{\overline{X} - \mu_0}{S/\sqrt{n}} \qquad (\alpha = 0{,}05)$$

$$Z = \frac{890 - 1000}{220/\sqrt{50}} = -3.535 \quad \text{vs} \quad -Z_\alpha = -Z_{0.05} = -1.645$$

Ho Rejection Region (RRHo)

$$Z > Z_\alpha \quad t > t_{\alpha, n-1}$$
$$Z < -Z_\alpha \quad t < -t_{\alpha, n-1}$$
$$|Z| > Z_{\alpha/2} \quad |t| > t_{\alpha/2, n-1}$$

(Minitab)

Test

Null hypothesis   Ho: $\mu = 1000$
Alternative hypothesis   H₁: $\mu < 1000$

Z-Value P-Value
-3.54   0.000 $p \leq 0.05$

Given that $-3.535 < -1.645$ ($p \leq 0.05$), there is sufficient evidence to reject Ho. In other words, we reject the hypothesis that the average operational [shipping] cost is greater than or equal to 1,000 USD.

2. Hypothesis testing and CI for means

Exercise: Hypothesis testing and CI for means

- The following table shows 50 data points for a filling station:

74.030	73.994	74.002	73.998	73.988	74.009	74.000	73.994	73.984	74.001
73.995	74.004	73.992	74.000	74.004	73.995	73.994	74.006	74.012	73.999
73.988	73.983	74.024	74.002	74.010	73.985	74.006	74.003	74.010	73.989
74.002	74.006	73.996	73.967	74.015	74.008	73.984	73.995	74.002	74.008
73.992	74.012	74.007	74.014	73.982	73.998	74.000	74.000	74.010	73.984

Using a 99% confidence interval:

- Determine if we can confirm that standard deviation is less than 0.010 ml.

- Calculate the confidence interval for the standard deviation of the process.

- Determine if we can confirm that the average volume is greater than 73.8 ml.

- Calculate a confidence interval for average volume.

3. Hypothesis Testing and CI for difference of means

Ho Rejection Region (RRHo)

$$Ho: \mu_1 = \mu_2 \qquad Ha: \mu_1 > \mu_2$$

$$Z > Z_\alpha \quad t > t_{\alpha, n_1+n_2-2}$$

$$\mu_1 < \mu_2$$

$$Z < -Z_\alpha \quad t < -t_{\alpha, n_1+n_2-2}$$

$$\mu_1 \neq \mu_2$$

$$|Z| > Z_{\alpha/2} \quad |t| > t_{\alpha/2, n_1+n_2-2}$$

Different samples sizes, known variances, and equal to the populations'

a) $(n_1, n_2) \geq 30$

$$Z = \frac{\overline{X}_1 - \overline{X}_2}{\sqrt{\dfrac{S_1^2}{n_1} + \dfrac{S_2^2}{n_2}}}$$

$$CI = \overline{X}_1 - \overline{X}_2 \pm Z_{\alpha/2} \sqrt{\frac{S_1^2}{n_1} + \frac{S_2^2}{n_2}}$$

Different sample sizes, unknown population variance

b) $(n_1, n_2) < 30$

Unknown but equal variances

b1) $\sigma_1 = \sigma_2$

$$t = \frac{\overline{X}_1 - \overline{X}_2}{S_P \sqrt{\dfrac{1}{n_1} + \dfrac{1}{n_2}}}$$

$$CI = \overline{X}_1 - \overline{X}_2 \pm t_{\alpha/2, n_1+n_2-2} \, S_P \sqrt{\frac{1}{n_1} + \frac{1}{n_2}}$$

Average standard deviation

$$S_P = \sqrt{\frac{(n_1 - 1)S_1^2 + (n_2 - 1)S_2^2}{n_1 + n_2 - 2}}$$

3. Hypothesis Testing and CI for difference of means

Different sample sizes, unknown population variance

b) $(n_1, n_2) < 30$

Unknown and different variances (Welch's t-test)

b2) $\sigma_1 \neq \sigma_2$

$$t = \frac{\overline{X}_1 - \overline{X}_2}{\sqrt{\dfrac{S_1^2}{n_1} + \dfrac{S_2^2}{n_2}}}$$

$$CI = \overline{X}_1 - \overline{X}_2 \pm t_{\alpha/2,\,gl}\sqrt{\frac{S_1^2}{n_1} + \frac{S_2^2}{n_2}}$$

Sample size for the CI:

$$n_1 = n_2 = \left(\frac{Z_{\alpha/2}}{E}\right)(S_1^2 + S_2^2)$$

Degrees of freedom (df) to determine RRHo.

$$df = \frac{\left(\dfrac{S_1^2}{n_1} + \dfrac{S_1^2}{n_2}\right)^2}{\dfrac{\left(\dfrac{S_1^2}{n_1}\right)^2}{n_1 - 1} + \dfrac{\left(\dfrac{S_2^2}{n_2}\right)^2}{n_2 - 1}}$$

3. Hypothesis Testing and CI for difference of means

Example: Hypothesis testing and CI for difference of means

A team seeks to compare the average operational [shipping] costs for March and April. A sample of 10 cost data points for March and 12 cost data points for April were selected:

Xavg. (March) = 1,050 USD　　　S (March) = 100 USD
Xavg. (April) = 990 USD　　　S (April) = 170 USD

Test the hypothesis of equality for average operational [shipping] costs.
Alpha = 5%.
Calculate CI.

3. Hypothesis Testing and CI for difference of means

$H_0: \mu_1 = \mu_2 \quad H_a: \mu_1 \neq \mu_2$ **Different sample sizes, we assume equal variances (since costs originate from the same process)**

$$t = \frac{\overline{X}_1 - \overline{X}_2}{S_P\sqrt{\dfrac{1}{n_1} + \dfrac{1}{n_2}}} \qquad S_P = \sqrt{\frac{(n_1 - 1)S_1^2 + (n_2 - 1)S_2^2}{n_1 + n_2 - 2}}$$

Test

Null hypothesis $\quad H_0: \mu_1 - \mu_2 = 0$
Alternative hypothesis $H_1: \mu_1 - \mu_2 \neq 0$

$$S_P = \sqrt{\frac{9(100)^2 + 11(170)^2}{10 + 12 - 2}} = 142.811$$

T-Value	DF	P-Value
0.98	20	0.338

$$t = \frac{1050 - 990}{142.811\sqrt{\dfrac{1}{10} + \dfrac{1}{12}}} = 0.9812$$

$$t_{\alpha/2, n_1 + n_2 - 2} = t_{0.025,20} = 2.086$$

→ Since 0.9812 is not greater than 2.086 (p-value > 0.05), then we do not reject the hypothesis of equality for the means of the two populations.

$$CI = 1050 - 990 \pm (2.086)(142.811)\sqrt{\frac{1}{10} + \frac{1}{12}}$$

$$= (-67.55, 187.55)$$

Estimation for Difference

Difference	95% CI for Pooled StDev	Difference
60.0	142.8	(-67.6, 187.6)

Given that the value is within the interval, we do not reject the hypothesis of equality for the means of the two populations.

Exercise:
Solve the same problem but now consider different variances and compare results.

3. Hypothesis Testing and CI for difference of means

Answer: Hypothesis testing and CI for difference of means

Using the Excel template:

Test statistic	Table statistic		P Value	Conclusion	Confidence interval	
T Test	t [α/2, gl calc]				Lower Limit	Upper Limit
1.03	2.10		0.3177	Ho is approved	-62.65	182.65

Using Minitab:

Test

Null hypothesis $H_0: \mu_1 - \mu_2 = 0$
Alternative hypothesis $H_1: \mu_1 - \mu_2 \neq 0$

T-Value	DF	P-Value
1.03	18	0.318

Estimation for Difference

95% CI for
Difference   Difference
60.0 (-62.7, 182.7)

Answer: t = 1.027, df = 18.19, CI: (−62.65, 182.65) → Same conclusion.

3. Hypothesis Testing and CI for difference of means

Not independent (paired observations):
Normal populations, small sample sizes.

$$Ho: \mu_d = 0 \qquad Ha: \mu_d \neq 0 \qquad \text{Reject Ho if} \quad |t| > t_{\alpha/2, n-1}$$

$$TS: t = \frac{\bar{d} - \delta}{\frac{S_d}{\sqrt{n}}}$$

d represents the difference(s) and *n* is the number of differences.

$$CI: \bar{d} \pm t_{\alpha/2, n-1} \left(\frac{S_d}{\sqrt{n}} \right)$$

3. Hypothesis Testing and CI for difference of means

Example: Paired observations

A team seeks to analyze the difference in processing time for two operators in an assembly line of electrical components. These times are taking in pairs, as it is expected than processing time increases throughout the work shift (due to tiredness). The results are captured in seconds and are summarized in the table.

Determine if both operators have equal processing times. Use a 95% CI.

Hour	Operator 1	Operator 2	Difference (1-2)
7:00	11.35	10.98	0.37
7:30	11.74	11.31	0.43
8:00	11.98	11.78	0.20
8:30	12.21	12.03	0.18
9:00	12.56	12.43	0.13
9:30	12.87	12.79	0.08
10:00	12.99	13.00	-0.01
10:30	13.31	13.35	-0.04
11:00	13.45	13.51	-0.06
11:30	13.57	13.69	-0.12
12:00	13.89	13.97	-0.08
12:30	14.05	14.03	0.02
13:00	14.33	14.31	0.02
13:30	14.90	14.93	-0.03
14:00	15.10	15.15	-0.05
14:30	15.32	15.39	-0.07
15:00	15.55	15.55	0.00
	Average		0.0571
	Standard Deviation		0.157590

3. Hypothesis Testing and CI for difference of means

Answer

Using Minitab:

Estimation for Paired Difference

N	Mean	StDev	SE Mean	95% CI for $\mu\_difference$
17	0.0571	0.1576	0.0382	(-0.0239, 0.1381)

$\mu\_difference$: population mean of (Sample 1 - Sample 2)

Test

Null hypothesis H_0: $\mu\_difference = 0$
Alternative hypothesis H_1: $\mu\_difference \neq 0$

T-Value	P-Value
1.49	0.155

Given that p-value > 0.05, we accept Ho. In other words, the equality of the time observed is validated by the confidence interval, which contains the value of 0.

4. Hypothesis testing and CI for one and two proportions

One proportion test

a) $n \geq 30, 0.1 \leq p \leq 0.9$

Ho Rejection Region (RRHo)

$$Ho: p = p_0 \qquad Ha: p > p_0 \qquad \boxed{\begin{array}{l} Z > Z_\alpha \\ \\ Z < -Z_\alpha \\ \\ |Z| > Z_{\alpha/2} \end{array}}$$

$$p < p_0$$

$$p \neq p_0$$

$$TS: Z = \frac{X - np_0}{\sqrt{np_0(1 - p_0)}} \qquad \hat{p} = \frac{X}{n}$$

$$CI: \hat{p} \pm Z_{\alpha/2} \sqrt{\frac{\hat{p}(1 - \hat{p})}{n}} \qquad X = \text{number of successes of the sample size.}$$

Difference between two proportions test

b) $(n_1, n_2) \geq 30$

Ho Rejection Region (RRHo)

$$Ho: p_1 = p_2 \qquad Ha: p_1 > p_2 \qquad \boxed{\begin{array}{l} Z > Z_\alpha \\ \\ Z < -Z_\alpha \\ \\ |Z| > Z_{\alpha/2} \end{array}}$$

$$p_1 < p_2$$

$$p_1 \neq p_2$$

$$TS: Z = \frac{\hat{p}_1 - \hat{p}_2}{\sqrt{\hat{p}(1 - \hat{p})\left(\frac{1}{n_1} + \frac{1}{n_2}\right)}} \qquad \hat{p}_1 = \frac{X_1}{n_1} \qquad \hat{p}_2 = \frac{X_2}{n_2}$$

$$CI: \hat{p}_1 - \hat{p}_2 \pm Z_{\alpha/2} \sqrt{\frac{\hat{p}_1(1 - \hat{p}_1)}{n_1} + \frac{\hat{p}_2(1 - \hat{p}_2)}{n_2}} \qquad \hat{p} = \frac{X_1 + X_2}{n_1 + n_2}$$

Example: Hypothesis testing and CI for proportions

A team wants to understand if a difference exists between the proportions of customer complaints for two **Bank of the Atlantic** branches. The number of complaints for branch 1 was 702 for a total 7,272 services performed, while branch 2 had 1,056 complaints for a total of 13,393 services offered. Use alpha of 5% and calculate the CI.

$$\text{Ho: } p_1 = p_2 \qquad \text{Ha: } p_1 \neq p_2$$

$$\hat{p}_1 = \frac{X_1}{n_1} \qquad \hat{p}_2 = \frac{X_2}{n_2} \qquad \hat{p} = \frac{X_1 + X_2}{n_1 + n_2}$$

$$\hat{p}_1 = \frac{702}{7272} = 0.0965 \qquad \hat{p}_2 = \frac{1056}{13393} = 0.0788 \qquad \hat{p} = \frac{702 + 1056}{7272 + 13393} = 0.0851$$

$$\text{TS: } Z = \frac{\hat{p}_1 - \hat{p}_2}{\sqrt{\hat{p}(1 - \hat{p})\left(\frac{1}{n_1} + \frac{1}{n_2}\right)}} \qquad Z = \frac{0.0965 - 0.0788}{\sqrt{0.0851(1 - 0.0851)\left(\frac{1}{7272} + \frac{1}{13393}\right)}} = 4.35$$

→ Given that 4.35 > 1.96 = $Z_{\alpha/2}$, we reject the hypothesis of equality for proportions of customer complaints for the two branches.

$$\text{CI: } \hat{p}_1 - \hat{p}_2 \pm Z_{\alpha/2} \sqrt{\frac{\hat{p}_1(1 - \hat{p}_1)}{n_1} + \frac{\hat{p}_2(1 - \hat{p}_2)}{n_2}}$$

$$= 0.0965 - 0.0788 \pm 1.96 \sqrt{\frac{0.0965(1 - 0.0965)}{7272} + \frac{0.0788(1 - 0.0788)}{13393}}$$

$$= (0.0095, 0.0259)$$

Since a value of zero (0) is not included within the interval, we *reject* the hypothesis for equality for proportions of customer complaints for the two branches.

4. Hypothesis testing and CI for one and two proportions

Using Minitab:

Estimation for Difference

Difference	95% CI for Difference
0.0176875	(0.009508, 0.025867)

CI based on normal approximation

Test

Null hypothesis	H_0: $p_1 - p_2 = 0$
Alternative hypothesis	H_1: $p_1 - p_2 \neq 0$

Method	Z-Value	P-Value
Normal approximation	4.24	0.000
Fisher's exact		0.000

Same results, same confidence interval. Therefore, we *reject* the hypothesis for equality for proportions of customer complaints for the two branches.

4. Hypothesis testing and CI for one and two proportions

Exercise: Hypothesis testing and CI for proportions

Analyze the proportion of defects for two different workstations:

- Workstation 1: 120 samples; proportion of defects is 0.15.

- Workstation 2: 200 samples; proportion of defects is 0.18.

Using a 99% confidence interval:

- Determine if we can conclude that proportions of defects for both workstations are equal.

- Define a confidence interval for the difference between the two proportions.

5. Hypothesis testing and CI for more than two proportions

$$Ho: p_1 = p_2 = p_3 = \cdots = p_k$$

Ha: At least one proportion is different

$$X^2 = \sum_{i=1}^{c} \frac{(fo_i - fe_i)^2}{fe_i}$$

Reject Ho if:

$$X^2 > X^2_{\alpha,,k-1}$$

$$fe = \frac{(\text{Row Total})\,(\text{Column Total})}{\text{Grand Total}}$$

of = observed frequency
ef = expected frequency
k = number of proportions to compare
c = number of cells

5. Hypothesis testing and CI for more than two proportions

Example

Determine if a difference exists between the number of defective units for three different work shifts. Use alpha = 5%. The following results were obtained:

WORK SHIFT	1	2	3	TOTAL
Defective Units (x)	30 (16.89)	10 (14.36)	8 (16.75)	48
Units Produced (n)	3251	2763	3223	9237
"Good" Units (n-x)	3221 (3234,11)	2753 (2748,64)	3215 (3206,25)	9189

$$X^2 = \frac{(30 - 16.89)^2}{16.89} + \cdots + \frac{(3215 - 3206.25)^2}{3206.25} = 16.144$$

$$X^2_{0.05,2} = 5.99$$

→ Since $X^2 = 16.144 > 5.99$, we can conclude that at least **one** of the three work shifts **is different** (number of defective units).

5. Hypothesis testing and CI for more than two proportions

Use Minitab (Statistics → Tables → Chi-Squared Test) to build a table summarizing defective vs. good units.

Rows: Worksheet rows   Columns: Worksheet columns

	Defect	Good	All
1	30	3221	3251
	16.9	3234.1	
2	10	2753	2763
	14.4	2748.6	
3	8	3215	3223
	16.7	3206.3	
All	48	9189	9237

Cell Contents
Count
Expected count

Chi-Square Test

	Chi-Square	DF	P-Value
Pearson	16.144	2	0.000
Likelihood Ratio	15.483	2	0.000

→ Since p-value < 0.05, we reject H0 and we can conclude that at least **one** of the three work shifts **is different** (number of defective units).

5. Hypothesis testing and CI for more than two proportions

Exercise

Analyze the proportion of defective units for three different work shifts in two workstations:

WORK SHIFT 1:
 Workstation 1: 120 samples; defective units: 8
 Workstation 2: 150 samples; defective units: 12

WORK SHIFT 2:
 Workstation 1: 100 samples; defective units: 6
 Workstation 2: 200 samples; defective units: 10

WORK SHIFT 3:
 Workstation 1: 180 samples; defective units: 11
 Workstation 2: 150 samples; defective units: 9

Use a 95% confidence interval to determine if we can conclude that the proportions of Defective units for all work shifts and all workstations is equal.

Analysis of variance (ANOVA)

Objectives

1. Understand the basic concepts related to analysis of variance.
2. Integrate analysis of variance with Six Sigma improvement projects.

Content

> Background
> What is ANOVA?
> Key elements
> Types of ANOVA

  * One-way ANOVA
  * One-way ANOVA with blocking
  * Two-way ANOVA
  * Two-way ANOVA with blocking
  * Three-way ANOVA

> Examples
> Exercises

Background

- ANOVA was developed by Sir Ronald Aylmer Fisher (1890-1962).

- Because of his poor eyesight, he had to visualize problems in geometric terms that could be presented graphically.

- In 1919 , he studied large data sets from his analysis of variation in harvests.

- In 1925, he published *Statistical methods for Researchers.*

- In 1935, he published *Design of Experiments*, which became an industry standard.

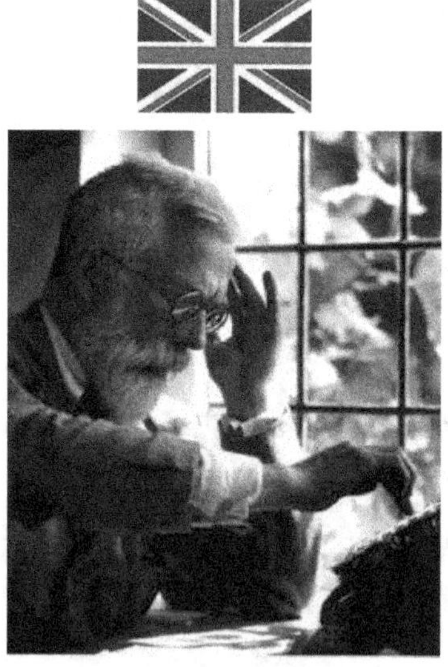

LSSI
LEAN SIX SIGMA INSTITUTE

What is ANOVA?

1. **ANOVA** is a breakdown of the total variation of data as follows:

   a. **Internal** or **natural** variation within groups.

   b. The variation **between groups** of means.

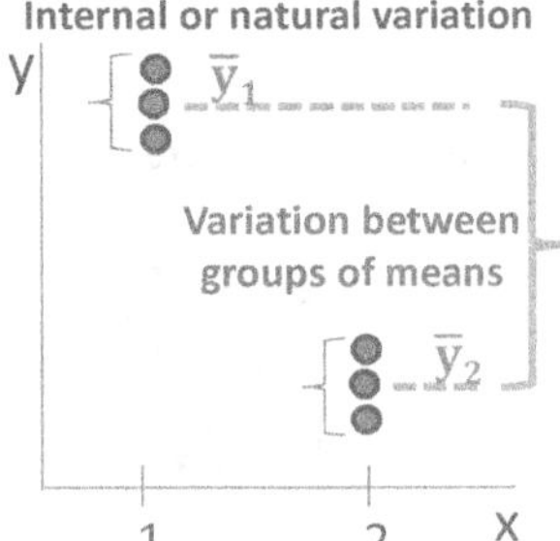

2. It compares these two types of variation:

$$F_{calc} = \frac{\text{Variation between groups of means}}{\text{Internal or natural variation}}$$

3. When comparing these two types of variation, ANOVA is used to determine whether there is a *difference* between the means being analyzed.

- ANOVA is a hypothesis test:

   Null hypothesis, H_0: all means* are the same.
   Alternative hypothesis, H_a: at least 1 mean is different.

- H_0 rejection region:

F-Distribution Chart

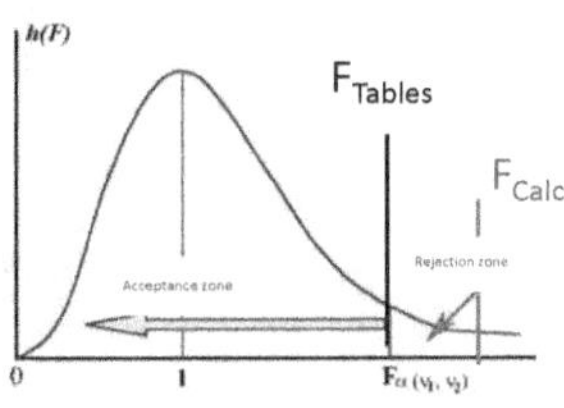

If $F_{calc} < F_{tables}$ (**p-value** > **0.05**): then we accept H_0, since means are the same.

If $F_{calc} \geq F_{tables}$ (**p-value** ≤ **0.05**): then we reject H_0, since at least 1 mean is $\neq$ (H_a).

** Means of the different groups or levels of factors.*

Key elements

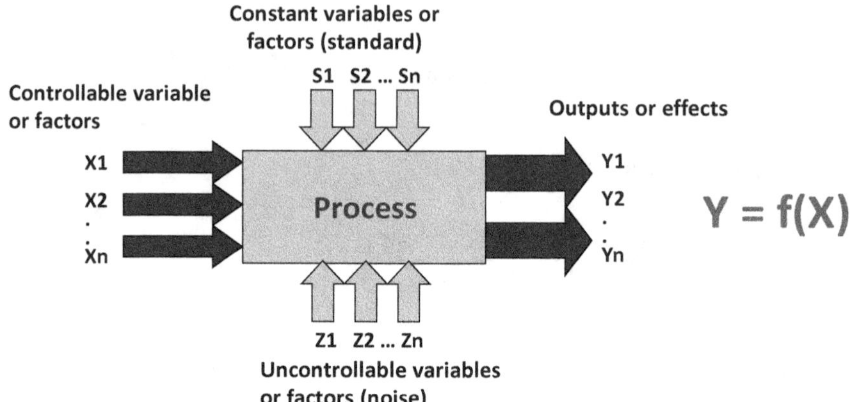

Key elements – example

<u>Cooking pancakes</u>

- **Factors**
  - Temperature
  - Amount of flour.
  - Amount of milk.
  - # of eggs.
  - Amount of sugar.
  - Cooking time

- **Levels**
  - Temperature: 200°, 210°, 220°
  - Flour: ½ kg, ¾ kg
  - Milk: ¼ L, ½ L
  - Eggs: 2, 3, 4
  - Sugar: 100 g, 200 g
  - Cooking Time: 5 min, 8 min

- **Noise factors**
  - Altitude.
  - Humidity

- **Treatments**
  - All combinations
    $2^4 \times 3^2 = 144$

Basic concepts for a correct analysis

- **Replication:** Used to obtain an estimate of the experimental error and determine if specific factors influence the results.

- **Randomization:** Used to neutralize sources of variation.

- **Blocking:** Used to eliminate the effect of nuisance variables on the experiment.

Key elements

1. **Include non-statistical knowledge:** It is important to consult with experts on the subject matter who can contribute their input and feedback. This non-statistical knowledge is highly valuable for selecting factors, determining levels and interpreting results.

2. **Keep the experiment design and analysis as simple as possible:** Do not overuse complex and sophisticated statistical tools. Is it best to use simple design and analysis methods.

3. **Consider both the statistical and practical significance:** This is important because we sometimes find solutions that optimize a result, but that are not economically feasible or sustainable in the long term.

4. **Conduct iterative experiments:** Long experiments are inconvenient and often impractical. They often are not necessary because solutions may appear sooner in the experimental process. It is recommended that you limit your contribution of resources to no more than 25% for the initial experiment in order to reserve enough resources for the final experiment.

Types of ANOVA

1. One-way ANOVA

2. One-way ANOVA with blocking

3. Two-way ANOVA

4. Two-way ANOVA with blocking

5. Three-way ANOVA

1. One-way ANOVA

- A one-way ANOVA is used to investigate the effect of different levels of one factor (x) with respect to the mean of a response variable (y).

- In the following example, we will determine if the manufacturing process (x) influences the length of screws (y).

Resulting screw length from each manufacturing process:

Process	Replicates 1	2	3	Average Yi
A	2.05	2.03	2.02	2.03333
B	1.98	1.99	2.00	1.99000
C	2.07	2.05	2.05	2.05667

Avg. Y   2.02667

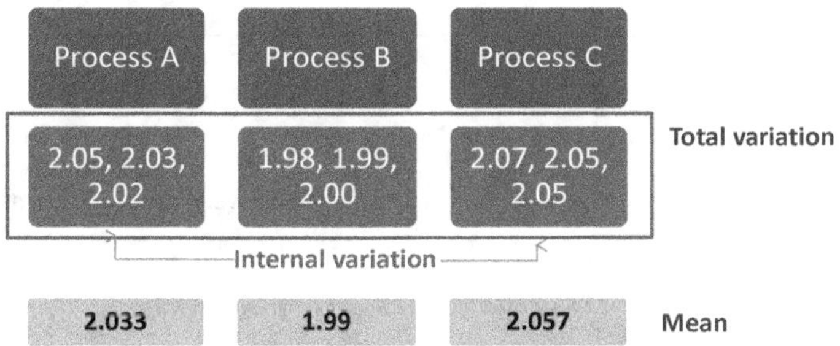

- Is the difference seen on the box plot significant?

- You can use ANOVA to answer this question.

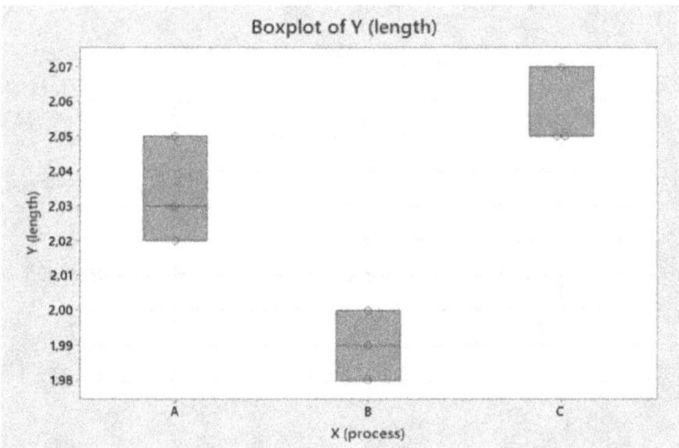

Procedure: ANOVA table

Sources of variation	SS	df	MS	F
Treatments (t)	SSt	$a - 1$	MSt = SSt / a-1	MST / MSE
Error (E)	SSE	N - a	MSE = SSE / N-a	
Total	SST	N - 1		

SS = Sum of squares
df = Degrees of freedom
MS = Mean square
F = Comparison of variation (error) within and between groups (treatments)

Using the data from the screws exercise:

Sources of variation	SS	Df	MS	F
Treatments (t)	0.006867	2	0.003433	22.08
Error (E)	0.000933	6	0.000156	
Total	0.00780	8		

$> F_{0.05,\,2,\,6} = 5.14$

Microsoft Excel Worksheet

Analysis of variance

Source	Df	Adj. SS	Adj. MS	F-value	P-value	
Process (x)	2	0.006867	0.003433	22.07	0.0017	< 0.05
Error	6	0.000933	0.000156			
Total	8	0.007800				

Minitab

When comparing F_0 to the F-value (5.14) or to the p-value (0.0017), we see that:

$$F_{calc} > F_{tables} \text{ and p-value} < 0.05$$

→ Therefore, we conclude that the process variable **does** affect the mean length of the screws.

ANOVA assumptions

The dependent variable (Y) must be continuous, on an interval scale or a ratio scale.

- **Normality:** The distributions of the residuals are normal.
- **Homoscedasticity:** Homogeneity of variances.
- **Independence** of observations.

Errors are independent and normally distributed.

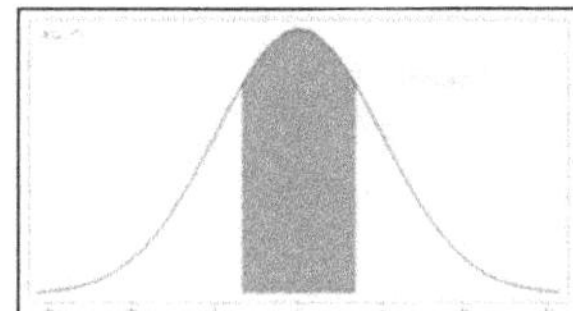

$$\varepsilon \sim N(0,\sigma^2)$$

Example 1: One-way ANOVA

We want to know whether the number of employees performing a picking function at **Logistics Company** affects the average time it takes to perform this process. In this case, the factor is a discrete quantitative variable, from which 5 levels were tested, and 5 replicates were performed. Picking time was measured and recorded in minutes. The results were as follows:

No. of Employees	Replicates				
	1	**2**	**3**	**4**	**5**
5	9.0	8.7	9.1	8.5	8.8
6	7.3	7.6	7.2	7.5	7.7
7	5.6	5.8	5.3	5.3	5.1
8	4.9	4.8	4.8	5.0	5.0
9	5.2	5.1	5.0	4.9	5.3

- **What is the problem?**

  - As process improvement analysts, we want to know if the number of employees assigned to the task affects picking time.

  - It is important to always plot the data.

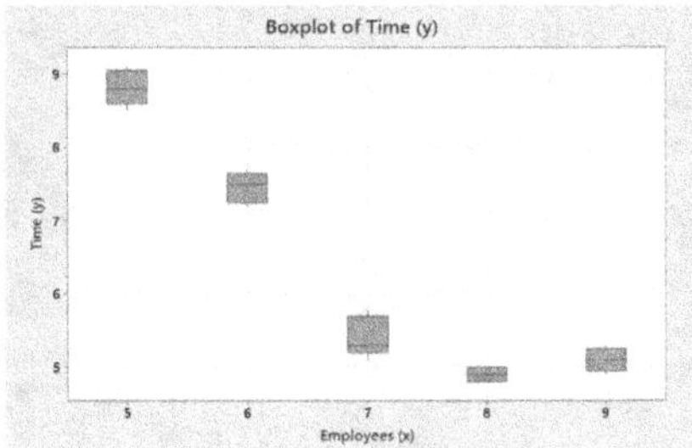

Normality

- Test for normality by graphing the residuals in a *normal probability plot*.

- If the residuals tend to follow a straight line, then they are normally distributed.

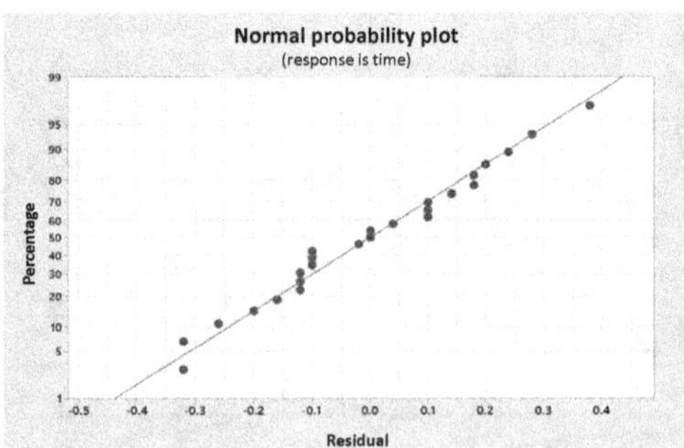

LSSI
LEAN SIX SIGMA INSTITUTE

Constant variance

- One way to test for constant variance (i.e., constant variances among treatments) is by graphing the residuals vs. the fitted values plot.

- If the points on the graph are distributed fairly evenly above and below the central line, then the variance is considered constant.

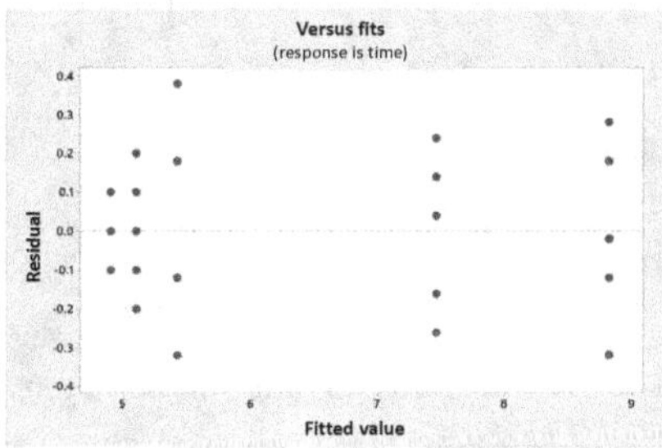

Independence

- Test if there is independence between the data and the order in which the data was collected. To test independence, we must graph the residuals vs the observation order.

- If there is a tendency or pattern when graphing the residuals vs. the observation order, there is no independence. If there are random fluctuations, then this means there is independence.

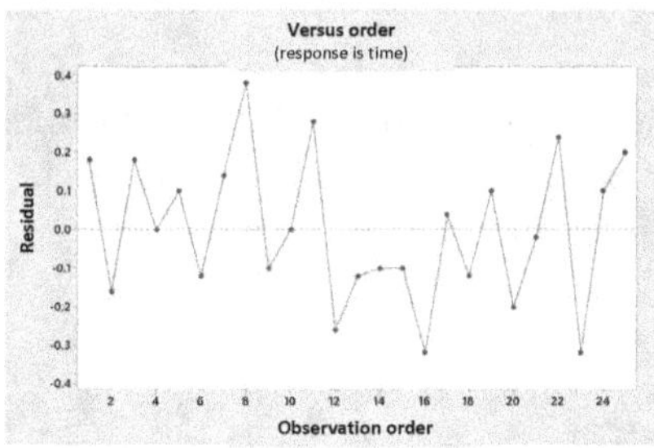

Example 2: One-way ANOVA

Source of Variation	SS	dF	MS	F	F-table
Treatments/Number of Employees	59.312000	4	14.828000	349.717 >	2.866
Error	0.848000	20	0.042400		
TOTAL	60.160000	24			

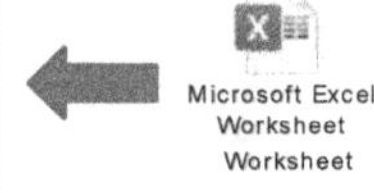
Microsoft Excel
Worksheet
Worksheet

Analysis of variance

Source	Df	Adj. SS	Adj. MS	F-value	P-value
Operators	4	59.3120	14.8220	349.72	0.000 < 0.05
Error	20	0.8480	0.0424		
Total	24	60.1600			

Minitab

$F_{calc} > F_{tables}$ **and p-value < 0.05** → the number of employees variable **does** affect the time it takes to perform the picking process.

* Assumptions are validated.

We can conclude that the number of operators is indeed a significant factor when it comes to the time it takes to perform the picking process.

It is important to clarify that, through ANOVA, we can only determine if a factor is significant or not. The optimal level for each factor will be covered and identified during the improve phase.

LSSI
LEAN SIX SIGMA INSTITUTE

Exercise: One-way ANOVA

- We want to know whether temperature affects glass density during a manufacturing process. Tests were performed, and the following data was collected:

Temperature	Density		
1	4.5	7.8	6.7
2	3.8	5.6	9.1
3	7.6	4.6	7.6
4	3.5	3.5	4.8

- What can you conclude after performing an ANOVA?

Answer

Source of Variation	SS	df	MS	F	F-table	Conclusion
Treatments	13.609167	3	4.536389	1.329	< 4.066	Not Significant
Error	27.3	8	3.4125			
TOTAL	40.909167	11				

Microsoft Excel Worksheet

Analysis of variance

Source	Df	Adj. SS	Adj. MS	F-value	P-value	
Temperature	3	13.61	4.536	1.33	0.331	> 0.05
Error	8	27.30	3.413			
Total	11	40.91				

Minitab

$F_O < F_{tables}$ **and p-value > 0.05** → The temperature variable **does not** affect glass density.

* Assumptions are validated.

2. One-way ANOVA with blocking

When conducting experiments, it is common to find other variables that are not of interest, but are yet present and could influence the results. Therefore, it is necessary to neutralize or block the effect of these variables.

Example: One-way ANOVA with blocking

- Let's suppose that in our previous example regarding screws we had 3 suppliers and each process used a different supplier's raw material.

- In this case, the difference in length might have more to do with the differences in raw materials than the different processes [A, B and C] themselves. As such, there is an additional variable (raw material) in the experiment that we need *to block* in order to adequately compare the processes.

The following data on screws length is provided to us:

Process	A	B	C	
1	2.05	1.98	2.07	Supplier 1
2	2.08	2.04	2.10	Supplier 2
3	1.99	1.97	2.02	Supplier 3

Answer

Using: 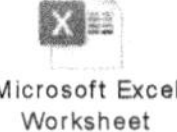
Microsoft Excel Worksheet

Source of Variation	SS	dF	MS	F	F-table	Conclusion
Processes	0.00687	2	0.003433	18.7273	6.94	**Significant**
Suppliers/Blocks	0.00960	4	0.004800	26.1818	6.94	**Significant**
Error	0.00073	4	0.000183			
TOTAL	**0.01720**	**8**				

Given that for both the treatments and the blocks, **F > F-tables**, we can conclude that the processes and the blocks have a significant effect on the response variable.

The influence of the blocks must be removed before we can draw any conclusions about the processes. In order to do such, we can use a single raw material for all processes or match the specifications of all three.

Using: Minitab

```
Analysis of variance: Length
Source        Df    Adj. SS    Adj. MS    F-value    P-value

Processes      2    0.006867   0.003433    18.73      0.009    < 0,05    Significant
Block          2    0.009600   0.004800    26.18      0.005    < 0.05    Significant
Error          4    0.000733   0.000183
Total          8    0.017200
```

Given that both **p-values < 0.05**, we can conclude that the processes (with these levels) and the blocks do have a significant effect on the response variable.

Same conclusion: the influence of the blocks must be removed before drawing conclusions about the processes.

- When we calculate ANOVA without blocking, then the **SST** (0.006867) is the same for the two ANOVA calculations (with and without blocking). This means that the variation between treatments (processes) is not free from the effect of different suppliers (blocking). The **SSE,** however, would vary if we take blocking into account.

- **Was the blocking effective?** When we can compare **MSBL** (mean square between blocks) to **MSE** (mean squared error), if MSBL is at least 2 to 2.5 larger than MSE, then the answer is yes.

Analysis of variance

Source	Df	Adj. SS	Adj. MS	F-value	P-value
Process (x)	2	0.006867	0.003433	18.73	0.009
Supplier (Block)	2	0.009600	0.004800	26.18	0.005
Error	4	0.000733	0.000183		
Total	8	0.017200			

$$\frac{.004800}{.000183} = 26.23 > 2 - 2.5$$

→ Yes, blocking was effective

Exercise: One-way ANOVA with blocking

In the **Logistics Company** case, the team wants to determine if the picking procedure is a significant factor affecting the picking process time. The following table shows picking time (in minutes); replicate 1 was performed based on the previously established procedure for the picking process and replicate 2 was performed following a new procedure that is being tested.

No. of Operators	Process A	Process B
5	9.0	8.8
6	7.3	7.7
7	5.6	5.1
8	4.9	5.0
9	5.2	5.3

Answer

Using: 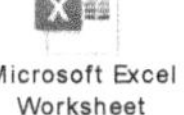
Microsoft Excel
Worksheet

Source of Variation	SS	dF	MS	F	F-table	Conclusion
Treatments	23.97400	4	5.993500	102.4530	6.39	**Significant**
Block	0.00100	1	0.001000	0.0171	7.71	**Not Significant**
Error	0.23400	4	0.058500			
TOTAL	**24.209**	9				

The blocked factor (picking procedure) is not significant, so we conclude that only the number of operators has an influence on process time.

Using: Minitab

Analysis of variance: Picking

Source	Df	Adj. SS	Adj. MS	F-value	P-value		
No. of Operators	4	23.9740	5.99350	102.45	0.000	**< 0.05**	Significant
Process (BLOCK)	1	0.0010	0.00100	0.02	0.902	**> 0.05**	Not Significant
Error	4	0.2340	0.05850				
Total	9	24.2090					

Same conclusion: the blocked factor (picking procedure) is not significant, so we conclude that only the number of operators has an influence on process time.

3. Two-way ANOVA

The two-way ANOVA test is a method that is used to evaluate the effect that two factors may have on a response variable and to help us identify if the *interaction* between the factors is significant.

Example: Two-way ANOVA

Assume that only two variables are involved in the process of manufacturing projection lamps.

A: **Filling pressure** (1,000, 1,100, 1,200 psi)   x1

B: **Type of gas** (N2, ArN2)   x2

We want to know if these variables influence the *light output* (lumens) of the lamps.

Type of Gas (B)	Filling Pressure (A)		
	1,000	1,100	1,200
N2	88	91	87
N2	89	91	88
ArN2	92	87	95
ArN2	94	90	93

Answer

Using: 
Microsoft Excel
Worksheet

Source of Variation	SS	dF	MS	F	F-table		Conclusion
Factor (A)	2.667	2	1.33333	0.842	5.143		Not Significant
Factor (B)	24.083	1	24.08333	15.211	5.987		Significant
Interaction (AB)	44.667	2	22.33333	14.105	5.143		Significant
Error	9.500	6	1.58333				
TOTAL	80.917	11					

The type of gas (B) and the AB interaction is significant. We need to further investigate the effect of Pressure (A), even though it did not show up as significant.

Using: Minitab

Analysis of variance

Source	Df	Adj. SS	Adj. MS	F-value	P-value	
Filling pressure (A)	2	2.667	1.333	0.84	0.476	Not Significant
Type of gas (B)	1	24.083	24.083	15.21	0.008	Significant
Filling pressure (A) * Type of gas (B)	2	44.667	22.333	14.11	0.005	Significant
Error	6	9.500	1.583			
Total	11	80.917				

Same conclusion.

Exercise: Two-way ANOVA

- We want to test the efficiency of two types of powder produced during two different shifts by measuring the *light output* from the 75W incandescent bulbs.

- The following data was obtained from previous testing:

  X1   Powder

  X2   Shift

  Y   Light output

Shift	Powder			
	1		2	
1	56	65	72	78
2	58	60	63	67

Conclusion _______________________________________

Answer

Using:  Microsoft Excel Worksheet

Source of Variation	SS	dF	MS	F	F-table	Conclusion
Factor (A)	210.125	1	210.12500	12.270	7.709	Significant
Factor (B)	66.125	1	66.12500	3.861	7.709	Not Significant
Interaction (AB)	36.125	1	36.12500	2.109	7.709	Not Significant
Error	68.500	4	17.12500			
TOTAL	380.875	7				

Using: Minitab

Analysis of variance

Source	Df	Adj. SS	Adj. MS	F-value	P-value	
Powder (A)	1	210.13	210.13	12.27	0.025	Significant
Shift (B)	1	66.13	66.13	3.86	0.121	Not Significant
Powder (A) * Shift (B)	1	36.13	36.13	2.11	0.220	Not Significant
Error	4	68.50	17.13			
Total	7	380.88				

4. Two-way ANOVA with blocking

During this analysis, and in addition to identifying if the factors and their interactions are significant, we will also use *blocking* to identify if the *noise* variables are significant.

Example: Two-way ANOVA with blocking

- In the light output (lumens) exercise we studied the following two factors:

  A: **Filling pressure** (1,000, 1,100, 1,200 psi)

  B: **Type of gas** (N2, ArN2)

Let's assume that 2 operators were performing the measurements and that because of time constraints they were each able to obtain only 6 measurements. It Is believed that there is a difference in the way the operators performed the measurements, i.e., there is an additional variable (operator method) that we want to neutralize (block) so that it does not interfere with the experiment.

One condition must apply. Block sizes must be equivalent to ab, where a and b are the number of levels of factors A and B, respectively.

	Operator 1			Operator 2		
	Filling Pressure (A)			Filling Pressure (A)		
Type of Gas (B)	1,000	1,100	1,200	1,000	1,100	1,200
N2	88	91	87	89	91	88
ArN2	92	87	95	94	90	93

Answer

Using: 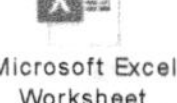
Microsoft Excel
Worksheet

Source of Variation	SS	dF	MS	F	F-table	Conclusion
Factor (A)	2.667	2	1.333	0.899	5.786	Not Significant
Factor (B)	24.083	1	24.083	16.236	6.608	Significant
Blocks	2.083	1	2.083	1.404	6.608	Not Significant
Interaction (AB)	44.667	2	22.333	15.056	5.786	Significant
Error	7.417	5	1.483			
TOTAL	80.917	11				

Was the blocking effective?   MSBL / MSE = 2.083/1.483 = 1.40 < 2.5

We can conclude that the significant variables are Type of Gas (B) and its interaction with Filling pressure (AB). Additionally, we can see that there is not a significant difference between the operators when we observe the p-value and when we compare MSBL to MSE (since it is not at least 2.5 times larger).

Using: Minitab

Analysis of Variance

Source	Df	Adj. SS	Adj. MS	F-value	P-value	
Filling pressure (A)	2	2.667	1.333	0.90	0.464	Not Significant
Type of gas (B)	1	24.083	24.083	16.24	0.010	Significant
Operat (BLOCK)	1	2.083	2.083	1.40	0.289	Not Significant
Filling pressure (A) * Type of gas (B)	2	44.667	22.333	15.06	0.008	Significant
Error	5	7.417	1.483			
Total	11	80.917				

Was the blocking effective?   MSBL / MSE = 2.083/1.483 = 1.40 < 2.5

Same conclusion.

Exercise: Two-way ANOVA with blocking

- Let's suppose that we can perform one more replicate and a 3rd operator is assigned the task to conduct the measurements.

	Operator 1			Operator 2			Operator 3		
	Filling Pressure (A)			Filling Pressure (A)			Filling Pressure (A)		
Type of Gas (B)	1,000	1,100	1,200	1,000	1,100	1,200	1,000	1,100	1,200
N2	88	91	87	89	91	88	72	75	65
ArN2	92	87	95	94	90	93	48	46	54

Answer

Using:  Microsoft Excel Worksheet

Source of Variation	SS	dF	MS	F	F-table	Conclusion
Factor (A)	283.111	2	141.556	1.363	4.103	Not Significant
Factor (B)	3.556	1	3.556	0.034	4.965	Not Significant
Blocks	2290.111	2	1145.056	11.025	4.103	Significant
Interaction (AB)	323.111	2	161.556	1.556	4.103	Not Significant
Error	1038.556	10	103.856			
TOTAL	3938.444	17				

In this case, blocking is significant, so we cannot draw conclusions about the factors. Moreover, the results are different compared to those from the previous test. Therefore, it is important to standardize the operators' method for performing measurements.

Using: Minitab

Analysis of variance

Source	Df	Adj. SS	Adj. MS	F-value	P-value	
Factor A	2	283.11	141.56	1.36	0.300	Not Significant
Factor B	1	3.56	3.56	0.03	0.857	Not Significant
Blocks	2	2290.11	1145.06	11.03	0.003	Significant
Interaction (A) and (B)	2	323.11	161.56	1.56	0.358	Not Significant
Error	10	1038.56	103.86			
Total	17	3938.44				

Same conclusion.

5. Three-way ANOVA

It is a method used to evaluate the effect that three factors may have on a response variable and to help us identify if the *double interactions* (all the combinations of two factors) are significant.

It is important to note that, given the calculations made, the triple interaction should not be taken into account. This is what is known as an ignorable interaction or factor.

Example: Three-way ANOVA

An experiment is carried out by a computer expansion card manufacturer to determine if the temperature in the three critical processes (and their interactions) are significant regarding the percentage of broken cards produced. The results from this experiment are as follows:

Temp: Engraving	Temp: Soldering	Temp: Water	Percentage of broken cards	
			R1	R2
- 3 ° C	60 ° C	20 ° C	0.040	0.032
- 1 ° C	60 ° C	20 ° C	0.012	0.008
- 3 ° C	98 ° C	20 ° C	0.036	0.028
- 1 ° C	98 ° C	20 ° C	0.000	0.000
- 3 ° C	60 ° C	70 ° C	0.020	0.020
- 1 ° C	60 ° C	70 ° C	0.000	0.016
- 3 ° C	98 ° C	70 ° C	0.016	0.008
- 1 ° C	98 ° C	70 ° C	0.004	0.004

Answer

Using: Microsoft Excel Worksheet

Source of Variation	SS	dF	MS	F	F-table	Conclusion:
Factor (A)	0.001521	1	0.001521	52.448	5.318	Significant
Factor (B)	0.000169	1	0.000169	5.828	5.318	Significant
Factor (C)	0.000289	1	0.000289	9.966	5.318	Significant
Interaction (AB)	0.000001	1	0.000001	0.034	5.318	Not Significant
Interaction (AC)	0.000361	1	0.000361	12.448	5.318	Significant
Interaction (BC)	0.000001	1	0.000001	0.034	5.318	Not Significant
Interaction (ABC)	0.000025	1	0.000025	0.862	5.318	Not Significant
Error	0.000232	8	0.000029			
TOTAL	0.002599	15				

The three temperatures: Engraving, soldering, and water (A, B, and C), as well as the interaction between the engraving temperature with the water temperature (AC) are significant.

Using: Minitab

Analysis of variance

Source	Df	Adj. SS	Adj. MS	F-value	P-value	
Temp: Engraving (A)	1	0.001521	0.001521	52.45	0.000	Significant
Tem: Soldering (B)	1	0.000169	0.000169	5.83	0.042	Significant
Temp: Water (C)	1	0.000289	0.000289	9.97	0.013	Significant
Temp: Engraving (A) * Temp: Soldering (B)	1	0.000001	0.000001	0.03	0.857	Not Significant
Temp: Engraving (A) * Temp: Water (C)	1	0.000361	0.000361	12.45	0.008	Significant
Temp: Soldering (B) * Temp: Water (C)	1	0.000001	0.000001	0.03	0.857	Not Significant
Temp: Engraving (A) * Temp: Soldering (B) * Temp: Water (C)	1	0.000025	0.000025	0.86	0.380	Not Significant
Error	8	0.000232	0.000029			
Total	15	0.002599				

Same conclusion.

Exercise: Three-way ANOVA

- Experiments are conducted at a plastics company to determine if three factors are significant in the percentage of good quality (acceptable) products. These three factors are temperature, molding time, and type of raw material (sieved and unsealed). The results are as follows:

Temperature	Molding Time	Raw Material	Percentage of good products	
			R1	R2
90	8	Unsealed	76.4	76.9
130	8	Unsealed	76.3	76.9
90	15	Unsealed	80.4	81.0
130	15	Unsealed	77.9	76.9
90	8	Sieved	84.4	84.6
130	8	Sieved	84.7	84.5
90	15	Sieved	82.7	83.2
130	15	Sieved	85.0	84.7

Answer

Using: 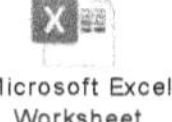
Microsoft Excel
Worksheet

Source of Variation	SS	dF	MS	F	F-table	Conclusion
Factor (A)	0.00000	1	0.00000	0.000	5.318	Not Significant
Factor (B)	6.00250	1	6.00250	22.439	5.318	Significant
Factor (C)	146.41000	1	146.41000	547.327	5.318	Significant
Interaction (AB)	0.00250	1	0.00250	0.009	5.318	Not Significant
Interaction (AC)	4.00000	1	4.00000	14.953	5.318	Significant
Interaction (BC)	14.06250	1	14.06250	52.57	5.318	Significant
Interaction (ABC)	3.42250	1	3.42250	12.794	5.318	Significant
Error	2.14000	8	0.26750			
TOTAL	176.04000	15				

Molding time and raw material (B and C), the interaction between temperature and raw material (AC) and the interaction between molding time raw material (BC) are each significant (i.e., all factors have influence over the result).

Using: Minitab

Analysis of variance

Source	Df	Adj. SS	Adj. MS	F-value	P-value	
Temperature (A)	1	0.000	0.000	0.00	1.000	**Not Significant**
Molding Time (B)	1	6.003	6.003	22.44	0.001	**Significant**
Raw Material (C)	1	146.410	146.410	547.33	0.000	**Significant**
Temp (A) * Molding Time (B)	1	0.003	0.003	0.01	0.925	**Not Significant**
Temp (A) * Raw Material (C)	1	4.000	4.000	14.95	0.005	**Significant**
Molding Time (B) * Raw Material (C)	1	14.063	14.063	52.57	0.000	**Significant**
Temp (A) * Molding Time (B) * Raw Material (C)	1	3.423	3.423	12.79	0.007	**Significant**
Error	8	2.140	0.268			
Total	15	176.040				

Same conclusion. The triple interaction is not taken into account.

Correlation

For every cause, there is an effect. The secret is to identify it

Objectives

1. Understand the basic concepts of correlation analysis.
2. Develop correlation diagrams for a set of variables and identify their relationship.
3. Apply the correlation graphics correctly for any project and for all kinds of processes (service, manufacturing, sales, logistics, finance, etc.).

Content

> Introduction
> What is correlation?
> What is it used for?
> Correlation diagram
> Types and strength of relationship
> Interpretation of results
> When is it used?
> Procedure
> Example
> Exercise
> Checklist: Reviewing the analyze phase

Introduction

There are many situations in which it is necessary to identify how one variable interacts with another, and where we can answer questions such as:

- How are the two variables related to each other?

- How does their relationship affect the outcome?

In order to achieve this, we use **simple correlation analysis.**

Important considerations:

- Correlation indicates the strength of a linear relationship between two variables.

- It does not assume a "causal" relationship between the two variables.

- Should be used in conjunction with graphical techniques.

- The correlation coefficient **(r)** indicates the strength of the relationship.

What is correlation?

Correlation aims to determine the strength of the relationship between two variables of a process – instead of using a variable to predict the other one's value. Example: speed and training.

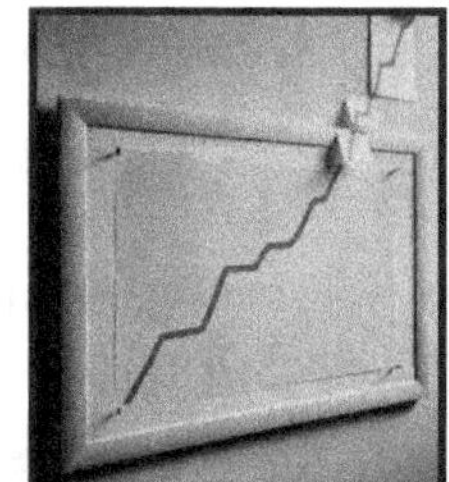

- Financial statements are completed on time when those responsible for preparing them are better trained.

- The better training cooks receive at a restaurant, the faster they can prepare meals.

- The more training hours an assembly worker received, the faster she can assemble each unit.

Correlation

- Correlation – or regression – is used to analyze quantitative variables.

- Recall that the purpose of Six Sigma is to solve and understand the equation:

$$Y = f(x)$$

Where:

- **Y** is the expected value of a process (quality, speed, cost, etc.).

- **X** represents all the variables that are required in a process (people, machines, materials, information, etc.).

- It is used to explain, predict, optimize, and control **Y** based on a specific configuration of **X**'s.

Correlation diagram

- It is a simple graph with two numeric variables (X, Y).

- It helps to visualize how the two variables are related to each other.

- For example:

  - Analyzing whether a group of students' height (X) and weight (Y) are related.

  - Understand the relationship between a process input variable (X) such as speed, temperature, or humidity and the value of a quality characteristic (Y) of the product or service (e.g., weight, size, etc.).

Types and strength of relationship

Types of relationship

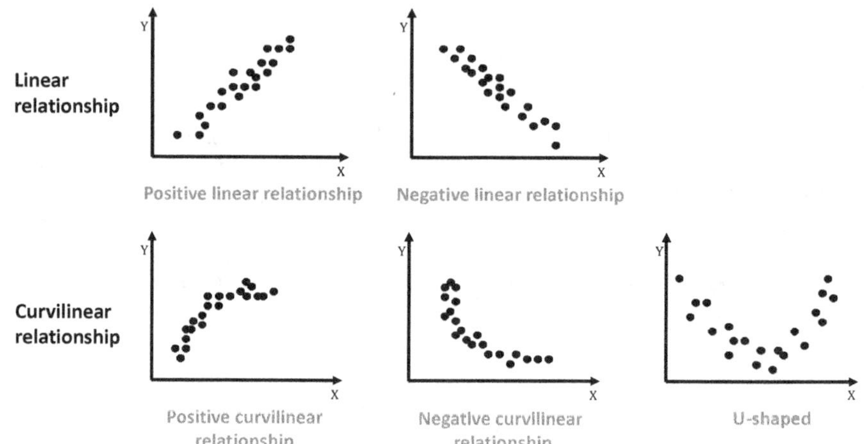

Linear relationship

Curvilinear relationship

Strength of relationship

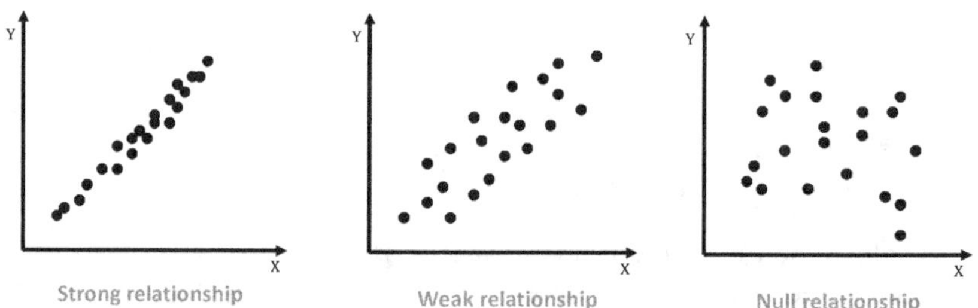

Interpretation of results

According to the Western Electric (1956) *Statistical Quality Control Handbook*, it is important to consider that:

1. Even if a strong relationship is observed, it does not necessarily imply causality. The cause-effect relationship is established from knowledge of the process.

2. If there is no significant relationship, then this might mean that there is no actual correlation between the two variables, or that the range of data is insufficient.

Interpretation of Pearson correlation coefficient

▶ The range of correlation coefficient values r include:
  ▶ Between -1 and 1 ($-1 \leq r \geq 1$).

Criteria	Interpretation
r is close to 1	Strong positive linear correlation
r is close to -1	Strong negative linear correlation
r is close to -0.85 or 0.85	Strong linear correlation
r is close to -0.50 or 0.50	Moderate or weak linear correlation
r is equal or less than -0.30 or 0.30	Linear correlation practically non-existent
r is close to or equal to zero	Null linear relationship between X and Y

Causality vs. chance (coincidence)

Causality implies a **cause-effect relationship** between variables, while **chance does not**.

Examples

a) Pressure vs. temperature

b) Summer energy consumption vs. ambient (room) temperature
(Montgomery & Peck, 1992)

c) Number of storks vs. number of births (in the last 100 years)

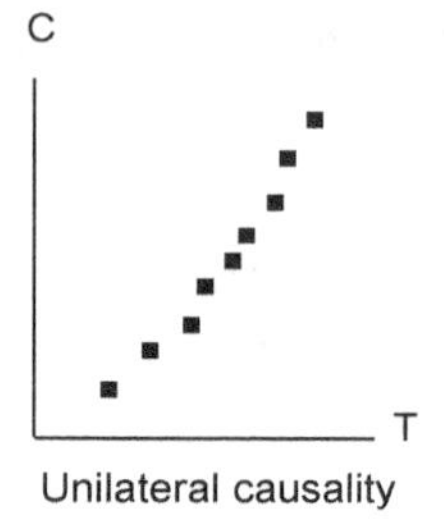

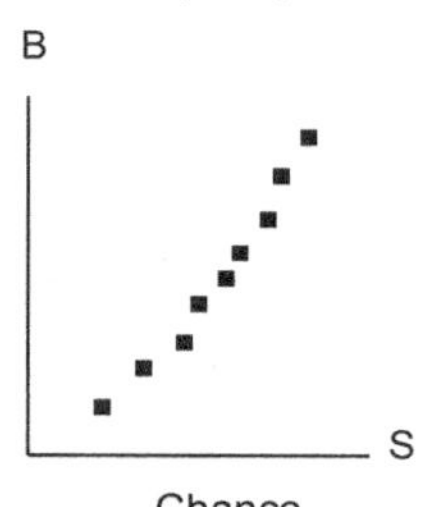

When there is no *causality*, the prediction model can be used to predict the process — but not to control it.

When is it used?

- Analyze phase:

  - To understand the relationship of variables (X's) in relation to the expected result (Y). It provides the work team with knowledge about the potential variables that can be improved. Example: a material (X) vs. the delivery speed (Y).

  - To identify the relationship between input variables (X's). Example: team performance with respect to the team members' training level.

- Improvement phase:

  - To validate the improvement actions between input variables (X's) and results (Y's).

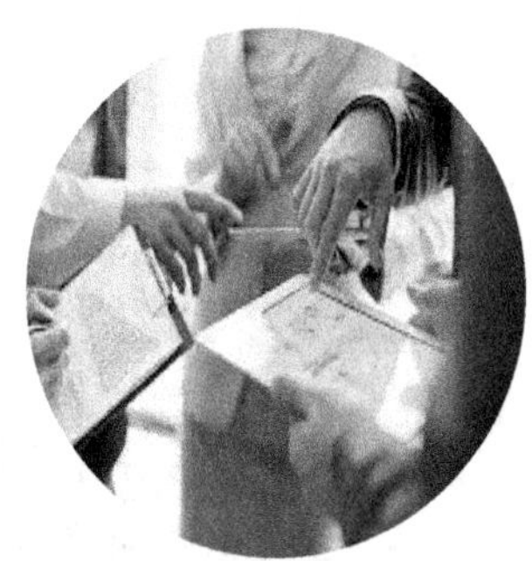

LEAN SIX SIGMA INSTITUTE

Procedure

1. Define the objective of the analysis.
2. Identify the variables:
   - Input and output.
   - Input and input.
   - Output and output.
3. Build a table that includes the variables.
4. Build scatter plots.
5. Determine an equation for the prediction line.
6. Interpret the results.

How long does it take?

- The time is variable according to the number of variables to evaluate and especially to the time needed to obtain the data.

- Once the data have been obtained, one to two hours should be allocated to – as a team – perform the analysis, establish a correlation level, and make decisions about the variables that have a real impact on the results of the process.

Examples

Example 1

Paul Evans's team at **Logistics Company** wants to prove the hypothesis formed when elaborating an Ishikawa Diagram. The hypothesis identifies the company's product inventory shortages as the root cause of late or incomplete deliveries. In order to prove this, the team analyzes the relationship between the number of shortages per week as well as the OTIF metric (percentage of on-time, in-full deliveries). The following table contains the data concerning these two variables:

Week	Shortages	OTIF	Week	Shortages	OTIF
7	10	88.0	13	0	99.8
8	6	93.9	14	1	99.1
9	5	95.5	15	2	97.0
10	8	90.5	16	7	92.2
11	7	92.6	17	11	85.8
12	3	96.3	18	8	90.9

1. **Objective:** Determine the relationship that exists between product inventory shortages (input variable) and on-time, in-full deliveries (output variable).

2. **Variables:**
   - Input: Product shortages
   - Output: On-time, in-full deliveries

3. **Table:**

Week	Shortages (X)	OTIF (Y)
7	10	88
8	6	93.9
9	5	95.5
10	8	90.5
11	7	92.6
12	3	96.3
13	0	99.8
14	1	99.1
15	2	97
16	7	92.2
17	11	85.8
18	8	90.9

4 and 5. Graph and determine the equation for the prediction line:

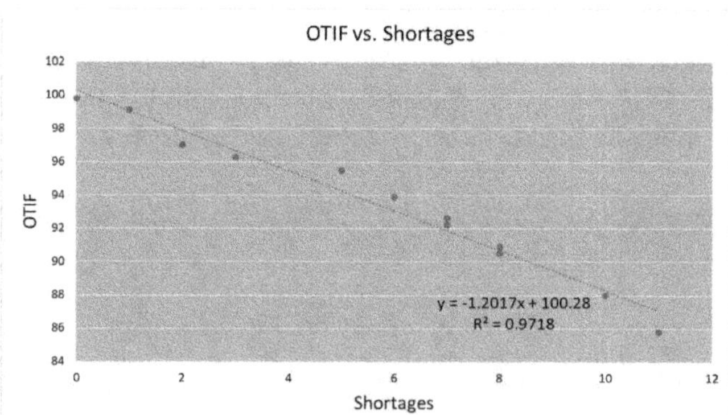

6. Interpret the results:

- There is a strong negative relationship between the two variables (if shortages increase, then OTIF decreases).

- The equation for the prediction line is: OTIF = −1.2018 shortages + 100.28.

    - The first-term [negative] coefficient indicates that OTIF decreases by 1.2018 units for each additional unit increase in shortages.

    - In this case, zero is within the measurement range of shortages (X's), so the second term of the equation indicates that the OTIF metric would be approximately 100% if the number of shortages was 0 (if zero is not found within the X's interval, then this coefficient is not significant.).

- The coefficient of determination is: R^2 = 97.18%.

    - The coefficient of determination indicates a strong relationship, since 97.18% of the variation in the OTIF metric is explained by the variation in shortages. For the relationship to be considered strong, this coefficient must be greater than or equal to 80%.

Example 2

In a manufacturing process, we wish to determine the type and strength of the relationship between the hardness of a part (Y) and the time it takes to solidify (X).

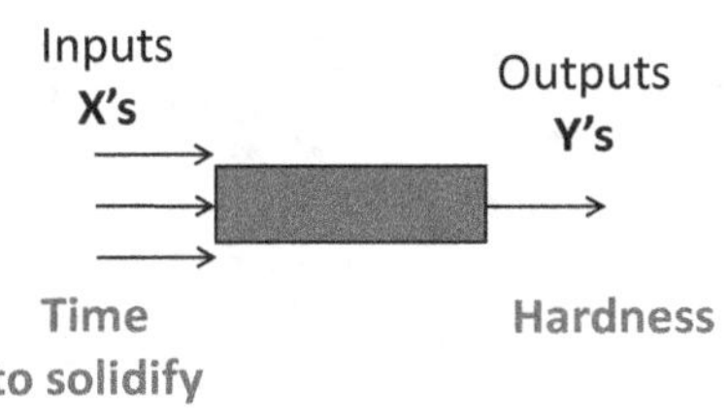

T-Solid (X)	Hardness (Y)
10	4.5
11	4.2
12	3.8
13	3.6
14	3.4
15	3.0
16	2.9
17	2.4
18	2.2
19	2.1
20	1.8

1. **Objective:** Determine the relationship between time to solidify (input variable) and hardness (output variable or CTQ).

2. **Variables:**

   - Input: Time to solidify
   - Output: Hardness

3. **Table:**

T-Solid (X)	Hardness (Y)
10	4.5
11	4.2
12	3.8
13	3.6
14	3.4
15	3.0
16	2.9
17	2.4
18	2.2
19	2.1
20	1.8

4 and 5. Graph and determine the equation for the prediction line:

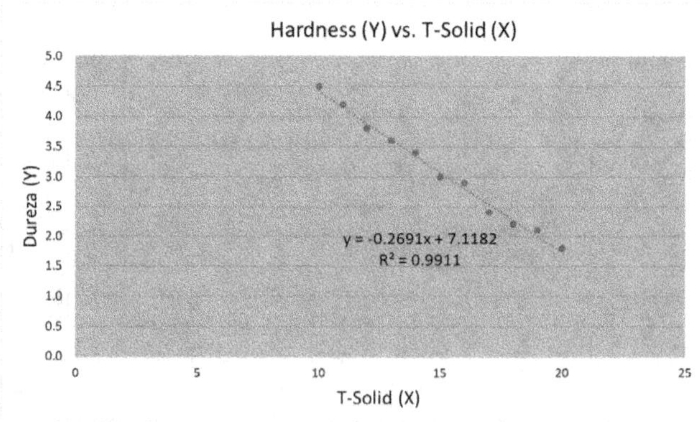

6. **Interpret the results:**

   Hardness decreases by 0.2691 units for each additional unit increase in time. Since the data does not include X = 0, the constant 7.11 is not significant.

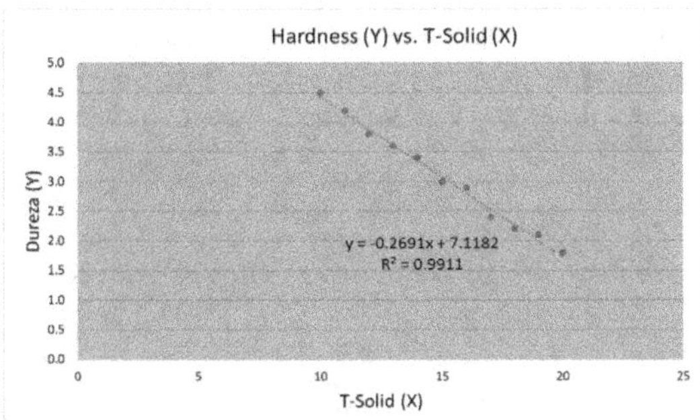

   The R-squared value indicates the proportion of variability that is explained or represented by the regression model.

99.1% of the variability is explained by time to solidify.

Build a scatter plot using the following information of pre-heating temperature and hardness. Determine the type and strength of the correlation between the two variables.

Temp	Hardness
390	1.5
391	1.8
392	2.1
393	2.3
394	2.6
395	3.1
396	3.4
397	3.7
398	3.9
399	4.2
400	4.5

Checklist: Reviewing the analyze phase

- Once the activities of the analyze phase have been completed – and before into the improve phase – the improvement team must verify if the objectives were met. The following checklist can be used to do so:

Review: Analyze Phase

Project: ____   Date: __________

	Yes	No
1.- Processes have been examined and bottlenecks, disparities, and redundancies that could contribute to the problem at hand have been identified.	☐	☐
2.- Analysis has been conducted to evaluate the added value and cycle time of each step in the process - identifying non-value-added activities where resources are wasted.	☐	☐
3.- Data has been analyzed in order to evaluate process performance, stratify the problem, and identify sources of variation and potential root causes.	☐	☐
4.- Evaluation has been conducted to determine whether the project should focus on process improvement or process design or redesign.	☐	☐

Process improvement:

	Yes	No
5.- Root cause hypotheses that explain the problem at hand have been developed.	☐	☐
6.- Root cause hypotheses have been evaluated and verified, and the team ensured that all possible root causes were covered.	☐	☐

Process design or Redesign:

	Yes	No
7.- The team has identified all process requirements in order to design or redesign a process that is both more effective and more efficient.	☐	☐

Introduction to design of experiments

16

Objectives

1. Understand the basic concepts of experimental design.
2. Develop experimental designs to identify critical factors that affect the process.
3. Conduct experiments and predict the effect of changes.

Content

> Background
> What is Design of Experiments (DoE)?
> DoE applications
> Classification of DoE
> Experimental methodology
> Exercise

Background

- Sir Ronald Aylmer Fisher developed this technique in the 1920s, when he was responsible for statistics and data analysis at the Rothamsted agricultural station.

- Fisher formed the opinion that experiments conducted to collect data on agriculture had many flaws. With the collaborative efforts of many scientists and researchers from diverse fields, Fisher developed the ideas and methods that are now known as *design of experiments (DoE)*.

What is Design of Experiments (DoE)?

An experiment is a test or a series of tests in which we manipulate or change input variables (factors) of a system or process so that we can *observe* the changes on the output (effects).

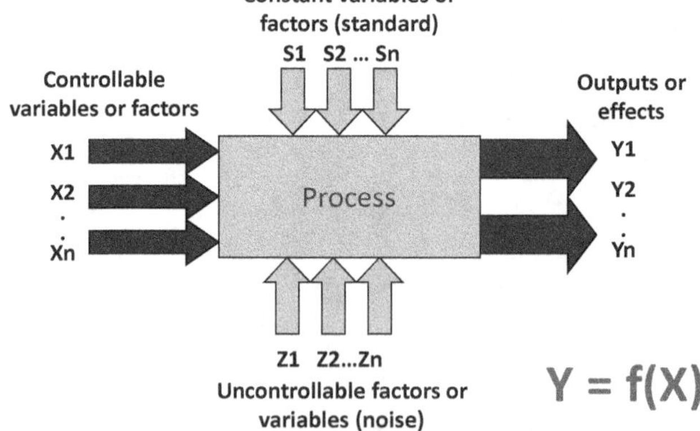

Variables, factors and levels

All processes include different types of variables or factors:

Important considerations:

- What quality characteristics will be measured?
- What controllable factors should be included in the experiment?
- How many levels should each factor have?
- What type of experimental design is the most appropriate?

Defining output variable(s)

- Is the output quantitative or qualitative?

- Objective: Improving variation or centrality?

- What is the baseline (mean or sigma)?

- Is the output under statistical control?

- Does the output vary with respect to time?

- How much change in the output do we want to detect?

- Is the output normally distributed?

- Is the measurement system appropriate?

- Are there multiple outputs?

Basic concepts

- **Experimental design:** The formal plan to conduct an experiment is called "experimental design". The plan may include the selection of response variables, factors, levels, blocks and treatments and the use of certain tools, including planned grouping, randomization, repetition and/or replication.

- **Response variable:** The characteristic of the product, service, or process whose value you are interested in improving through an experiment.

- **Factors:** The influence of factors or inputs (which may be either controlled or uncontrolled variables), on the response (output) is studied during these types of experiments. A factor can be quantitative such as degrees or time, or qualitative such as different machines or operators.

- **Level:** The levels are the different values of a factor that are studied in the experiment.

  - **Quantitative factors:** e.g., temperature. If the experiment is being conducted at two different temperatures, then the temperature factor has two levels.

  - **Qualitative factors:** e.g., cleanliness (clean or not clean).

- **Treatment:** A factor at a specified level. For example: Temperature at 250 degrees for factor A.

- **Treatment combination:** A set of factors and their levels. The number of treatment combinations in a complete experiment is a result of the total number of levels and total number of factors in the experiment.

- **Design matrix:** Table that will show all possible combinations of high and low levels for each factor, including replicates.

Three basic principles

1. Randomization: The order of the experiments must be random. Randomizing the test runs neutralizes sources of variation that may be present during the experiment. These sources of variation are generally unknown and can be numerous. For example, worker fatigue may be present during the experiment or during measurements. Other examples include, changes in voltage, changes in humidity, etc.

2. Repetition: It is recommended to replicate the experiment. In doing so, you can obtain an estimate of the error to understand how well the designed experiment represents the process and to compare the factors and determine if they are significant.

3. Blocking: Occasionally, there may be variables in an experiment whose effect is not intended to be tested and could affect or cover up the influence of variables that are of interest in the experiment. In this case, it is necessary to neutralize or block the effect of such nuisance variables.

DoE applications

«DoE can be considered part of the scientific method and is one of the ways to understand the functioning of systems and processes.»

D. Montgomery

- Experimental design is a fundamental tool used in industrial engineering to **improve** process performance.

- It also has a wide application in the development and design of **new** processes.

- The task of the analyst/engineer/person responsible for the process is to **obtain, document,** and **transfer knowledge** of the product, service, or process.

Real knowledge is better than theoretical knowledge.

Experimental objectives

> **The objective is usually stated in terms of the effects of the inputs on the outputs.**

The following are examples of potential objectives when conducting an experiment:

- Determine the effects of *variation del material* or *input* in product or service reliability.
- Determine the effects of different types of (cheaper to more expensive) inputs on product or service performance.
- Determine the impact of *operator variation* on product quality
- Determine the *sources of variation* of a *critical process;* in other words, the cause-effect relationship between process inputs and product or service quality characteristics.
- Determine the equation that *models* the process.

Process characterization vs. process optimization

- In a characterization experiment, the goal is typically to determine the most influential variable that affects the response

- In an optimization experiment, the goal is to determine a design or operating region in which the important factors lead to the best possible response.

- For example, if the response is performance, you would find the maximum performance region. If the response is variability, then you would find the minimum variability region.

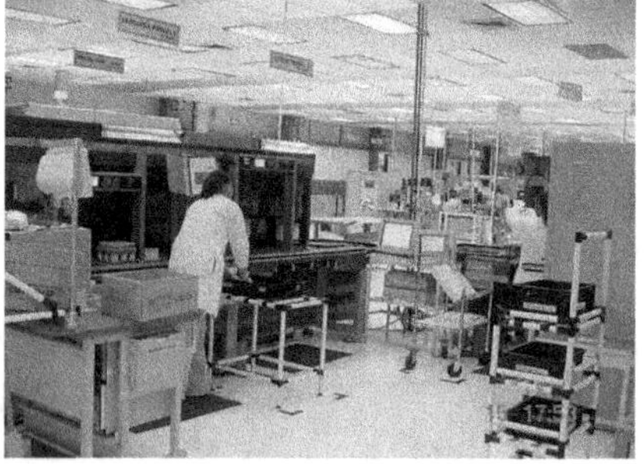

LSSI
LEAN SIX SIGMA INSTITUTE

Applications to processes

The following are basic objectives for applying DoE to processes:

1. Improving process performance.

2. Minimizing variability in the output parameters of a process.

3. Reduction of lead time.

4. Reduction of total costs.

Applications to products and services

Another important application of DoE is in the design and improvement of new products and services:

1. Evaluation and comparison of products and services.

2. Evaluation of alternative materials and inputs.

3. Reduction of development time (product launch/time to market).

4. Reduction in global costs.

Characterization of a process: Example

- A liquid welding machine is used as part of the process for manufacturing printed circuit boards. The machine cleans the boards, preheats them and then they pass through a liquid welding wave by means of a transporter.

- The circuit boards' manufacturing process has a 1% defect level.

- The engineer responsible for the process could use a designed experiment to determine which machine parameters influence the occurrence of defects.

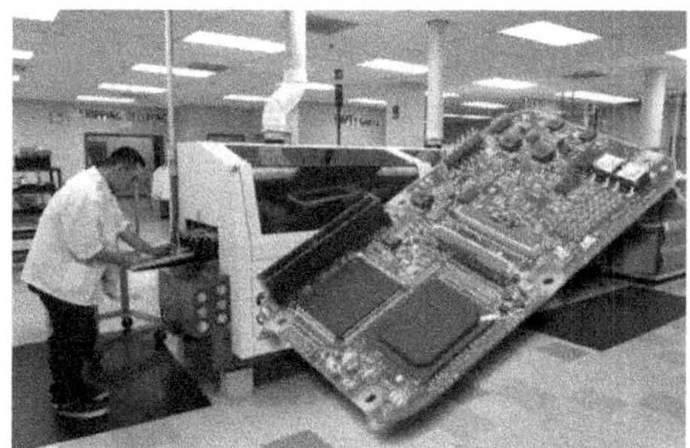

There are various variables that can be controlled in the machine:

1. Temperature
2. Transporter speed
3. Type of fluid
4. Fluid gravity
5. Weld depth
6. Transporter angle

Other factors that could be controlled for testing purposes:

1. Circuit board thickness
2. Operator
3. Production speed
4. Time when tests will be conducted

Product design: Example

- Experimental design can be applied to the product design process.

- It is based on a given characteristic. For example, tension of spring.

  A team of engineers considers that the tension of a spring is a function of the following factors:

  1. Distance moved by the cylinder.
  2. Height of the spring.
  3. Distance from the spring to the pivot.

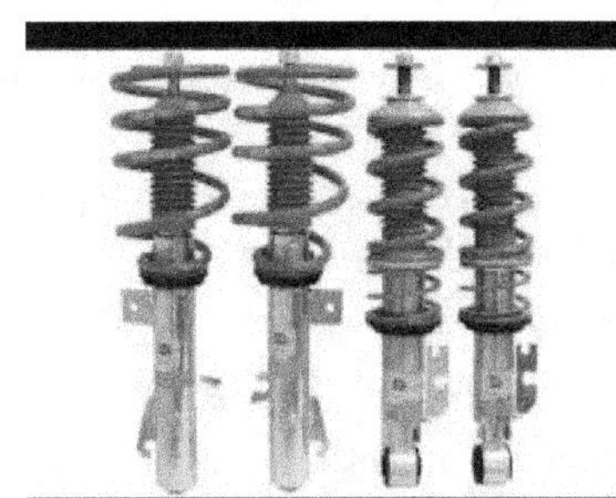

Classification of DoE

1. Designs to compare 2 or more treatments.
   - Completely randomized designs.
   - Randomized block designs.
   - Greco Latin and Latin square designs.

2. Designs to study the effects of various factors on the response(s).
   - **2^k factorial designs.**
   - **3^k factorial designs.**
   - 2^{k-p} fractional factorial designs.

3. Designs to obtain the optimal operational setting of the process.

   1st order designs
   - **2^k and 2^{k-p} factorial designs**
   - Plackett-Burman designs
   - Simplex designs

   2nd order designs
   - Central Composite Designs (CCD)
   - Box-Behnken Designs (BBD)
   - **Response Surface Methodology (RSM)**

4. Robust designs.
   - Orthogonal arrangements

Stages in experimental design

- **Experimental planning**

  1. Experimental **objective or problem** statement: Find a problem that causes significant losses to the company or is of particular interest for research and development.

  2. Choice of **factors:** Determine which factors need to be studied or investigated according to their alleged influence on the response.

  3. Selection of **response** variable(s): Select the response variable(s) that will be measured and verify that it is measured reliably.

  4. Choice of experimental design: Select the **appropriate experimental design** based on the factors and experimental objective.

  5. **Plan** and organize the designed experiment.

  6. **Conduct** the experiment.

> **In many cases, more than 50 % of the total efforts need to focused on the experimental planning phase.**

- **Analysis**

  7. Perform statistical analysis using a spreadsheet, statistical software or by hand, generally using analysis of variance (ANOVA).

  8. Plot graphs to support your analysis and depict the effects of factor interactions.

- **Interpretation**

  9. You should **go beyond formal statistical analysis** and analyze what has happened during the experiment in detail, starting with comparing the initial hypotheses with actual results to observing the new things learned about the process. Verify assumptions and select the best treatment.

- **Conclusions**

  10. You will decide which measures to implement to ensure that the results of the experiment **are maintained** under the conditions of the product or process. Additionally, you should make a presentation to **share the results and accomplishments.**

Procedure: Documentation of the experiment

It is important to use and establish the designed experiment planning form as part of the internal documentation system to give formality to all experiments. As such, you are establishing a standardized way to record all improvement efforts through experiments.

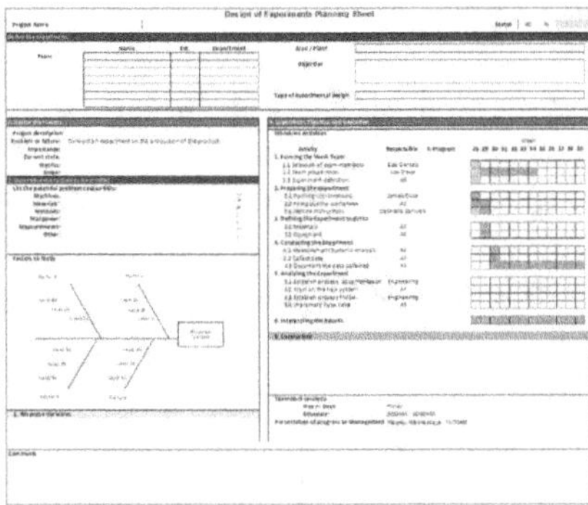

Tips

- **Use of non-statistical knowledge:** Use the knowledge of process experts to provide feedback on the study. Non-statistical knowledge is key to selecting **factors** and **levels** and **interpreting** results.

- **Keep the design and analysis as simple as possible:** Make sure not to misuse or overuse complex and sophisticated statistical tools. **Simple** design and analysis methods are always the best.

- **Keep in mind practical and statistical significance** since we sometimes find solutions that optimize the response, but are economically infeasible.

- **Designed experiments are usually iterative:** This avoids lengthy experiments and still produces the desired results. Be sure to use no more than 25 % of the resources for the initial experiment to reserve enough resources for future experiments.

Barriers to successful experimentation

- Unclear definition of problems.

- Unclear experiment objectives.

- Poor brainstorming.

- Failure to recognize the value of a designed experiment.

- Misperception that designed experiments are costly.

- Misperception that designed experiments are time-consuming.

- Lack of understanding of DoE strategies and tools.

- Lack of support from management.

- Expectation of immediate results.

- Lack of adequate consultancy.

LSSI
LEAN SIX SIGMA INSTITUTE

Helicopter dynamics

You want to build a helicopter prototype that will have the longest time in the air (flight time) once it has been released from a given height.

Test 3 design parameters according to the following specifications:

A: Length of the blades(2", 3")

B: Length of the body (2", 3")

C: Width of the body (1", 1.5")

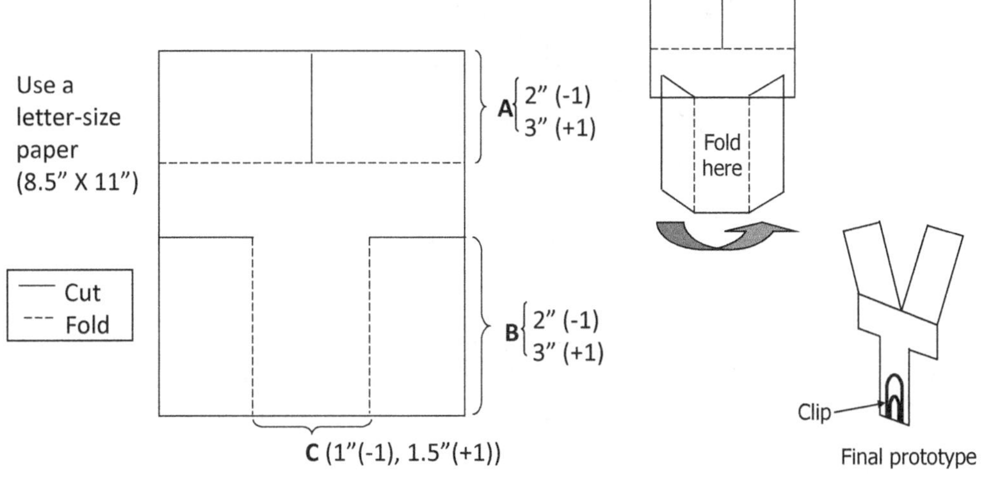

1. Create a design matrix and perform the experimental runs.

2. Conduct two genuine replicates. Release one helicopter at each experimental treatment and do not repeat the release of a helicopter twice in a row.

Perform the experimental runs
(the levels are in inches).

StdOrder	RunOrder	BLADES	LENGTH	WIDTH	TIME
13	1	2	2	1,5	
4	2	3	3	1,0	
3	3	2	3	1,0	
14	4	3	2	1,5	
5	5	2	2	1,5	
11	6	2	3	1,0	
15	7	2	3	1,5	
10	8	3	2	1,0	
2	9	3	2	1,0	
7	10	2	3	1,5	
16	11	3	3	1,5	
12	12	3	3	1,0	
1	13	2	2	1,0	
6	14	3	2	1,5	
9	15	2	2	1,0	
8	16	3	3	1,5	

Factorial experimental designs

Objectives

1. Understand the key concepts and terminology of factorial experimental designs.
2. Perform factorial designs to identify how changes in different variables can affect a process, product or service for improvements.

Content

> Factorial designs
> Sample size
> Types of factors
> Examples
> Exercises

Factorial designs

- Two-level experimental designs are a practical way to conduct experiments and are represented by a *design matrix.*

- A two-level full factorial design is represented as follows:

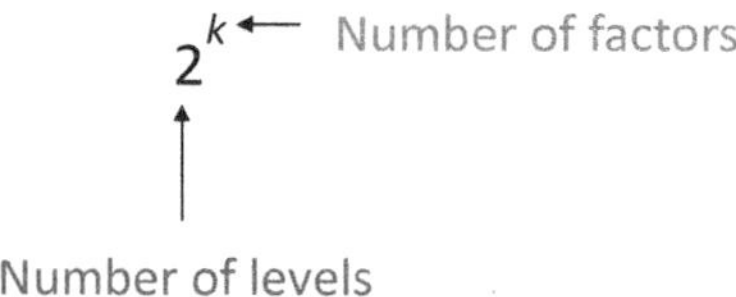

$$2^k = \text{Total number of combinations (experimental runs).}$$

With *full* factorial designs, *all* possible combinations (experimental runs) that can be formed with the selected levels are randomly executed in the process.

Examples:

k = 2 factors, each with 2 levels	2^2	4 experiments
k = 3 factors, each with 2 levels	2^3	8 experiments
k = 2 factors, each with 3 levels	3^2	9 experiments
k = 3 factors: 1 factor with 2 levels & 2 factors with 3 levels	$2^1 \times 3^2$	18 experiments

Note: The experiments do **not** include repetitions.

Sample size

- The total number of experiments depends on the repetitions. With ANOVA, for example, at least 2 replicates are needed to evaluate the significance of the factors.

- Schmidt and Launsby (1994) present practical methods to calculate sample sizes for designed experiments with two-level factors, and with either full or fractional factorials:

Design	# of runs	Replicates per run
2^2	4	9
2^3	8	5
2^4	16	3
2^5	32	2

Types of factors

Factors can be either qualitative or quantitative.

- Qualitative: Supplier, claims adjuster, provider of service, employee, location, materials, equipment, etc.

- Quantitative: Distance, speed, time, size, etc.

Example 1: 2^2 full factorial design

A 2^2 factorial experiment has been conducted to determine the effects that applying a surface coating (x_1) and a cutting fluid (x_2) may have on a part's surface. The low level for each of the variables represents the absence of technology (no coating and no fluid). The high level represents the use of technology. The response variable is the surface finish measured in microns (R-value) and the objective is to minimize it.

X_1	X_2	R_a
-	-	44
+	-	32
-	+	55
+	+	20

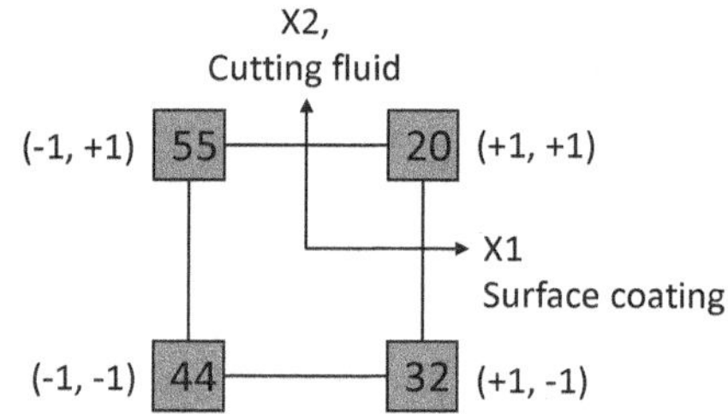

Questions:
What are the main effects? Is there an effect due to factor interaction?

Main effects plot

- The Y-axis represents the output or response (surface finish).

- The levels of the factors are represented on the X-axis.

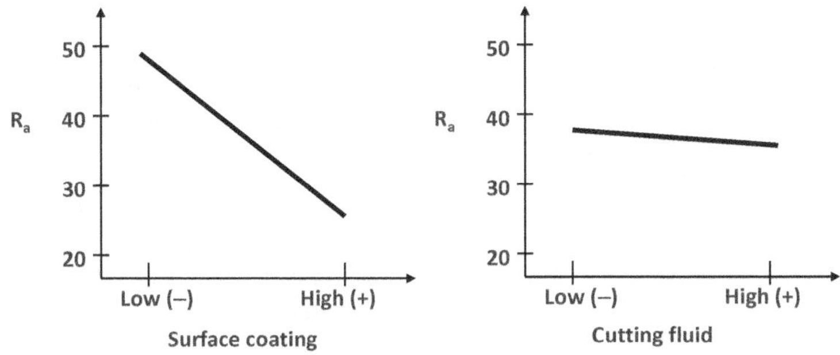

Which factor has the greatest effect?

Interaction plots

- The Y-axis is the output or response (surface finish).

- The levels of the factors are represented on the X-axis.

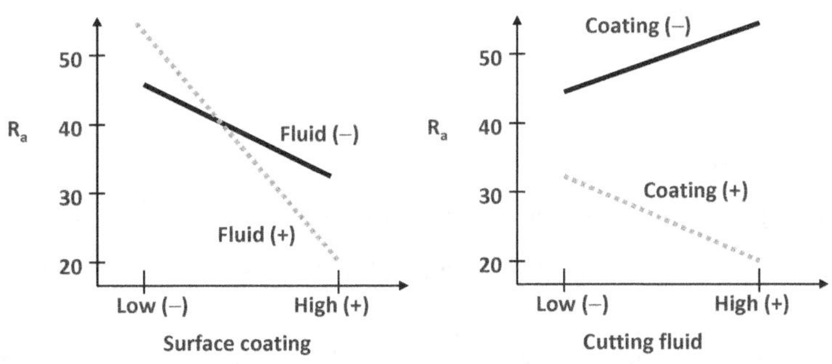

What is the difference between these two plots?

Interpretation of plots

- When there is an interaction, the lines have very different slopes and usually cross each other. When there is no interaction, the lines have similar slopes and are approximately parallel.

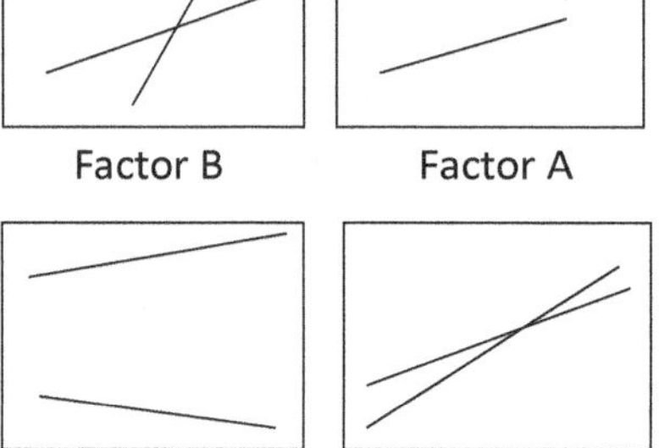

Factor B   Factor A

In this case there is an interaction: The effect on Y of increasing B is different depending on the level of A.

Factor B   Factor A

In this case there is no interaction: The effect on Y of increasing B is the same regardless of the level of A.

What is the conclusion?

- **Statistical conclusion:**
    - ✓ Applying surface coating has a greater effect on the surface finish than applying cutting fluid.
    - ✓ Interaction is significant.

- **Practical conclusion:**
    - ✓ Applying surface coating significantly improves the surface finish.
    - ✓ The application of cutting fluid does not have a significant effect on surface finish.
    - ✓ If we want to further improve surface finish, then we should use **both** surface coating and cutting fluid.

LSSI
LEAN SIX SIGMA INSTITUTE

Example 2

Bank of the Atlantic, in order to improve (reduce) service time, the CI team conducted the following two-way (or two-factor) experiment in one of the Bank's branches (as a pilot test):

1. TPM implementation for hardware and software (levels: before / after).

2. Preparation of standardized work manuals and training of personnel (levels: before / after).

		A Factor TPM for Hardware and Software	
		Before	After
B Factor	Before	9.35	7.99
Standardized		11.12	6.18
Work Manuals		10.33	8.02
and Training	After	4.55	3.01
		5.31	2.02
		4.03	1.77

- The previous table shows service time (three replicates per combination of treatments) before and after the implementation of each improvement – and aims to examine the effectiveness of these actions. The following analysis was conducted using Minitab.

- **Step 1. Analyze significant factors and previous assumptions:** The first step is to determine which factors (from those analyzed) are truly significant. This is done using the ANOVA table:

Source	Df	Adj. SS	Adj. MS	F-value	P-value
Model	3	107.674	35.8914	52.38	0.000
Linear	2	107.482	53.7408	78.42	0.000
TPM	1	20.541	20.5408	29.97	0.001
Training	1	86.941	86.9408	126.87	0.000
Two-term interactions	1	0.193	0.1925	0.28	0.610
TPM * Training	1	0.193	0.1925	0.28	0.610
Error	8	5.482	0.6853		
Total	11	113.156			

- As we can see, the two individual factors (TPM and training) reflect p-values < alpha = 0.05 (0.001 for TPM and 0.000 for training), which indicate that both have a significant influence on service time.

- The AB interaction (TPM * training) has a p-value = 0.610 > alpha = 0.05, so it is not significant.

Pareto chart:

- Minitab also provides us with a *Pareto chart* in which the significance of factors and interactions can be observed graphically.

- Bars whose lengths exceed the dotted vertical line indicate factors or interactions that are significant.

- We verify that A (TPM) and B (Training) are significant, while the AB interaction is not.

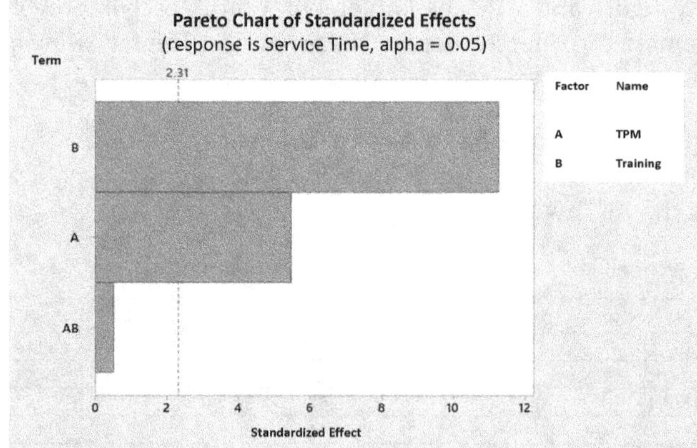

Before conducting the analysis for the optimal levels, we must verify that the residuals for each observation meet the following three conditions:

1. **Normality:** The distributions of the residuals are normal.

2. **Homoscedasticity:** Homogeneity of variance for the observations.

3. **Independence** of observations.

The method for performing this analysis was presented in the ANOVA module.

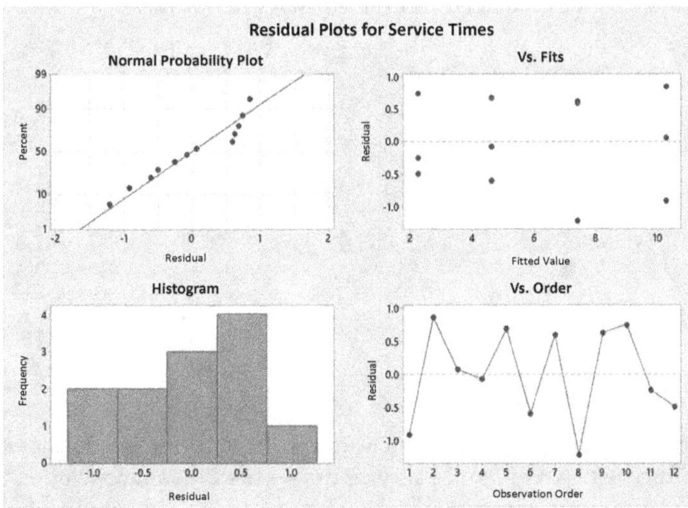

Using the plots obtained on Minitab, we can conclude that the experiment satisfies the tests for normality, homoscedasticity and independence.

- **Step 2. Determine optimal levels for each factor**
  In order to determine the optimal levels for each factor, we develop factorial graphs following these three rules:

  1. If the double interactions results show they are significant, then plot this interaction. The graphs for the corresponding individual effects are not needed. For example, if we determine that the interaction of factors B and C (B*C) is significant, then, to optimize the response, we should plot only this interaction graph. The plots of the individual effects of factors B and C are not needed.
  2. If there are individual significant effects that have not shown significant double interactions, then these should be plotted individually.
  3. If the experiment has three factors or more, the triple and greater [quadruple, quintuple] interactions should not be presented on a graph or plotted – even if they showed to be significant in the initial analysis. These interactions should be considered "ignorable" since it is possible that they can be denoted as significant without being so (and vice versa) – due to the calculations conducted.

- The corresponding chart(s) in this case are only the main effects plot, as the interaction is not significant.

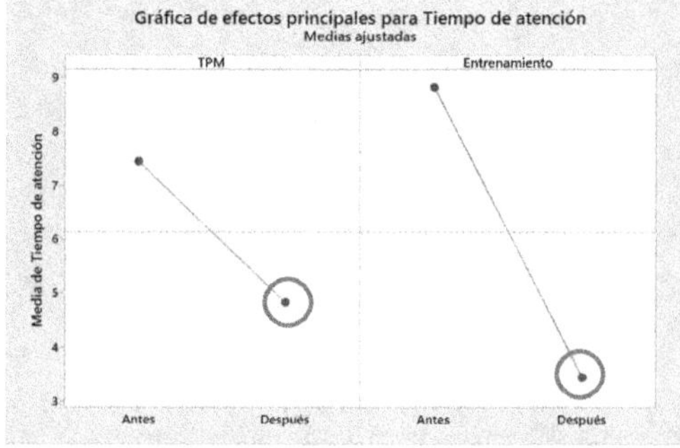

Following the factorial graphs (and the Minitab optimizer) – and considering that the objective of the test is to minimize service time – the CI team concludes the following:

- A lower service time is achieved when implementing TPM for hardware and software.

- A lower service time is achieved when personnel is trained with standardized manuals and procedures.

Therefore, the team will proceed to implement these improvements at the enterprise level.

Example 3

- An engineer is designing a battery that will be used in a device that is subject to extreme temperature variations.

- The only design parameter that can be selected at this point is the material of the plate (the battery's anode).

- Once the device is produced and used in the field, the engineer has no control over the potential temperatures that the battery is exposed to. She knows from experience, however, that environmental temperature affects battery life and that she can control the temperature in the lab for final testing.

The engineer decides to test three different plate materials at three different temperatures that are consistent with the environment in which the battery will be used : −15, 70 and 125 °F.

Four batteries will be tested at each combination of materials and temperatures. All 36 runs are performed randomly.

The following table shows the results of the experiment on battery life (in hours).

1. What effects do the type of material and temperature have on battery life?

2. Is there a material that will **prolong battery life independent of changes in temperature?**

Type of Material	Temperature (°F)											
	-15				70				125			
A	130	155	74	180	34	40	80	75	20	70	82	58
B	150	188	159	126	136	122	106	115	25	70	58	45
C	138	110	168	160	174	120	150	139	96	104	82	60

- **Step 1. Analyze significant factors and previous assumptions**

Analysis of variance

Source	Df	Adj. SS	Adj. MS	F-value	P-value
Model	8	59416	7427.0	11.00	0.000
Linear	4	49802	12450.6	18.44	0.000
Type of Material	2	10684	5341.9	7.91	0.002
Temperature	2	39119	19559.4	28.97	0.000
Two-term interactions	4	9614	2403.4	3.56	0.019
Type of Material * Temperature	4	9614	2403.4	3.56	0.019
Error	27	18231	675.2		
Total	35	77647			

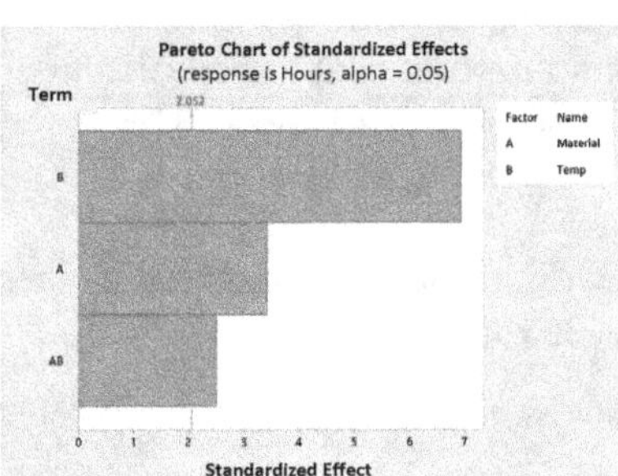

We can conclude that:

- There is a significant interaction between the type of material and temperature.

- Additionally, the main effects of material type and temperature are also significant.

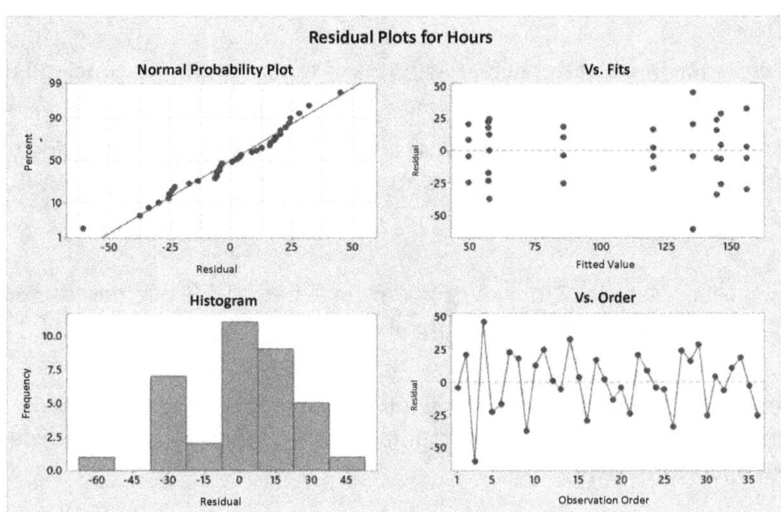

Using the plots above, we can conclude that the experiment meets the tests for Normality, Homoscedasticity, and Independence.

- **Step 2. Determine optimal levels for each factor**

  - In this case, since the interaction is significant, we only need to draw the factorial interaction plot in order to find the optimum level.

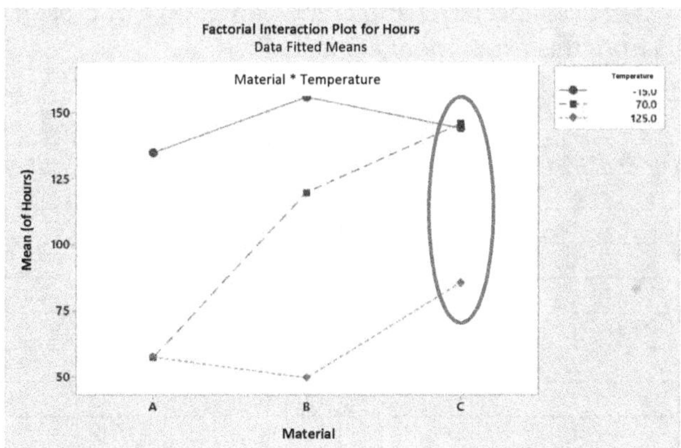

In order to **maximize** battery life, regardless of temperature, we conclude that:

- Material C should be used for low and medium temperatures. By using this material, the average battery life is approximately between 144 and 145.7 hours.

- When using Material C, however, the average battery life decreases to 85.5 hours when exposed to **high** temperatures.

- Therefore, the R&D team will continue its search for a different material that can extend battery life at high temperatures and that is relatively independent of temperature itself.

Example 4

- An experiment is carried out by a computer expansion card manufacturer to determine if the temperature in the three critical processes (and their interactions) are significant regarding the **percentage** of broken cards produced. The results from this experiment are as follows:

Temp: Engraving	Temp: Soldering	Temp: Water	Percentage of broken cards	
			R1	R2
- 3 ° C	60 ° C	20 ° C	0.040	0.032
- 1 ° C	60 ° C	20 ° C	0.012	0.008
- 3 ° C	98 ° C	20 ° C	0.036	0.028
- 1 ° C	98 ° C	20 ° C	0.000	0.000
- 3 ° C	60 ° C	70 ° C	0.020	0.020
- 1 ° C	60 ° C	70 ° C	0.000	0.016
- 3 ° C	98 ° C	70 ° C	0.016	0.008
- 1 ° C	98 ° C	70 ° C	0.004	0.004

- **Step 1. Analyze significant factors and previous assumptions**

Analysis of variance

Source	Df	Adj. SS	Adj. MS	F-value	P-value
Model	7	0.002367	0.000338	11.66	0.001
Linear	3	0.001979	0.000660	22.75	0.000
Temp: Engraving	1	0.001521	0.001521	52.45	0.000
Tem: Soldering	1	0.000169	0.000169	5.83	0.042
Temp: Water	1	0.000289	0.000289	9.97	0.013
Two-term interactions	3	0.000363	0.000121	4.17	0.047
Temp: Engraving * Temp: Soldering	1	0.000001	0.000001	0.03	0.857
Temp: Engraving * Temp: Water	1	0.000361	0.000361	12.45	0.008
Temp: Soldering * Temp: Water	1	0.000001	0.000001	0.03	0.857
Three-term interactions	1	0.000025	0.000025	0.86	0.380
Temp: Engraving * Temp: Soldering * Temp: Water	1	0.000025	0.000025	0.86	0.380
Error	8	0.000232	0.000029		
Total	15	0.002599			

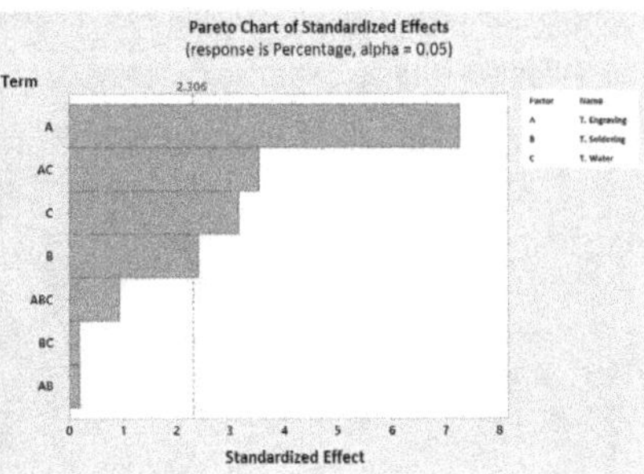

We can conclude that:

- The three individual factors (Temperatures for engraving, soldering and water) are significant.

- The AC interaction (engraving temperature * water temperature) is also significant.

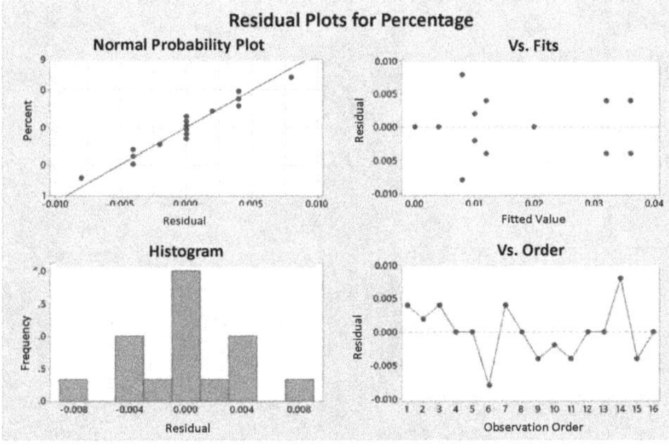

Using the plots above, we can conclude that the experiment meets the tests for normality, homoscedasticity, and independence.

- **Step 2. Determine optimal levels for each factor**

  - In this case, since the AC interaction is significant, only the Factorial Interaction Plot for these two factors is needed. It is not necessary to plot these two factors individually.

  - Factor B needs to be plotted individually, since it is also significant.

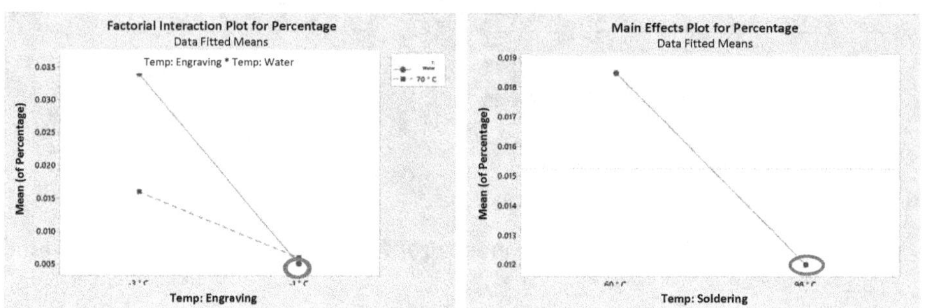

In order to **minimize** the percentage of broken cards, we conclude that the best combination is:

Engraving temperature:	−1°C
Soldering temperature:	98°C
Water temperature:	20°C

Multi-response prediction

Variable	Value
Temp: Engraving	- 1 °C
Temp: Soldering	98 °C
Temp: Water	20 °C

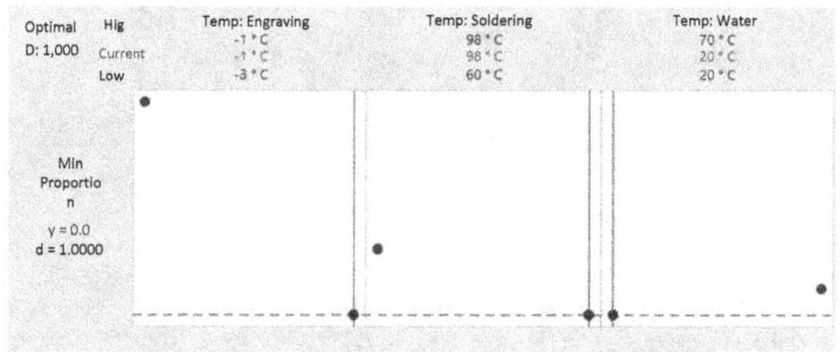

Exercise 1

- The continuous improvement team at **Logistics Company** wants to justify the recent purchase of three different types of software: 1. To analyze demand, 2. To plan routes, and 3. To optimize loading and unloading. The team runs tests with and without the use of the software in order to evaluate its impact on OTIF (on-time and in-full). The results are summarized in the table below. What is the best combination? Is the purchase of each software justified?

A Factor Level Demand Analysis Software	B Factor Level Route Planning Software	C Factor Level Loading & Unloading Software	Weekly OTIF (Percent)				
			1	2	3	4	5
Without Software	Without Software	Without Software	97.00	97.12	96.45	95.31	96.55
With Software	Without Software	Without Software	98.90	98.45	98.07	97.45	97.80
Without Software	With Software	Without Software	97.94	96.50	95.56	98.60	98.70
With Software	With Software	Without Software	99.12	99.21	98.99	99.03	99.87
Without Software	Without Software	With Software	95.40	93.21	95.32	93.45	95.78
With Software	Without Software	With Software	98.76	98.77	98.97	98.06	99.03
Without Software	With Software	With Software	98.08	98.77	98.05	98.21	97.76
With Software	With Software	With Software	98.05	98.02	97.31	98.05	98.32

Exercise 2 (practical): Full factorial

- A company conducts an experiment to determine what are the critical factors that affect the dissolution time of a tablet.

- The factors are the following:

    - Tablet brand

    - Type of water

    - Stirring

    - Water level

- The levels of the exercise are as follows:

    - Tablet brand: e.g., Bayer, generic

    - Type of water: Sparkling, tap

    - Stirring: With stirring, without stirring (using a spoon)

    - Water level: High, low (mark the glass)

- Each team will perform their own designed experiment, using these factors and levels, and present their data and results to the group.

Statistical process control

Controlling improvements and variation

Objectives

1. Understand the types of statistical control charts.
2. Correctly select the type of control chart.
3. Develop control charts for any type of process.

Content

> Background
> What is statistical process control?
> What are they used for?
> Benefits
> Elements
> When to use them?
> Procedure
> Examples
> Exercises
> Re-calculation of control limits

Background

- Statistical Process Control (SPC) was developed in 1924 by Dr. Walter Shewhart from Bell Labs.

- SPC helps detect variation from special causes through "out-of-control signals." These "out-of-control signals" alert us that the process is out of control, but cannot tell us why.

  - First Shewhart Control Charts – 1931
  - Deming – 1975 and 1982
  - Moen and Nolan – 1987
  - Nolan and Provost – 1990

What is statistical process control (SPC)?

- **SPC** is a fundamental tool used to study **variation.** It uses statistical signals to monitor process yield and lead to improvements.

- Its primary function is to determine in a definite manner if the results obtained from real-time measurements are in accordance with initial hypotheses.

What is a control chart?

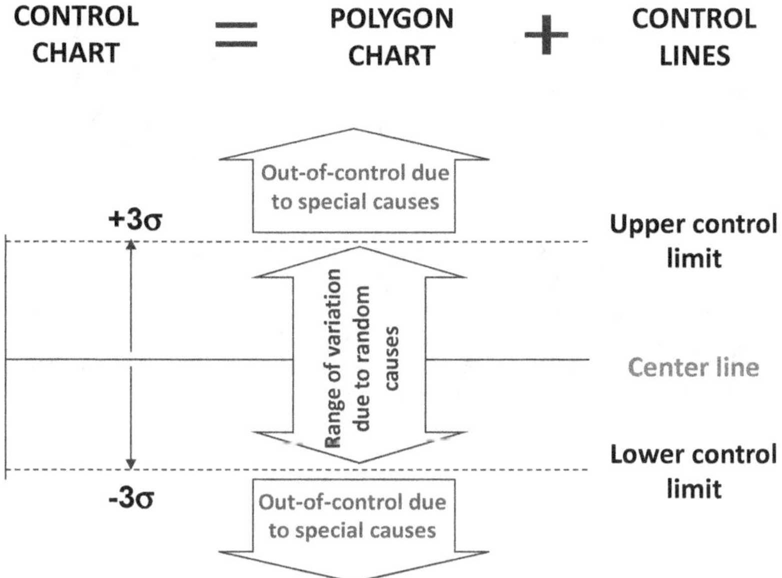

- Definition

Statistical tools that depict the behavior of a process quality characteristic with respect to time.

- Objective

To analyze, improve, and control processes.

Walter A. Shewhart (1931)

Statistical Process Control (SPC)

SPC (X's or Y's) without proper training = waste.

- SPC (X's or Y's) with trained operators, but without authority or decision-making power = waste of time.

  Operators have been trained and they understand the rules of SPC, but management does not allow them to stop and investigate the causes.

- SPC (X's or Y's) with trained operators and staff that respects rules = **success.**

  When everyone understands the rules of SPC and the graph shows a problem, everyone will accept to stop in order to identify the special cause and eliminate it.

Requirements

Before implementing control charts, the following requirements should be met:

Stability:	Normality:
If no special causes are detected, the process is considered to be stable.	Data should follow a normal distribution.
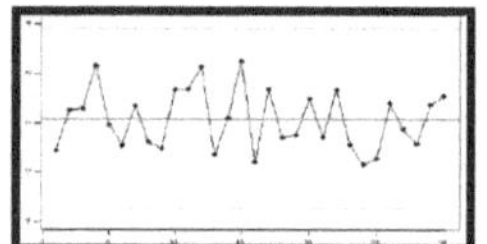	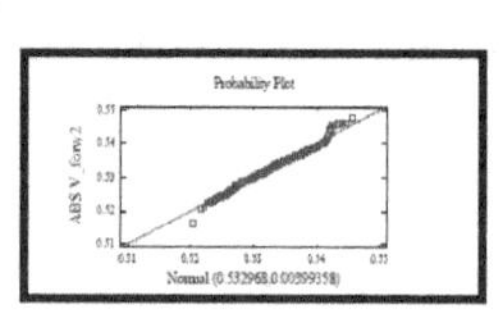

LSSI
LEAN SIX SIGMA INSTITUTE

What are they used for?

- Control charts are used to depict measured values taken from a process, and to monitor and control the process as well.

- Control charts incorporate upper and lower control limits that identify the natural limits of random variability in a process. These limits **SHOULD NOT** be compared to the customer's specification limits.

- Control charts help to identify the non-natural (non-random) tendencies of process variables.

- The actions taken to correct non-random tendencies are the key to the successful application of SPC.

Control charts

- Control charts are used to distinguish between common causes and special causes of variation.

- Control charts indicate when to improve a process and when not to.

- Overacting when a process is stable causes more variation.

Benefits

- Helps us understand if the process is under statistical control.

- Proven technique used to improve productivity.

- Effective method for preventing defects.

- Prevents unnecessary adjustments to the process.

- Can be used for both attribute and variable data.

- Provides a database that can be used to improve the process, measure its capability, and help make better decisions.

- Provides real-time process monitoring.

- Helps us to understand long-term process performance.

- Provides more knowledge and a better understanding of the process.

Elements

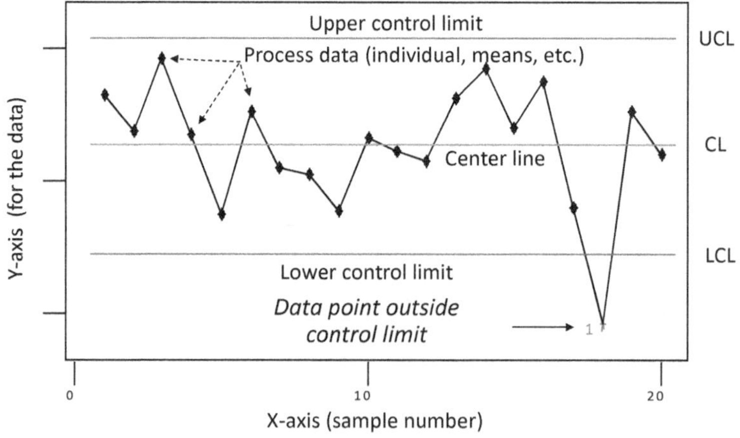

Basic concepts

- **Common causes**
  Refers to the random variability due to the combination of effects that are not easy to identify. A process that includes only common causes is considered to be under statistical control.

- **Special causes**
  The variability assignable to causes that are possible to identify, correct, and eliminate. A process that includes special causes is not under statistical control.

All processes have variation.

Types of control charts

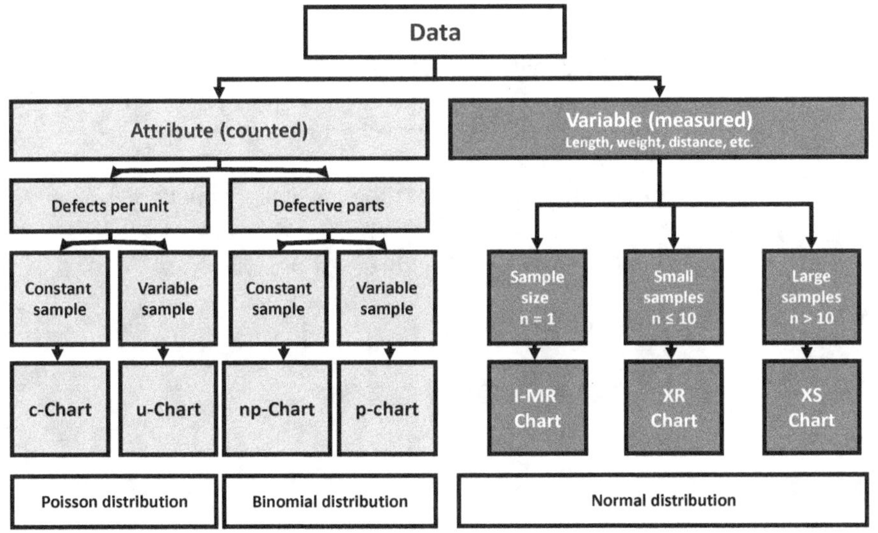

When to use them?

- When **analyzing** process performance (capability studies).

- When you want to **improve** process performance (identify causes of variation, prevent problems).

- When you want to **maintain** process performance (timely adjustments).

Procedure

1. Select a quality characteristic.

2. Select the type of control chart to use.

3. Define the sampling method and collect the data.

4. Calculate the control limits.

5. Plot the control chart.

6. Analyze the state of the process.

Chemical Manufacturing. The improvement team wants to monitor the weight of container caps for a plastic molding process. The weight specifications for the lids is from 60.00 to 67.50 grams.

1. Select a quality characteristic

- Continuous variable

- Normality assumption

- Independence assumption

Example – In this case, our continuous variable is weight [of plastic caps].

2. Select the type of control chart

Types of control charts

There are two general types of control charts:

- **Variable data control charts:**

  - X – R (average and range)
  - X – S (average and standard deviation)
  - I – MR (individuals and moving range)

- **Attribute data control charts:**

  - *p* (proportion of defects)
  - *np* (number of defective units)
  - *c* (number of defects)
  - *u* (number of defects per unit)

Example: Juliana Wilson's team at Chemical Manufacturing concludes that the variable data (weight of the lids), with sampling by subgroups of 5 pieces each corresponds with the X – R (Average and Range) chart.

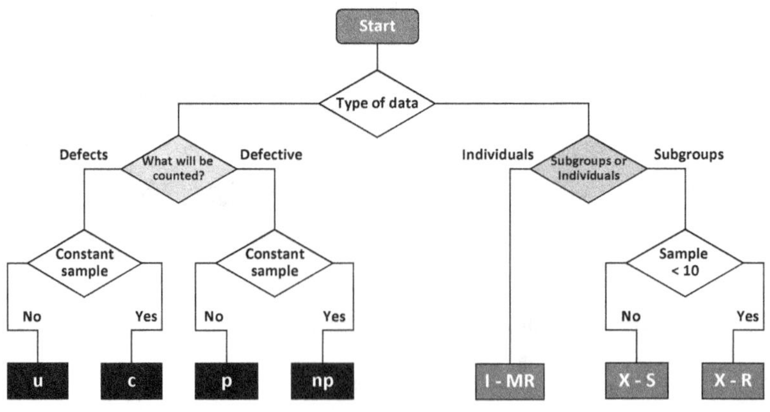

3. Define the sampling method and collect the data

- Organize data into subgroups.

- Homogenous sample.

- Sampling method:
  - Instant method
  - Period method

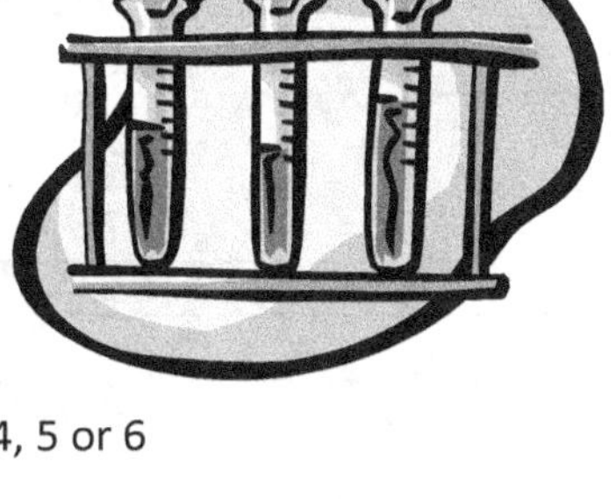

- Sample size:
  - Detection of moderate to large changes n = 4, 5 or 6
  - Detection of small changes, n = 7, 8 , 9 or 10
  - If n > 10, then use an X – S chart

- Frequency:
  - On average, there should be 1 out of 25 data points outside the control limits. If there are more, then increase the sampling frequency.

- Number of samples:
  - 20 subgroups with n = 5, or 25 subgroups with n = 4 (100 observations)

Example: 60 data points were collected from the plastic molding production line.

- Sample size n = 5
- Frequency = Every hour

Weight was recorded using the following table:

Sample	Hour	Weight (g)				
1	07:00	62.45	62.58	63.38	62.02	63.11
2	08:00	64.17	63.34	62.33	62.21	63.57
3	09:00	64.78	63.92	62.80	62.10	63.86
4	10:00	63.92	63.70	62.37	62.88	63.88
5	11:00	63.77	63.80	64.83	63.45	65.32
6	12:00	63.15	63.04	63.22	62.73	64.27
7	13:00	63.09	64.34	64.27	66.04	64.15
8	14:00	62.84	64.49	63.04	62.87	61.73
9	15:00	62.88	64.68	62.74	63.15	64.19
10	16:00	62.13	63.08	62.83	63.42	63.26
11	17:00	65.98	63.48	64.59	65.03	63.29
12	18:00	63.13	63.71	63.11	62.67	64.66

4. Calculate the control limits

$\overline{X} - R$ Ghart (Median and Range)		p Chart	u Chart
Means	Ranges	(proportion defective)	(density of defects)
$\begin{aligned} UCL &= \overline{\overline{x}} + A_2\overline{R} \\ CL &= \overline{\overline{x}} \\ LCL &= \overline{\overline{x}} - A_2\overline{R} \end{aligned}$	$\begin{aligned} UCL &= D_4\overline{R} \\ CL &= \overline{R} \\ LCL &= D_3\overline{R} \end{aligned}$	$\begin{aligned} UCL &= \overline{p} + 3\sqrt{\dfrac{\overline{p}(1-\overline{p})}{n}} \\ CL &= \overline{p} \\ LCL &= \overline{p} - 3\sqrt{\dfrac{\overline{p}(1-\overline{p})}{n}} \end{aligned}$	$\begin{aligned} UCL &= \overline{u} + 3\sqrt{\dfrac{\overline{u}}{n}} \\ CL &= \overline{u} \\ LCL &= \overline{u} - 3\sqrt{\dfrac{\overline{u}}{n}} \end{aligned}$
$\widetilde{X} - R$ Ghart (Median and Range)			
Means	Ranges		
$\begin{aligned} UCL &= \overline{\widetilde{x}} + m_3 A_2\overline{R} \\ CL &= \overline{\widetilde{x}} \\ LCL &= \overline{\widetilde{x}} - m_3 A_2\overline{R} \end{aligned}$	$\begin{aligned} UCL &= D_4\overline{R} \\ CL &= \overline{R} \\ LCL &= D_3\overline{R} \end{aligned}$	np Chart	c Chart
I – MR Chart	(Individuals)	(number of defective)	(quantity of defects)
Individuals	Ranges		
$\begin{aligned} UCL &= \overline{x} + 2.66\overline{R}_s \\ CL &= \overline{x} \\ LCL &= \overline{x} - 2.66\overline{R}_s \end{aligned}$	$\begin{aligned} UCL &= 3.27\overline{R}_s \\ CL &= \overline{R}_s \\ LCL &= \text{---} \end{aligned}$	$\begin{aligned} UCL &= n\overline{p} + 3\sqrt{n\overline{p}(1-\overline{p})} \\ CL &= n\overline{p} \\ LCL &= n\overline{p} - 3\sqrt{n\overline{p}(1-\overline{p})} \end{aligned}$	$\begin{aligned} UCL &= \overline{c} + 3\sqrt{\overline{c}} \\ CL &= \overline{c} \\ LCL &= \overline{c} - 3\sqrt{\overline{c}} \end{aligned}$

Constants used to calculate control limits

Sample size (n)	A_2	$m_3 \, A_2$	m_3	D_3	D_4	d_2	$1/d_2$	d_3
2	1.881	1.881	1.000	---	3.27	1.128	0.8865	0.853
3	1.023	1.187	1.160	---	2.57	1.693	0.5907	0.888
4	0.729	0.796	1.092	---	2.28	2.059	0.4857	0.880
5	0.577	0.691	1.198	---	2.11	2.326	0.4299	0.864
6	0.483	0.549	1.135	---	2.00	2.534	0.3946	0.848
7	0.419	0.509	1.214	0.08	1.92	2.704	0.3698	0.833
8	0.373	0.432	1.160	0.14	1.86	2.847	0.3512	0.820
9	0.337	0.412	1.223	0.18	1.82	2.970	0.3367	0.808
10	0.308	0.362	1.176	0.22	1.78	3.078	0.3249	0.797

Time	Samples of cap weight					Average	Range
	1	2	3	4	5		
1:00	62.45	62.58	63.38	62.02	63.11	62.71	1.36
2:00	64.17	63.34	62.33	62.21	63.57	63.12	1.96
3:00	64.78	63.92	62.80	62.10	63.86	63.49	2.68
4:00	63.92	63.70	62.37	62.88	63.88	63.35	1.55
5:00	63.77	63.80	64.83	63.45	65.32	64.23	1.87
6:00	63.15	63.04	63.22	62.73	64.27	63.28	1.54
7:00	63.09	64.34	64.27	66.04	64.15	64.38	2.95
8:00	62.84	64.49	63.04	62.87	61.73	62.99	2.76
9:00	62.88	64.68	62.74	63.15	64.19	63.53	1.94
10:00	62.13	63.08	62.83	63.42	63.26	62.94	1.29
11:00	65.98	63.48	64.59	65.03	63.29	64.47	2.69
12:00	63.13	63.71	63.11	62.67	64.66	63.46	1.99

	Averages	63.50	2.05

Example:

$$\textbf{UCL (X)} = X + A_2 R = 63.50 + 0.577(2.05) = \textbf{64.68}$$

$$\textbf{LCL (X)} = X - A_2 R = 63.50 - 0.577(2.05) = \textbf{62.32}$$

$$\textbf{UCL (R)} = D_4 R = 2.11(2.05) = \textbf{4.32}$$

$$\textbf{LCL (R)} = D_3 R = 0(2.05) = \textbf{0}$$

5. Plot the control chart

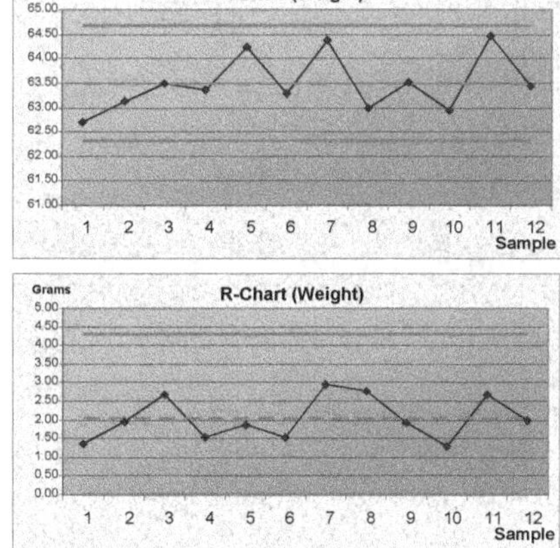

- Display both control charts on the same page.

- Display each data point along with any observations and additional information.

- **Do not include specifications.**

6. Analyze the state of the process

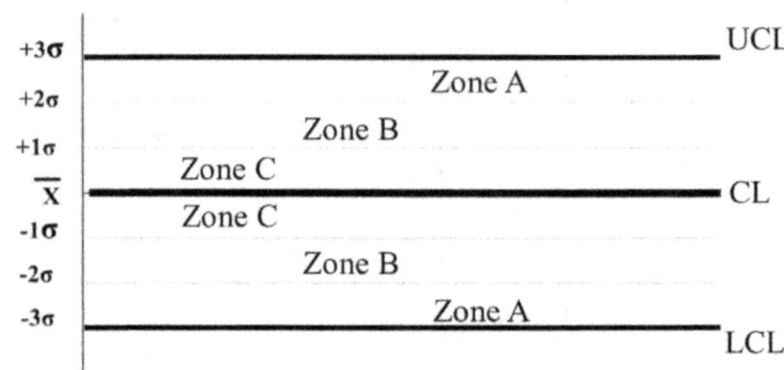

Consider the [upper or lower] half of a control chart and divide this area into thirds.

The empirical rule that the data must meet is:

- 60-75 % of the data fall between ± 1 sigma and the mean.
- 90-98 % of the data fall between ± 2 sigma and the mean.
- 99-100 % of the data fall between ± 3 sigma and the mean.

Interpretation of control chart patterns

Natural [or Normal] patterns have the following characteristics:

1. Most of the data points are close to the center line.
2. Few data points are close to the control limits.
3. None or an occasional data point is located outside of the control limits.

Unnatural patterns have the following characteristics:

1. The presence of data points outside the control limits is identified as an **instability** pattern.
2. The absence of data points near the control limits is identified as a **stratification** pattern.
3. An absence of data points near the center line is identified as a **mixture** pattern.
4. A series of 6 or more consecutive data points without a change in direction is identified as a **trend** pattern.

Patterns

1. Instability pattern

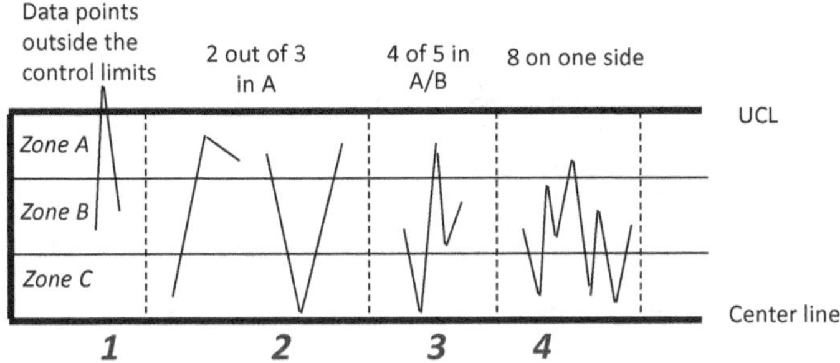

1. **Only one data point outside the center line** *(1).*
2. **Two out of 3 consecutive points in Zone A or beyond** *(2).*
3. **Four out of 5 consecutive points in Zone B or beyond** *(3).*
4. **Eight consecutive points in Zone C or beyond - RUN** *(4).*

2. Stratification pattern (closeness to the center line)

Occurs when 15 or more consecutive data points are in Zone C, either above or below the center line. The upward and downward variations are small compared to the control limits *(S).*

3. Mixture pattern (closeness to the control limits)

Occurs when eight consecutive data points are on both sides of the center line and none are in Zone C. This means there are lots of data points close to the control limits *(M).*

4. Trend pattern

A series of six or more consecutive data points, without a change in direction *(T).*

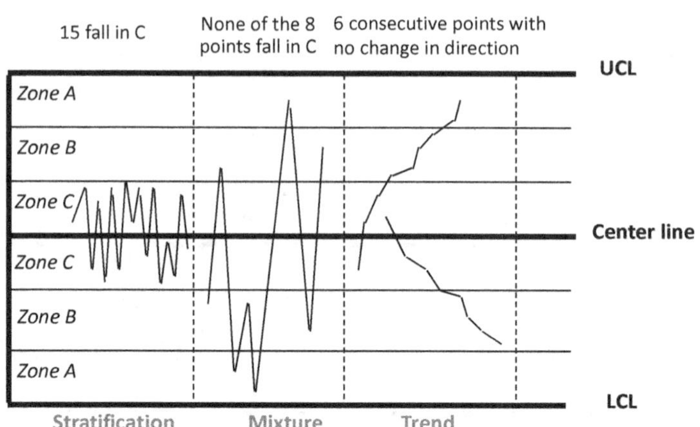

We do not detect any abnormal pattern for the plastic molding process. Therefore, we can conclude that the process is in statistical control.

A. Individuals – Moving Range Chart (I-MR)

Used for variable data by observing individual samples (i.e., n = 1).

Example: Bank of the Atlantic

In order to control the critical parameter, the Bank measures service time for the first customer who enters the branch in the morning and then for every 25 customers until the branch closes for the day. The results (in minutes) for the first day were recorded as follows:

Customer	1	2	3	4	5	6	7	8	9	10
Time	3,4	2,8	4,5	3,2	5,2	2,8	4,0	2,4	5,4	2,6

Customer	11	12	13	14	15	16	17	18	19
Time	3,8	2,6	2,9	5,0	3,7	4,2	2,1	4,6	3,2

- The following control charts were obtained using Minitab:

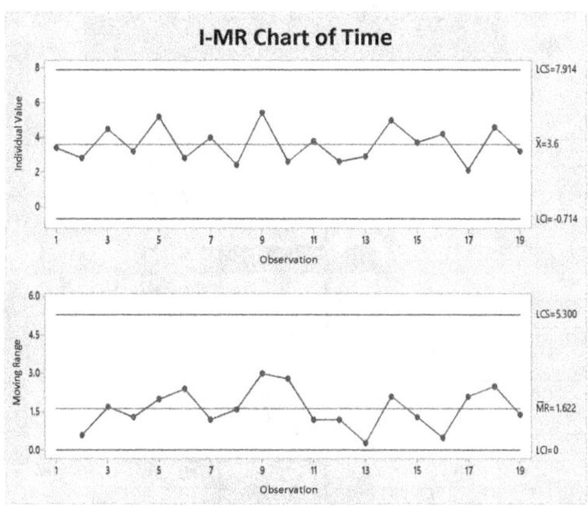

No abnormal patterns can be observed, which means service time at the branch is under statistical control. Monitoring will continue indefinitely in order to detect any significant variation and address the root cause immediately, which could include:

- Recently onboarded staff with little or no training.

- System failures that reflect maintenance issues.

B. Average and Range (XR)

- **Definition**

A statistical tool used to show the behavior of the mean (position) and variation (dispersion) of a process quality characteristic with respect to time. The control chart uses sample sizes between 2 and 10 and controls a continuous quality characteristic.

- **Objective**

Assess, improve, and control a quality characteristic from the perspective of *adjusting its mean* and *reducing* its variation relative to the *objective*.

Example

Example: We have *hardness* information *for 100* parts. The specifications are from 1 to 3 RC.

Sample	Hardness					Average	Range
1	1.855	1.162	1.606	2.010	1.929	1.712	0.849
2	2.020	1.473	1.502	2.471	1.518	1.797	0.998
3	2.378	1.525	1.743	2.693	1.492	1.966	1.202
4	1.644	1.870	1.703	1.745	1.640	1.720	0.230
5	2.189	2.281	1.854	1.645	1.801	1.954	0.637
6	1.828	1.093	1.943	2.594	1.971	1.886	1.501
7	2.614	1.976	1.649	1.827	2.179	2.049	0.966
8	2.298	2.533	2.681	1.548	2.233	2.259	1.133
9	1.971	2.280	1.817	2.333	1.773	2.035	0.560
10	1.823	2.060	2.290	1.471	1.364	1.802	0.925
11	2.431	1.267	1.737	2.011	2.061	1.901	1.163
12	1.956	1.811	1.770	1.863	1.420	1.764	0.537
13	2.047	1.231	2.805	1.926	1.988	1.999	1.574
14	2.241	2.095	1.723	2.036	2.703	2.159	0.980
15	1.966	1.715	2.175	1.517	2.686	2.012	1.170
16	2.351	1.790	2.416	2.305	1.985	2.170	0.627
17	1.630	2.433	2.726	2.330	2.207	2.265	1.095
18	1.833	1.575	2.039	1.492	1.838	1.756	0.547
19	1.941	1.788	2.077	1.607	1.376	1.758	0.700
20	1.883	2.220	1.581	2.290	1.105	1.816	1.185
					Average	1.939	0.9289

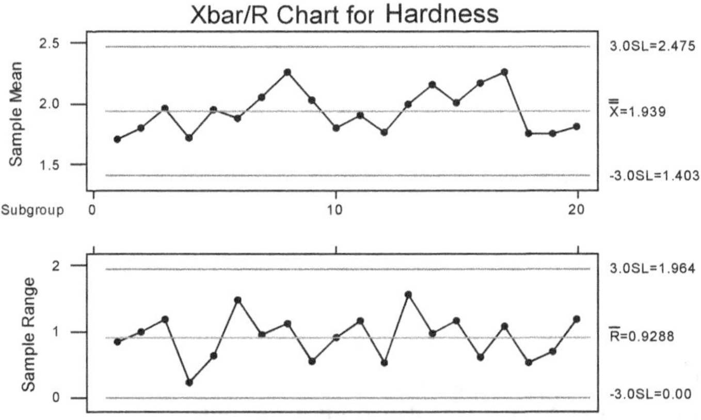

A stable process can be observed.

C. Mean and Standard deviation chart (XS)

This chart is used to control a continuous quality characteristic on sample sizes greater than 10.

Example: Chelsea Footwear

In order to detect variability and discrepancies for the cost of shoe soles, the product development team decides to use statistical process control in the shoe sole injection molding procedure and monitors the weight of soles to identify [and prevent] excess costs to the product. Since the molding machine has 12 cavities, the weight is verified by extracting a sample from each cavity (12 in total) every hour during an 8-hour work shift. The table on the following slide shows the data obtained:

Hour	Weight of soles per cavity (grams)											
	1	2	3	4	5	6	7	8	9	10	11	12
07:00	165	172	168	169	165	170	171	172	166	168	165	171
08:00	168	171	169	165	170	166	165	171	168	167	166	169
09:00	167	167	165	166	172	170	174	168	162	163	165	167
10:00	160	168	159	160	161	166	168	167	165	170	172	168
11:00	160	162	165	166	170	171	158	159	165	167	169	171
12:00	169	170	165	161	165	169	171	172	169	166	165	167
13:00	167	168	169	162	168	167	169	170	164	163	167	167
14:00	165	167	162	169	168	167	170	165	164	160	170	172
15:00	162	167	170	171	168	167	165	167	166	165	167	168

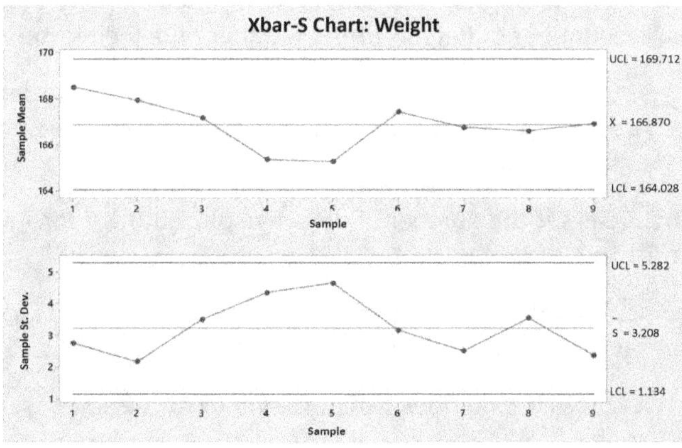

The charts reflect a stable process.

Chemical Manufacturing: Exercise

- Packaged weight is verified using samples of size n = 5, which are extracted from the operation every 30 minutes during the work shift. The following table represents the weights recorded:

Hour	Packaged Weight (lbs.)					Hour	Packaged Weight (lbs.)				
07:00	25.53	25.54	25.40	25.62	25.64	11:00	25.61	25.65	25.45	25.43	25.51
07:30	25.55	25.70	25.32	25.58	25.70	11:30	25.60	25.65	25.50	25.43	25.45
08:00	25.52	25.60	25.71	25.50	25.61	12:00	25.80	25.48	25.52	25.58	25.50
08:30	25.66	25.43	25.71	25.63	25.42	12:30	25.54	25.55	25.58	25.77	25.54
09:00	25.48	25.75	25.68	25.43	25.51	13:00	25.66	25.71	25.66	25.54	25.52
09:30	25.61	25.56	25.32	25.33	25.45	13:30	25.60	25.44	25.52	25.67	25.50
10:00	25.66	25.53	25.55	25.51	25.53	14:00	25.67	25.54	25.55	25.69	25.56
10:30	25.43	25.53	25.43	25.42	25.88	14:30	25.43	25.52	25.50	25.51	25.52

- **Control charts for attribute data** are used to measure discrete characteristics, i.e., measurable and countable on a scale of discrete values. For example, the number of defects or the number of defective items. Types of attribute data control charts:

  - **p-Chart:** Assesses the proportion or percentage of defective units. The size of sample **n** can be variable.

  - **np-Chart:** Assesses the number of defective units using a constant sample size, **n**.

  - **c-Chart:** Assesses the number of defects in well-defined units using a constant sample size, **n**.

  - **u-Chart:** Assesses the number of defects per unit. The size of sample **n** may be variable.

D. *p*-Chart: Example

We collected the following data on the manufacturing process for sinks:

Date	Units Produced (n)	Defective Units (X)	Proportion of defective units (p)	UCL (p)	LCL (p)
5-May	145	10	0.0690	0.182	0.029
6-May	236	1	0.0042	0.166	0.046
7-May	184	4	0.0217	0.174	0.038
8-May	122	6	0.0492	0.189	0.022
9-May	215	12	0.0558	0.169	0.043
10-May	218	35	0.1606	0.168	0.043
11-May	221	21	0.0950	0.168	0.044
12-May	149	32	0.2148	0.181	0.030
13-May	189	12	0.0635	0.173	0.039
14-May	156	22	0.1410	0.180	0.032
15-May	172	24	0.1395	0.176	0.035
16-May	125	35	0.2800	0.188	0.023
17-May	118	21	0.1780	0.191	0.021
18-May	164	19	0.1159	0.178	0.034
19-May	215	17	0.0791	0.169	0.043
20-May	248	21	0.0847	0.164	0.047
21-May	168	23	0.1369	0.177	0.035
22-May	159	24	0.1509	0.179	0.033
Sum	3204	339			

The control limits are calculated as follows:

$$\bar{p} = \frac{\sum X}{\sum n} = \frac{339}{3204} = 0.1058$$

$$UCL\ (p) = \bar{p} + 3\sqrt{\frac{\bar{p}(1-\bar{p})}{n}} \qquad LCL\ (p) = \bar{p} - 3\sqrt{\frac{\bar{p}(1-\bar{p})}{n}}$$

The graph is shown on the next slide. Western Electric (1956) recommends using sample sizes of 25, 50 or 100 for *p* and *np* charts. These charts are easier to interpret when the product of *np* is equal to 4 or 5.

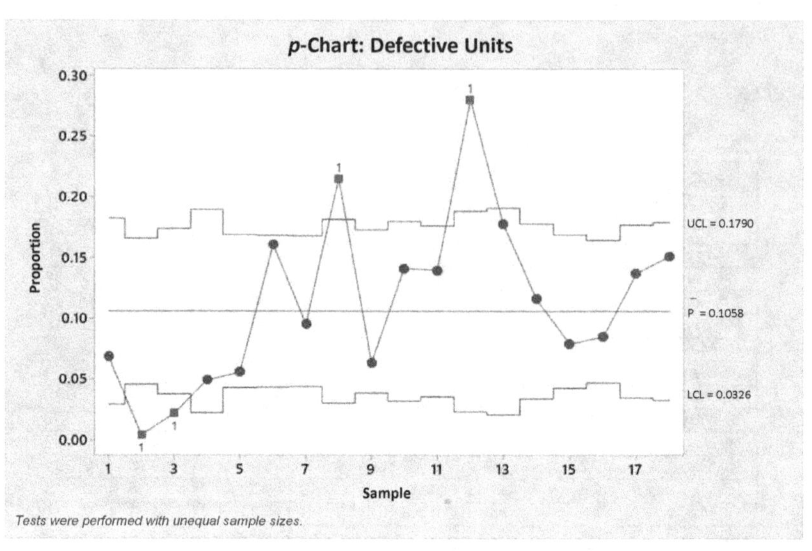

p-Chart: Conclusions

- We can observe two data points below the lower limit and two data points above the upper limit.

- The data points below the lower limit are batches with few defective products, which indicate that it would be convenient to examine the process performed and replicate it in order to decrease the proportion of such defective products.

- The data points above the upper limit indicate that there are factors causing a high percentage of defective products for these batches, which the team should examine.

- Note that the **p**-chart has variable control limits that change – since the sample size changes.

E. *np*-Chart: Example

- The **np**-chart serves the same purpose as the **p**-chart. The only difference is that the sample size **n** has to be constant for an **np**-chart. Instead of assessing the proportion of defects, the **np**-chart evaluates the number of defective units (**x = np**).

Example:

The following example is a modification of the previous example used for a **p**-chart and assumes a sample size of 100.

Date	Units Produced (n)	Units Defective (X)
5-May	100	10
6-May	100	1
7-May	100	4
8-May	100	6
9-May	100	12
10-May	100	35
11-May	100	21
12-May	100	32
13-May	100	12
14-May	100	22
15-May	100	24
16-May	100	35
17-May	100	21
18-May	100	19
19-May	100	17
20-May	100	21
21-May	100	23
22-May	100	24
Suma	1800	339

$$\overline{np} = \overline{X} = \frac{\Sigma X}{k} = \frac{339}{18} = 18.83$$

$$\text{UCL (np)} = \overline{np} + 3\sqrt{\overline{np}(1-\overline{p})}$$
$$= 18.83 + 3\sqrt{18.83(1-(18.83/100))}$$
$$= 30.56$$

$$\text{LCL (np)} = \overline{np} - 3\sqrt{\overline{np}(1-\overline{p})}$$
$$= 18.83 - 3\sqrt{18.83(1-(18.83/100))}$$
$$= 7.101$$

$$\overline{p} = \frac{\Sigma p}{k} = \frac{\Sigma(X/n)}{k}$$
$$= \frac{\Sigma X}{nk} = \frac{1}{n}(\overline{np})$$

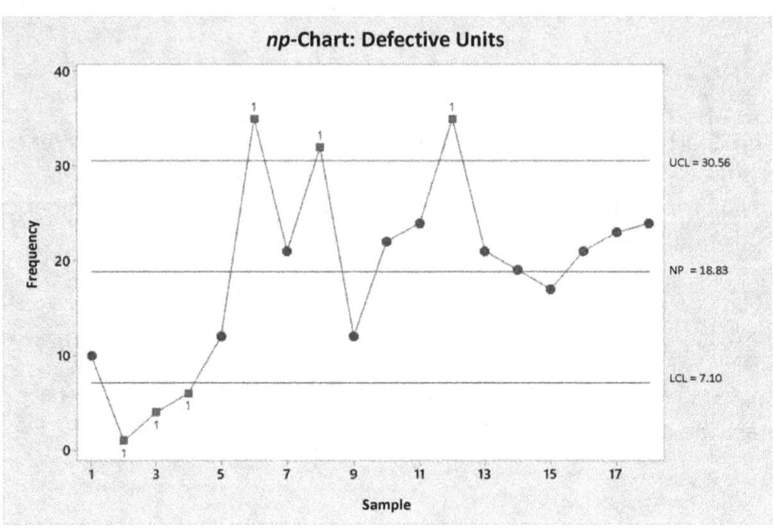

np-Chart: Conclusions

- We can observe three data points below the lower limit and three data points above the upper limit.

Same conclusions as the previous example:

- The data points below the lower limit are batches with few defective products, which indicate that it would be convenient to examine the process performed and replicate it in order to decrease the proportion of such defective products.

- The data points above the upper limit indicate that there are factors causing a high percentage of defective products for these batches, which the team should examine.

c-Chart and *u*-Chart

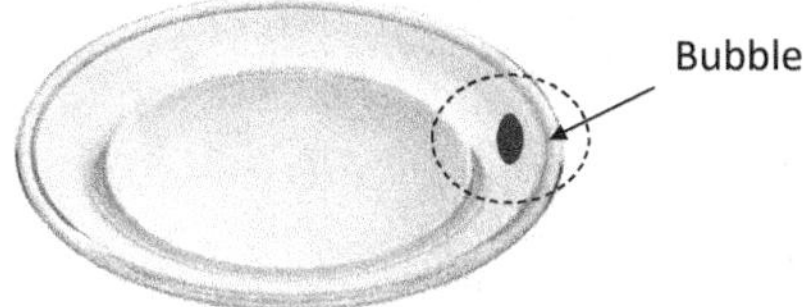

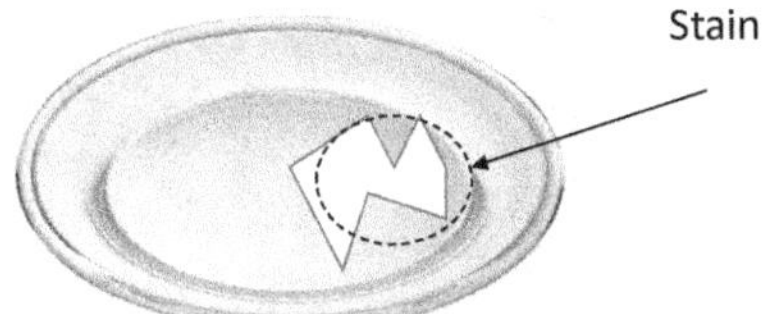

Defective ≠ Defects

Example:

Five crystal plates

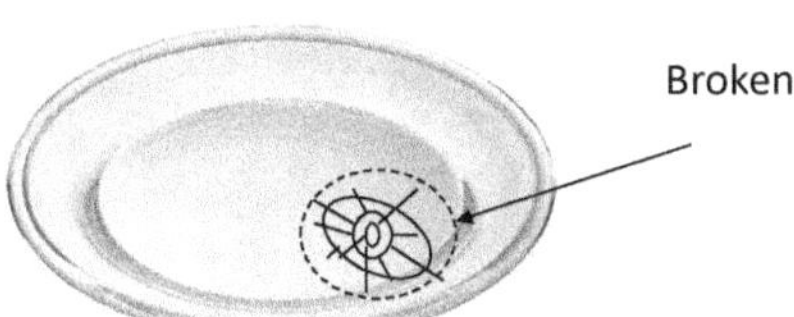

- Defective = 5
- Defects:

  - Bubble = 1

  - Stain = 3

  - Broken = 1

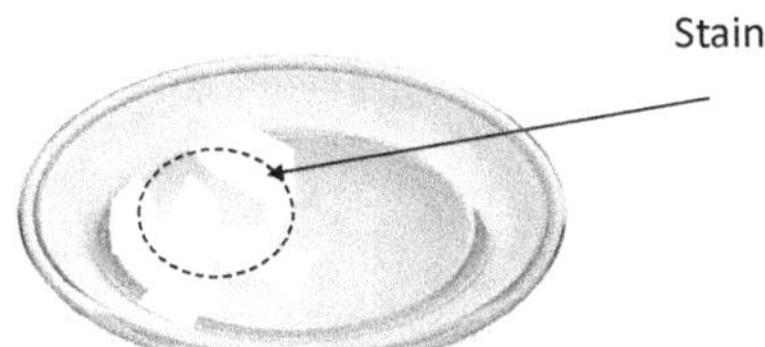

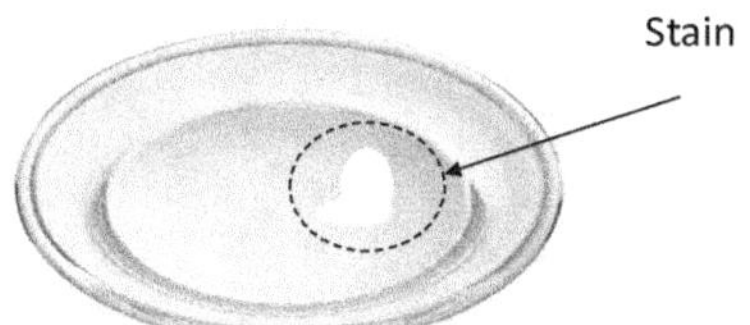

F. *c*-Chart: Example

The following data was collected on the number of defects found in a sample of 20 soda bottles:

Bottle Number	Number of Defects (c)	Bottle Number	Number of Defects (c)
1	3	11	2
2	2	12	0
3	4	13	1
4	0	14	5
5	1	15	2
6	2	16	5
7	1	17	4
8	5	18	3
9	6	19	6
10	1	20	2

$$\bar{c} = \frac{\sum c}{n} = \frac{55}{20} = 2.75$$

$$UCL(c) = \bar{c} + 3\sqrt{\bar{c}} = 2.75 + 3\sqrt{2.75} = 7.725$$

$$LCL(c) = \bar{c} - 3\sqrt{\bar{c}} = 2.75 - 3\sqrt{2.75} = -2.225 \rightarrow 0$$

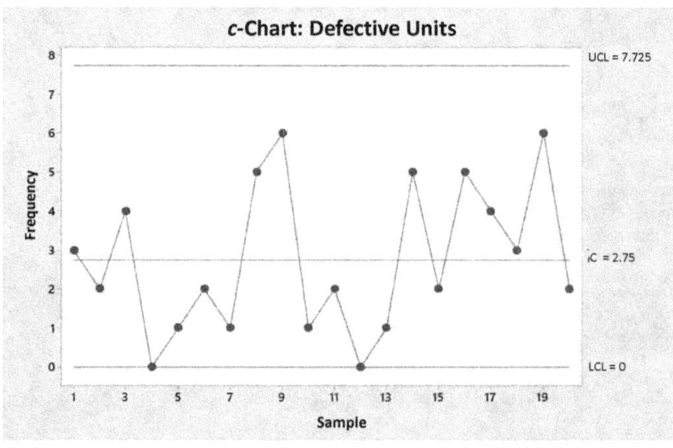

The process is under statistical control.

G. *u*-Chart: Example

- Assume that the sample size from the **c**-chart exercise was not one bottle, but instead a group of bottles.

- In this case, the Control Chart that we need to use is a **u**-chart.

- Consider the modified data from the *c*-chart example:

Number of Bottles	Number of Defects (c)	Average Defects (u)	Number of Bottles	Number of Defects (c)	Average Defects (u)
2	3	1.500	8	2	0.250
3	2	0.667	9	0	0.000
8	4	0.500	4	1	0.250
6	0	0.000	6	5	0.833
4	1	0.250	3	2	0.667
6	2	0.333	7	5	0.714
9	1	0.111	9	4	0.444
5	5	1.000	8	3	0.375
4	6	1.500	5	6	1.200
3	1	0.333	5	2	0.400

Similarly to the **p**-chart, the **u**-chart will also have variable control limits if the sample size is variable.

$$\bar{u} = \frac{\sum c}{\sum n} = \frac{55}{114} = 0.4825 \quad UCL\,(u) = \bar{u} + 3\sqrt{\frac{\bar{u}}{n}} \quad \underset{L}{LC}\,(u) = \bar{u} - 3\sqrt{\frac{\bar{u}}{n}}$$

$$UCL\,(u) = (0.4825) + 3\sqrt{\frac{(0.4825)}{(2)}} \quad LCL\,(u) = (0.4825) - 3\sqrt{\frac{(0.4825)}{(2)}}$$

Number of Bottles	Number of Defects (c)	UCL (u)	LCL (u)	Number of Bottles	Number of Defects (c)	UCL (u)	LCL (u)
2	3	1.956	- 0.991	8	2	1.219	- 0.254
3	2	1.686	- 0.721	9	0	1.177	- 0.212
8	4	1.219	- 0.254	4	1	1.524	- 0.559
6	0	1.333	- 0.368	6	5	1.333	- 0.368
4	1	1.524	- 0.559	3	2	1.686	- 0.721
6	2	1.333	- 0.368	7	5	1.270	- 0.305
9	1	1.177	- 0.212	9	4	1.177	- 0.212
5	5	1.414	- 0.449	8	3	1.219	- 0.254
4	6	1.524	- 0.559	5	6	1.414	- 0.449
3	1	1.686	- 0.721	5	2	1.414	- 0.449

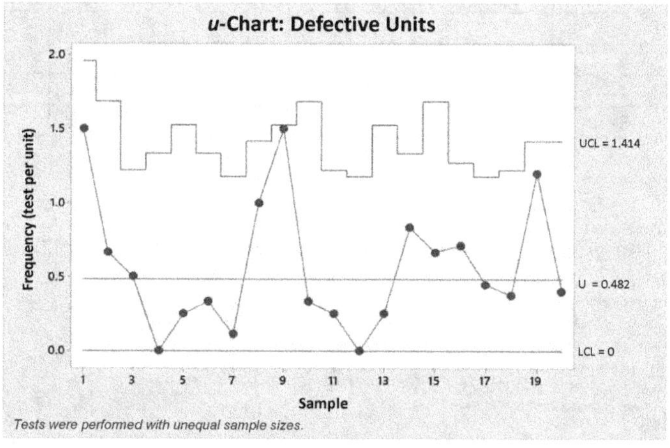

The process is under statistical control.

Attribute charts: Additional exercises

- **Exercise 1: Logistics Company.** Paul Evans's team is planning to implement a control chart for the number of incorrect invoices that are issued per week in relation to the number of orders sent. The following tables summarize the data that was collected:

Week	26	27	28	29	30	31	32	33	34	35
Orders Sent	615	595	606	692	584	612	655	632	678	599
Incorrect Invoices	3	1	2	0	1	3	4	2	0	1

Week	36	37	38	39	40	41	42	43	44	45
Orders Sent	632	650	675	594	587	625	633	651	668	606
Incorrect Invoices	3	2	3	3	4	2	3	8	1	1

Build the appropriate control chart and present your conclusion(s).

- **Exercise 2: Bank of the Atlantic.** James Roberts's team is using a control chart to monitor the number of mistakes detected at a branch during the month of November. The data was recorded in the following table. Note that more than one mistake can be counted while servicing the same customer.

Day	1	2	3	4	5	6	8	9	10	11	12	13
Customers Serviced	1,265	1,134	1,187	1,201	1,287	1,209	1,123	1,209	1,308	1,160	1,354	1,089
Mistakes	10	11	15	11	9	13	9	15	13	17	5	10

Day	15	16	17	18	19	20	22	23	24	25	26	27
Customers Serviced	1,398	1,123	1,198	1,132	1,098	908	1,190	1,231	1,109	1,212	1,255	1,099
Mistakes	15	11	8	5	19	11	9	13	21	15	12	7

Day	29	30
Customers Serviced	1,098	1,154
Mistakes	11	17

Build the appropriate control cChart and present your conclusion(s).

Re-calculation of control limits

According to Perry Regier (Dow Chemicals) all the following questions must have an *affirmative* answer in order to proceed with the re-calculation of control limits after a change has occurred:

a) Is the data behaving differently than in the past?
b) Do we know the reason for this change?
c) Is the new behavior desirable?
d) Is the new behavior expected to continue?

The number of data points necessary to start re-calculating control limits is two subgroups of sample size 4.

Wheeler (1998)

Control plan

Objectives

1. Introduce the concept of control.
2. Identify the elements that contribute to the successful control of a process.
3. Learn how to develop and document control plans.

Content

- > Introduction
- > What is a control plan?
- > What is it used for?
- > Key elements
- > When is it used?
- > Procedure
- > Example
- > Exercise

Introduction

- When we design a process and define the way in which it should work, it is also very important to define where in that process will a control plan be implemented – in order to ensure that it is performing as intended.

- Examples of processes where a control plan can be applied:

  Sales, Logistics, Accounting, Manufacturing, Services, etc.

- We usually use control plans in manufacturing; however, any critical process should use one.

What is a control plan?

- A tool that helps to ensure the stability of a process.

- A plan describing the long-term strategy to ensure improvements are effective and sustained.

- A list of all activities that should be performed to ensure the sustainment of process improvements.

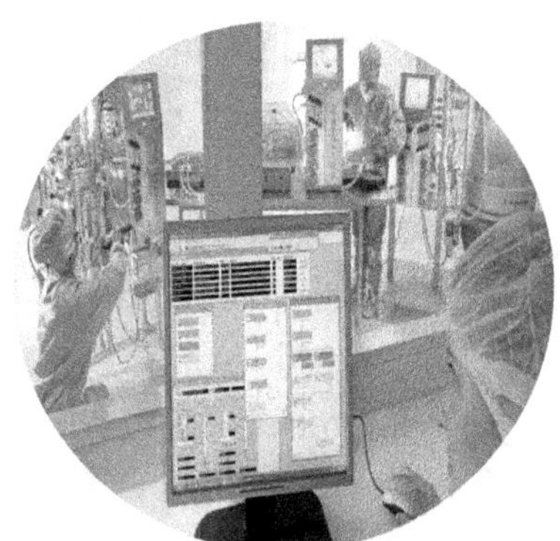

- To perform processes in a consistent manner – keeping in mind the target objectives and achieving them with the least possible variation.

- To minimize variation around the objectives/target values.

- To minimize the number of process interventions such as adjustments and/or over-control.

- To standardize process improvements.

- To highlight the areas in the organization that require additional training.

- To ensure that control measures are documented and included in the corresponding procedures.

- To include the necessary and required maintenance programs.

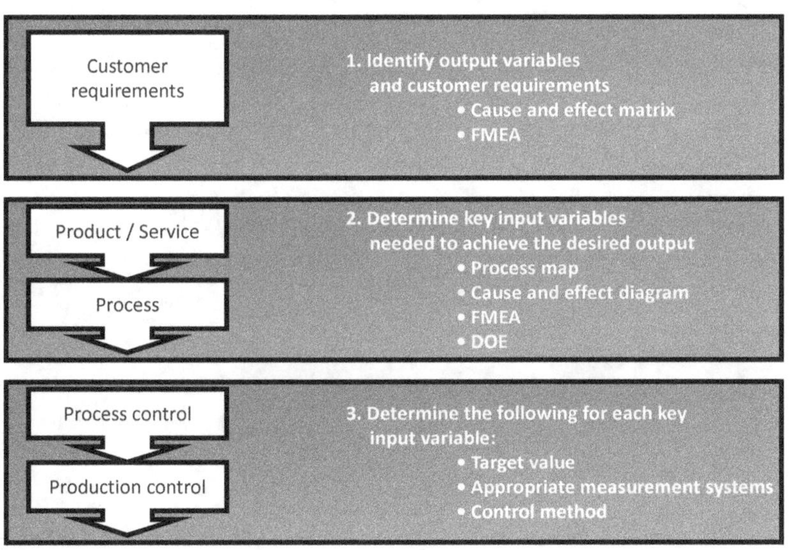

Contingency plan

- A procedure that indicates the activities to perform when there is an abnormal issue in the process.

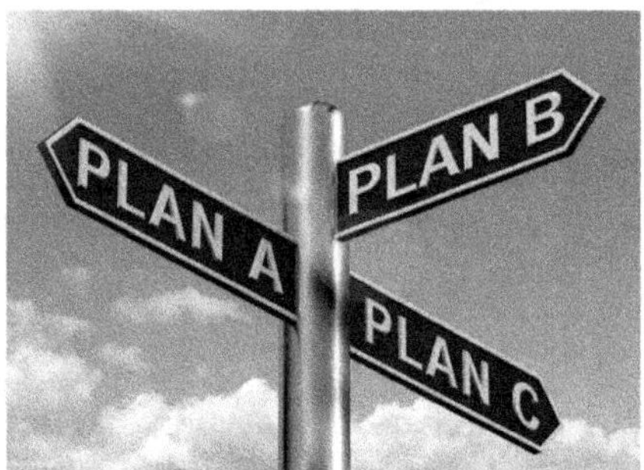

- In the **control phase** of a Lean Six Sigma project to evaluate the performance of an improved process.

- After a **process is designed** and in order to ensure adequate performance and continuously control it.

1. Include the general information.

2. Include process information.

3. Describe the measurement process.

4. Document the sampling process.

5. Document the decision-making process.

6. Obtain approval.

1. General information

- General data must be included that allow the document to be identified:

  - Date
  - Product
  - Process

- It is critical to the success of the project that the control plan is updated so that everyone has the same, relevant information.

- As you add more controls to the process, the control plan must be updated (along with its revision number).

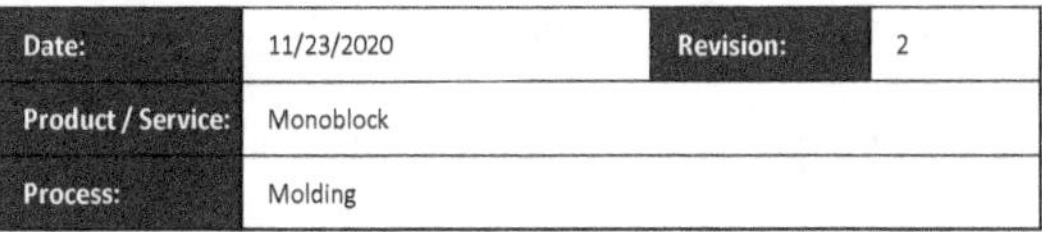

Date:	11/23/2020	Revision:	2
Product / Service:	Monoblock		
Process:	Molding		

2. Process information

Process				Measurement Process				Sampling			Decision-Making		
Process Step	What are we controlling?	Critical?	Input / Output	Specification limits / Requirements	Measurement method	Location	Control method	Sample size	Frequency	Who or what measures it?	Where is it recorded?	Corrective action	Doc. No.

- **Process steps.** List the critical process steps as identified in the FMEA.

- **What are we controlling?** Name of the input and output variables.

- **Are there any critical parameters?** Yes / No?

- **Input / Output.** Specify whether you are referring to an input or output variable. Initially, there might be more output than input variables. However, the goal is to control the inputs to ensure that the outputs are controlled.

3. Measurement process

Process				Measurement Process				Sampling			Decision-Making		
Process Step	What are we controlling?	Critical?	Input / Output	Specification limits / Requirements	Measurement method	Location	Control method	Sample size	Frequency	Who or what measures it?	Where is it recorded?	Corrective action	Doc. No.

- **Specification limits/Requirements.** Indicate the specification limits or the target values along with their tolerances. Include the unit of measurement.

- **Measurement method.** Describe the measurement system and include what machine(s) or equipment will be used.

- **Location.** Specify the location or control point in the process.

- **Control method.** What type of control method will be used (e.g., Automatic, SPC, etc.)?

4. Sampling

Process				Measurement Process				Sampling				Decision-Making	
Process Step	What are we controlling?	Critical?	Input / Output	Specification limits / Requirements	Measurement method	Location	Control method	Sample size	Frequency	Who or what measures it?	Where is it recorded?	Corrective action	Doc. No.

- **Sample size.** Select the sample size based on the measurement system, process capability and sampling cost.

- **Sample frequency.** Select the frequency based on the measurement system, process capability, operating costs, and operating requirements.

- **Who or what measures it?** The person or equipment that will be responsible for measuring at the required frequency.

5. Decision-making

Process				Measurement Process				Sampling				Decision-Making	
Process Step	What are we controlling?	Critical?	Input / Output	Specification limits / Requirements	Measurement method	Location	Control method	Sample size	Frequency	Who or what measures it?	Where is it recorded?	Corrective action	Doc. No.

- **Where is it recorded?** In what document and for what period of time?

- **Corrective action**

  - The actions that need to be taken when process measurements show the process is out of control.
  - Include the name of the person responsible for performing the corrective action.

- **Document number.** Include the corresponding document number for the information on each control point.

Corrective action rules

How can we measure if our decision-making rules are effective?

Corrective action rules should include the following:

- The person responsible for making the decision.
- The action to be performed.
- The process or parameter that needs to be modified.
- Where you will document the change.
- The person responsible for documenting the change.
- The criteria that leads to the action.
- The criteria for bringing up the issue.
- The data supporting this action.
- An evaluation of the action after it has been performed.
- Were the defined activities followed correctly?

The closer the decision maker is to the process, the more effective the solution.

6. Approval

- Approval is the most important part of the control plan because it indicates project buy-in from the people who will be responsible for following up on corrective actions.

- Why is it important to have project buy-in from the process owner?

  - Helps improvements become institutionalized.
  - Leads to improvements being extended to other processes.
  - Educates process engineers.
  - Enables Green/Black Belts to work on other improvement projects.

Approved by:	
Prepared by:	
Last revision date:	
Version:	

Relationship between FMEA and control plan

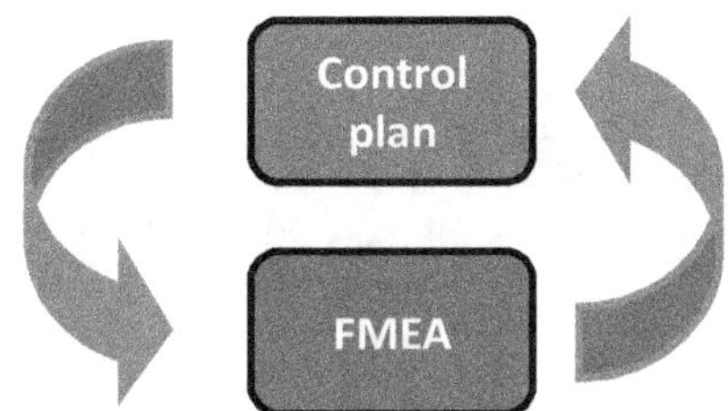

- FMEA should be the main source for identifying which variables to control and the initial evaluation of the current Control Plan.

- Controls that are included in the Control Plan need to be updated in the FMEA and the RPNs need to be recalculated.

Example – Chemical Manufacturing

Process				Measurement Process				Sampling			Decision-Making		
Process Step	What are we controlling?	Critical?	Input / Output	Specification limits / Requirements	Measurement method	Location	Control method	Sample size	Frequency	Who or what measures it?	Where is it recorded?	Corrective action	Doc. No.
Packaging	Net weight of package	Yes	Output	25.000 to 26.000 kilograms	Packaging area scale	Packaging	XR Chart	5 packages	Every 30 minutes	Packaging employee	Operation log	If weight > UCL, then analyze stirring speed, verify correct nozzle diameter, and adjust loading speed. If weight is < LCL, then stop the operation and notify the quality assurance inspector to verify granulometry of the product. For all cases, verify the first 5 units after any adjustment. If the problem continues to exist, then stop the operation and notify the production supervisor. The employee must document the actions performed in the operation log.	EN-035

Example – Bank of the Atlantic

Process				Measurement Process				Sampling			Decision-Making		
Process Step	What are we controlling?	Critical?	Input / Output	Specification limits / Requirements	Measurement method	Location	Control method	Sample size	Frequency	Who or what measures it?	Where is it recorded?	Corrective action	Doc. No.
Customer care at bank teller window	Customer care time	Yes	Output	Less than 6 minutes	Chronometer	Reception	I - MR Chart	1 Customer	Every 25 walk-in customers	Receptionist	Customer care time log	If time recorded > UCL, then notify manager to analyze the cause.	PR-055

Example – Logistics Company

Process				Measurement Process				Sampling			Decision-Making		
Process Step	What are we controlling?	Critical?	Input / Output	Specification limits / Requirements	Measurement method	Location	Control method	Sample size	Frequency	Who or what measures it?	Where is it recorded?	Corrective action	Doc. No.
Invoicing	Incorrect invoice	Yes	Output	Less than 0.006%	Customer complaint	Invoice issuance	p-Chart	100%	Weekly invoices	Customer service	Complaint log	If percentage > UCL, then inform the team during weekly meeting so that an analysis is conducted to identify the cause and correct the issue. Employee responsible for Customer service documents actions in the complaint log.	SC-025

Example – Chelsea Footwear

Process				Measurement Process				Sampling			Decision-Making		
Process Step	What are we controlling?	Critical?	Input / Output	Specification limits / Requirements	Measurement method	Location	Control method	Sample size	Frequency	Who or what measures it?	Where is it recorded?	Corrective action	Doc. No
Prototype production	Real vs. estimated cost of material	Yes	Output	Less than 100%	Cost objects	Production	I - MR Chart	Pilot lot at 100 %	Every production of a unit	New product development employee	Product documentation	If real cost > estimated cost, then notify the New product development manager to evaluate changes in material.	PR-055

Develop a step in the process control for a process that you are directly involved or familiar with.

Date:		Revision:	
Product / Service:			
Process:			

Process				Measurement Process				Sampling			Decision-Making		
Process Step	What are we controlling?	Critical?	Input / Output	Specification limits / Requirements	Measurement method	Location	Control method	Sample size	Frequency	Who or what measures it?	Where is it recorded?	Corrective action	Doc. No.

Glossary

accuracy of a measurement system
Defined in relation to its closeness (bias) with respect to an objective: greater proximity implies a good degree of accuracy. It is the difference between the average of the measurements and a reference value, known as a standard measurement.

analyze
Third phase of the DMAIC methodology where the primary objective is to identify the significance of the variables as it relates to a process.

baseline
The initial state of a gauge or metric. Must be expressed in units and based on long term information (at least the last three months).

blocking
Technique used to minimize or remove the effects of a few important nuisance variables in an experiment. For example, if you think that ambient temperature is a nuisance variable, tests must be conducted at the same time of day.

box plot diagram
A tool that permits the graphical comparison of the location and variations of various processes, product categories, or services.

business case
Tool used to identify areas of problems or improvement. Additionally, it provides a description of the characteristics of a situation and an estimate of the potential value of implementation.

champion
Owner of the process where the improvement project will be carried out. It's where the main benefits of the projects will be seen. Their responsibility is to maintain the team focused on the achievement of the objectives and be the link to the direction of the company. They must also attend all improvement meetings.

cluster sampling
The population is divided into subgroups that are very similar to each other. Typically, there is more variation within the subgroup than between subgroups. The variability within the subgroup is very similar to that of the entire population. It is recommended to take a cluster or subgroup and check all the elements of said subgroup.

continuous data
Data that can be measured by its input, for example: weight of containers or service time.

control
The fifth and final phase of the DMAIC methodology. Objectives include: standardizing new methods, document lessons learned, develop methods that ensure the continuation of improvements, determine and measure the impact, deliver projects to the champion, and transfer knowledge to other processes or services.

control charts
Tools that show the behavior of a certain quality parameter of a process with respect to time. The control charts for variables are:
- X - R_m (individuals and moving ranges).
- X - R (means and ranges).
- X - S (means and standard deviations).

The control cards for attributes are:
- np (proportion of defective units in samples of constant size).
- p (proportion of defective units in samples of variable size).
- c (number of defects per unit in constant size samples).
- u (number of defects per unit in variable size samples).

control plan
Document that provides an overview on the strategies that will be used to ensure that the main processes, product, or service are controlled through detection and prevention actions.

controllable inputs (C)
Can be changed to see the effects on the output variables. Oftentimes called "knob" variables because they can be turned or adjusted. Examples are temperature, number of analysts, etc.

controlled variation
Known as a common cause, it is a stable pattern or consistent variation throughout time (predictable).

correlation diagram
A graph showing the relationship between two variables.

critical inputs (X)
Inputs that statistically have been shown to have an impact on the output variables.

critical to quality (CTQ)
Referred to as the key characteristics of quality of a certain product or service.

critical to quality (CTQ) tree
Diagram-based tool that helps translate the customer needs and understand more about the specific, available, and measurable performance requirements needed to fulfill those needs.

cross-functional diagram
This diagram provides a graphical perspective of the process stages, with a special emphasis on the responsibilities and interdepartmental relations.

defects
Units that do not comply with specifications.

defects per million opportunities (DPMO)
A key measurement in Six Sigma and represents the defects or errors observed in a product, process, or service per million opportunities

define
The first phase in the DMAIC methodology. Its objectives include defining the project, determining the customers' needs, and obtaining the approval of the company to realize the project.

descriptive statistics
The collection, description, visualization, and summary of data.

design of experiments
Set of active techniques that manipulate a process in order to provide the information that is required to improve it. These planned experimentation methods help to learn the multiple factors that impact the quality of a service, product, or process.

disaggregate
Consists of dividing a process into the subprocesses that make it up. Allows for a deeper and more detailed analysis. Analyzes the systematic relationship between various subprocesses.

discrete data
Data that can only be counted in integral values. For example: amount of defective parts or number of late parts.

discrimination or resolution
It is the technological ability of a measurement system to be able to adequately differentiate between the values of the parameters of a measurement. The resolution should be 10X the tolerance limit.

DMAIC
A methodology for the implementation of improvement events structured in five distinct phases in which it gets its name: define, measure, analyze, improve, and control.

experiment
Change in operating conditions of a system r process in order to measure the effect of the change in one or more properties of the product or service.

experimental design
Formal plan for conducting an experiment. Includes the selection of variables of response, factors, levels, blocks, and the use of certain tools such as planned grouping, randomization, or repetition.

experimentation
Carry out carefully planned changes, noting the results. This process is to keep performing until you reach an optimal level.

factorial design
Experimental design in which all the possible combinations that can be formed with the selected levels are randomly executed.

factors
Are those controllable variables whose effect on the output variables you want to analyze. These can be qualitative (type of raw material, color of a fabric) or quantitative, both discrete (number of people, number of pieces) and continuous (process time, temperature, pressure.)

fishbone diagram
A graphical tool obtained from brainstorming possible causes of a problem. The causes are listed in an organized way which makes it easier to separate problems and possible areas of improvement.

Gantt
Weekly plan in which the activities are listed for each of the DMAIC phases, with estimated times.

histogram
presentation (using bars) of the frequency distribution of a set data, in which you can observe how data is distributed, accumulation or central tendency, and dispersion or variability.

hypothesis tests and confidence intervals
A statistical procedure used to make a decision based on a sample, determined by the value that the true population parameter may have: mean, variance, proportion, difference between means or proportion.

improve
Fourth phase of the DMAIC methodology. The objectives are to propose new conditions in the processes to optimize their performance and achieve the objectives, establish the benefits associated with the proposed solution, investigate and resolve failure modes, and implement and validate improvement efforts.

inferential statistics
Deals with the generation of models, inferences, and predictions. It's a combination of descriptive statistics and probability.

Kano model
Tool used to identify customer needs. It classifies the characteristics of the product or

service into three categories: must-be, primary satisfiers, and delighters.

leader
They are the guide of the team. They make sure that objectives are met. Tasks include organizing meetings, planning activities, and reporting progress to the champion and sponsor(s). Ensures that the team fulfills the tasks at hand and follows up.

levels
The values that will be assigned to each factor in an experiment. Each factor should be assigned at least two different levels and the total number will depend on the information you want to obtain.

mean
Arithmetic average.

measure
Second phase of the DMAIC methodology. Objectives in this stage include describing the process at a detailed level, evaluating measurement systems, collecting process data, classifying data, and performing initial measurements to verify process performance and estimate the baseline.

measurement system
Consists of the operations, procedures, calibrators or measuring instruments, additional support equipment, software, and personnel responsible for obtaining a measurement.

measurement system analysis (MSA)
The methodology that identifies and quantifies the different causes of variation that affect the measurement system which can cause an error. In other words, the variation in the measurements caused by the variation of the part being measured and the system itself.

median
Once the data has been ordered from smallest to largest, it is the data that divides them in half (50 % of the data are below this value and 50 % are above).

mode
The value that appears most often in a set of data values.

multi-vari chart
a visual way of presenting variability through a series of charts. Its objective is to present the different facets of variation.

objective
A specific declaration of the desirable outcomes of a project. Objectives should be described in measurable terms (numbers).

opportunities
The total number of possibilities to produce a defect in a process (manufacturing, service, accounting, operations, etc.) that can generate an undesirable result.

Pareto diagram
A Pareto chart is a type of chart that displays numerical and categorical data represented by both bars and a line graph, where individual values are represented in descending order by bars, and the cumulative total is represented by the line. It is used to quickly visualize what causes or what values in a given situation are the most important and, therefore, which ones must be addressed as a priority, in order to solve the problem or improve the situation.

population
Set of elements with a common characteristic. Used to obtain general information.

potential capacity index (Cp or Pp)
The comparison between the specification limits (tolerance) and the process limits, regardless of location or centrality of the process.

precision
Ability of a measurement system to obtain the same results when a part is measured

multiple times. The precision is expressed in terms of the standard deviation.

process map (PMAP)
Tool used to document the flow of a process. Very similar to a flow chart, the only difference is that in this case, the input variables *(X)* and output variables *(Y)* are included.

process performance
An indicator that allows us to understand how the process is actually performing and helps us find a baseline.

project letter
Document that contains the definition of the Six Sigma project. It should include the business case, problem definition, the project's purpose (CTQs), objectives, indicators, deliverables, scope, roles and responsibilities, and necessary resources.

project scope
The reach of the project in terms of the area or process to be improved, the specific operation, the geographic area, etc.

quality
Set of properties inherent to a product or service that grant enough capacity to satisfy implicit or explicit needs. The quality of a product or service is also understood as the perception that the
the customer has the same.

quality drivers
They are defined as the factors that must be present in order to deliver a product or quality service.

quality function deployment (QFD)
Tool used to develop a complete understanding of all factors that must be carried out to create a design of quality. It consists of translating the requirements of the clients (WHATs) in technical requirements of design, execution, and control (the HOWs).

random sampling
Used when the variation is equal throughout all samples of *n* experimental units. It's usually characterized by its imperial selection.

range
Measurement of the variability of a set of data that is the result of the difference between the largest and smallest data in the sample.

real capacity index (Cpk or Ppk)
The comparison between the specification limits (tolerance) and the process limits, taking into account the location or centrality of the process.

repeatability
the variation in the measurements obtained by a single user using the same measuring instrument to measure identical characteristics on the same parts. This variation is due to the measuring instrument.

repeatability and reproducibility studies
Statistical methodology to evaluate a measurement system. Assigns values to repeatability and reproducibility, which are compared against a standard to determine if the system is capable of providing reliable measurements.

replicas
Number of times each experiment will be repeated. The higher the number of replicas, the more accurate the results.

reproducibility
Variation in the average of the measurements tests made by different users using the same measuring instrument when they measure identical characteristics in the same parts. This variation is attributable to the operation testers or measurement procedure.

response variable
The outputs (must be quantifiable) that are going to be measured to observe the effect

that the change in the output has on the input variables.

sample
Representative portion of the population taken to obtain information on the whole.

sample population
Random selection of units of a population.

sigma level
Metric indicating compliance with a product, process, or service in relation to customer specifications.

SIPOC diagram
This diagram provides a graphical overview of the stages of a process in conjunction with key vendors, inputs, outputs, and users. It is a tool that allows you to analyze a process relative to its parameters in order to fully understand its impact in the value chain.

Six Sigma
Work philosophy and business strategy based on a focus on the customer, efficient management of data and methodologies, and robust designs which allow to significantly reduce variability in processes and achieve a minimum level of defects.

sponsor(s)
Member(s) of top management whose main responsibility is to remove obstacles and make strategic decisions for the team to achieve objectives. Attend advancement meetings when requested.

stability of a measurement system
The ability of a system to show consistency in measurements over time.

standard deviation
Measurement used to quantify the variation or dispersion of a set of data, equivalent to the square root of the variance. It is represented by the lowercase Greek letter Sigma (σ) or the Latin letter (s).

standard operation (S)
A standard procedure, instrument, or material to develop a process.

stratify
Classify and analyze data according to the different sources from which they come, for example: machines, batches, suppliers, shifts, branches, points of sale, days of the week, etc.

statistical process control
Tool utilized in the study of the variation and the use of statistical signals to monitor or improve the performance of a process.

statistics
A branch of mathematics that refers to the collection, study, and interpretation of obtained data.

stratified sampling
Stratified sampling is a method of sampling from a population which can be divided into subpopulations and then randomly selected. This occurs when there is more variation between start than within stratum.

systematic sampling
Starts with a unit taken at random and then sampled every *n* units thereafter.

tree diagram
Diagram showing the cause and effects relationships, taking into account all the variables that influence a given problem or situation.

uncontrollable inputs
Inputs which are impossible to control; for example, the environment. Identifying them is useful because they can affect our processes and we should try to minimize its impact.

uncontrolled variation
Known as a special cause, it is a pattern that changes over time (unpredictable).

unit
Any individual member of a population.

variance
Measurement that is used to quantify the variation or dispersion of a set of numerical data, equivalent to the sum of the mean squared, divided by the number of measurements minus one.

variation
Dispersion of a particular characteristic with respect to a target value.

variation analysis
Tool used to mathematically analyze the significance of the sources and causes of variation of a process.

voice of the customer (VoC)
Client's expression regarding their needs.

Manual de gestión aduanera. Normativas y procedimientos clave del comercio internacional

Pedro Coll

Productos y servicios inteligentes y sostenibles

Llorenç Guilera, Antoni Garrell

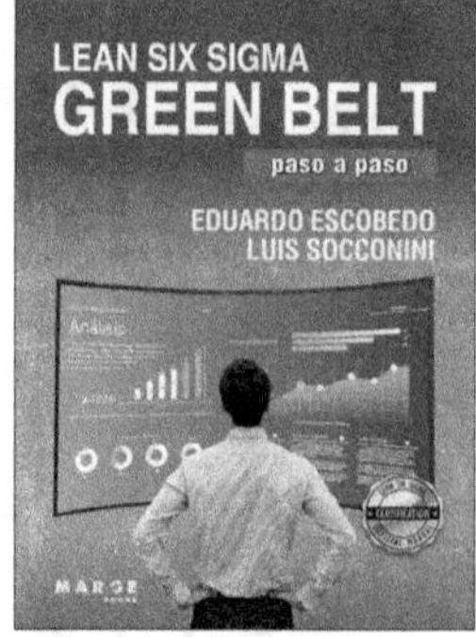

Lean Six Sigma Green Belt, paso a paso

Luis Socconini, Eduardo Escobedo

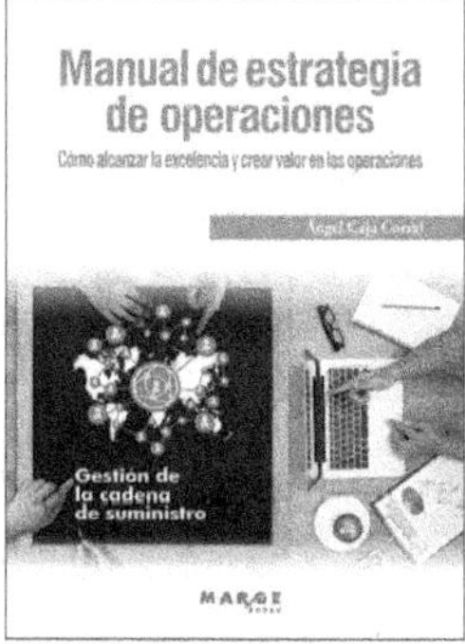

Manual de estrategia de operaciones

Ángel Caja Corral

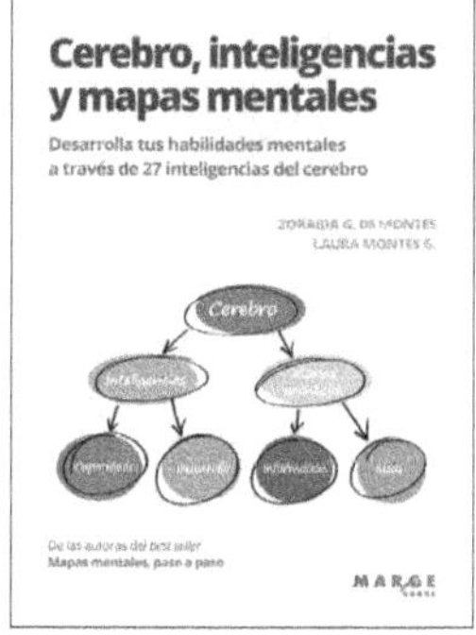

Cerebro, inteligencias y mapas mentales

Zoraida G. de Montes, Laura Montes G.

Manual del comercio electrónico

Eva María Hernández Ramos, Luis Carlos Hernández Barrueco

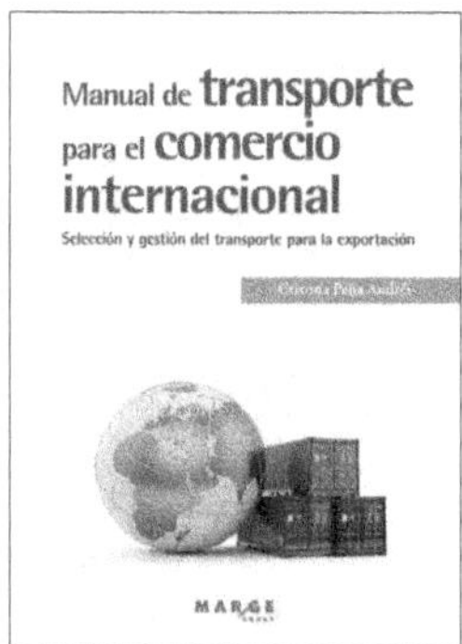

Manual de transporte para el comercio internacional

Cristina Peña Andrés

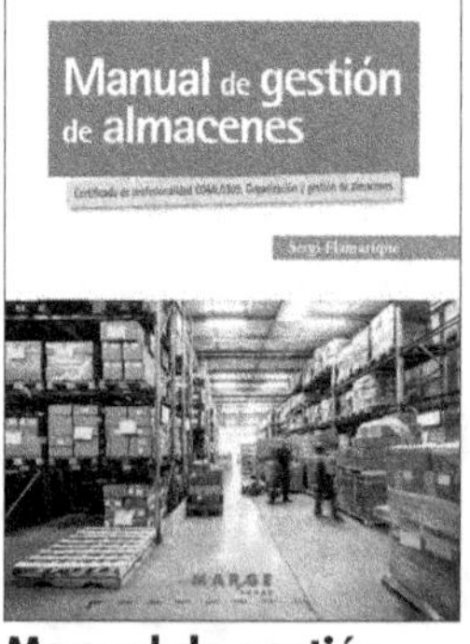

Manual de gestión de almacenes

Sergi Flamarique

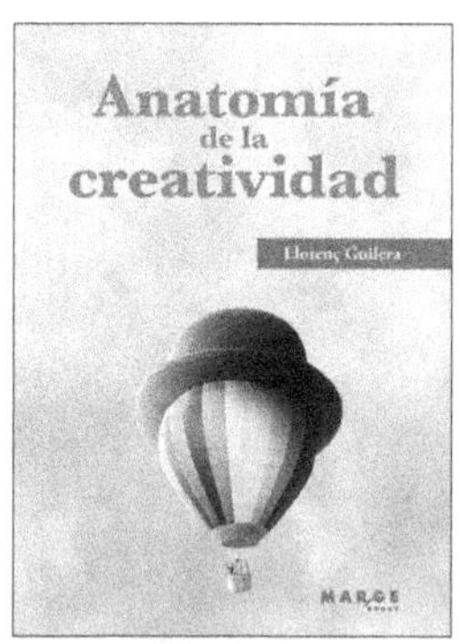

Anatomía de la creatividad

Llorenç Guilera Agüera

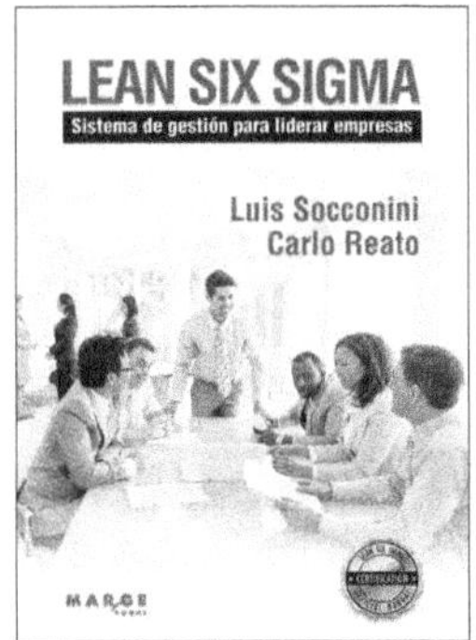

Lean Six Sigma. Sistema de gestión para liderar empresas
Luis Socconini, Carlo Reato

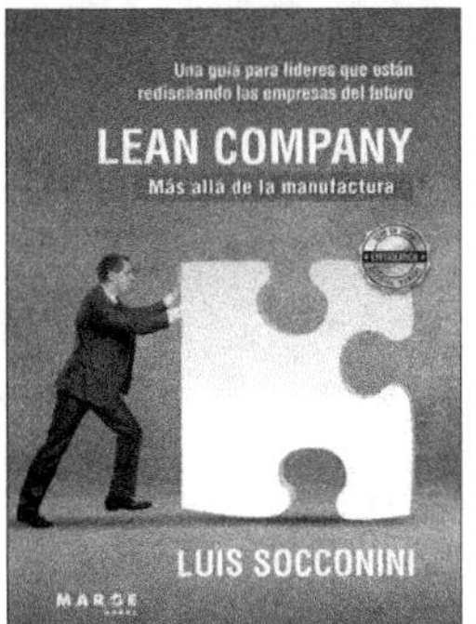

Lean Company. Más allá de la manufactura
Luis Socconini

El proceso de las 5'S en acción
Luis Socconini, Marco Barrantes

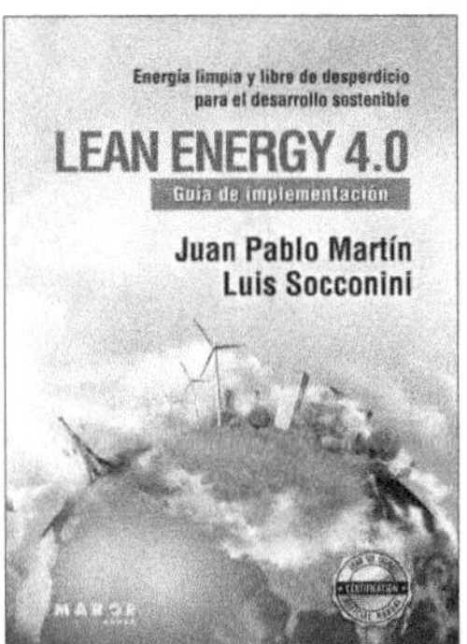

Lean Energy 4.0. Guía de Implementación
Luis Socconini, Juan Pablo Martín

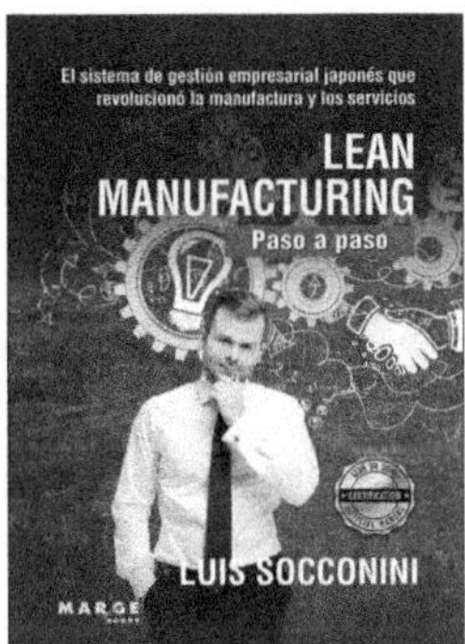

Lean Manufacturing. Paso a paso
Luis Socconini

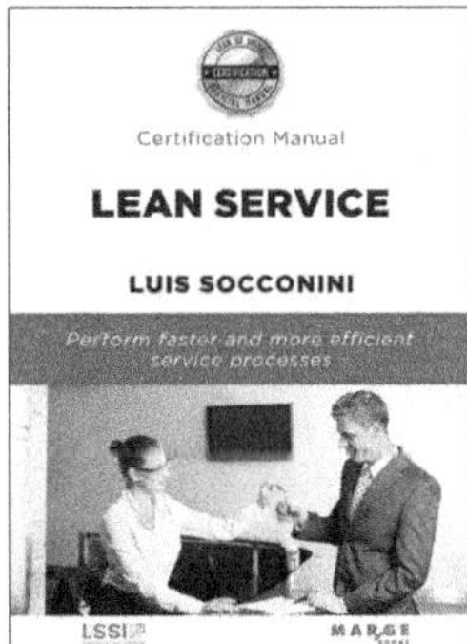

Lean Services. Certification Manual
Luis Socconini

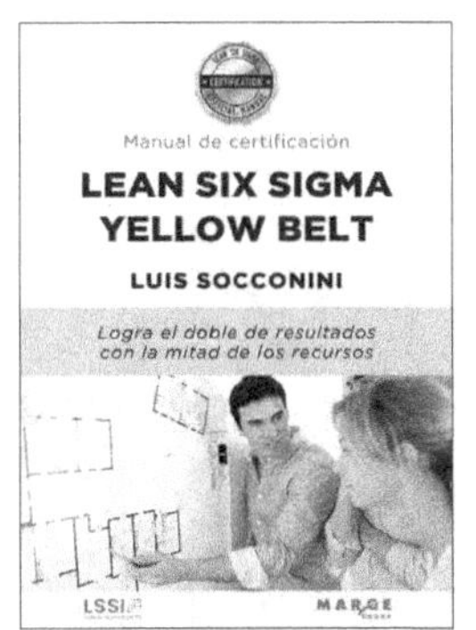

Lean Six Sigma Yellow Belt. Manual de certificación
Luis Socconini

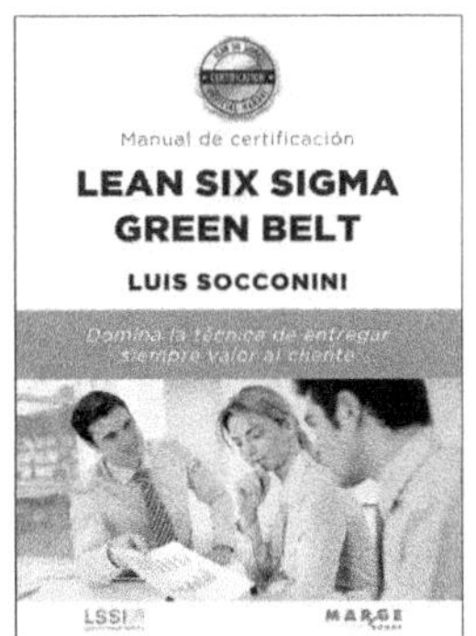

Lean Six Sigma Green Belt. Manual de certificación
Luis Socconini

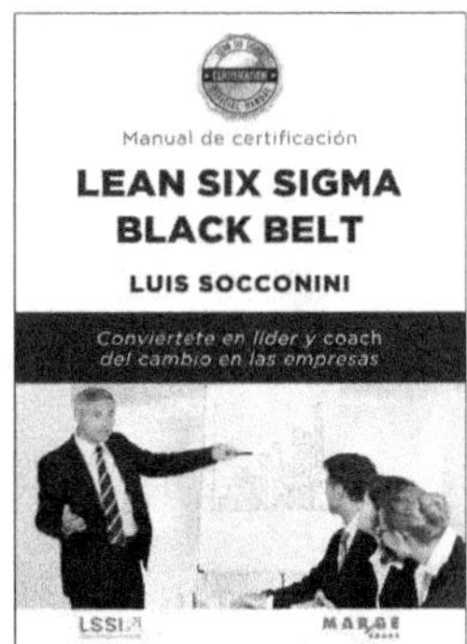

Lean Six Sigma Black Belt. Manual de certificación
Luis Socconini

València, 558 – 08026 Barcelona – Tel. +34-931 429 486 – marge@margebooks.com – www.margebooks.com